THE CHAMBER OF MAIDEN THOUGHT

Literature is recognised as having significantly influenced the development of modern psychoanalytic thought. In recent years psychoanalysis has drawn increasingly on the literary and artistic traditions of western culture and moved away from its original medical–scientific context. *The Chamber of Maiden Thought* (Keats's metaphor for 'the awakening of the thinking principle') is an original and revealing exploration of the seminal role of literature in forming the modern psychoanalytic model of the mind.

The crux of the 'post-Kleinian' psychoanalytic view of personality development lies in the internal relations between the self and the mind's 'objects'. Meg Harris Williams and Margot Waddell show that these relations have their origins in the drama of identifications which we can see played out metaphorically and figuratively in literature, which presents the self-creative process in aesthetic terms. They argue that psychoanalysis is a true child of literature rather than merely the interpreter or explainer of literature, illustrating this with some examples from clinical experience, but drawing above all on close scrutiny of the dynamic mental processes presented in the work of Shakespeare, Milton, the Romantic poets, Emily Brontë and George Eliot.

The Chamber of Maiden Thought will encourage psychoanalytic workers to respond to the influence of literature in exploring symbolic mental processes. By bringing psychoanalysis into creative conjunction with the arts, it enables practitioners to tap a cultural potential whose insights into the human mind are of immense value.

Meg Harris Williams is a writer, artist and English scholar, with a lifelong psychoanalytic education. **Margot Waddell** took a doctorate in English literature before training as a psychotherapist; she is now a Principal Child

THE CHAMBER OF MAIDEN THOUGHT

Literary origins of the psychoanalytic model of the mind

Meg Harris Williams and
Margot Waddell

Tavistock/Routledge
London and New York

First published in 1991
by Routledge
11 New Fetter Lane, London EC4P 4EE

Simultaneously published in the USA and Canada
by Routledge
a division of Routledge, Chapman and Hall Inc.
29 West 35th Street, New York, NY 10001

© 1991 Meg Harris Williams and Margot Waddell

Typeset by NWL Editorial Services, Langport,
Somerset, TA10 9DG

Printed and bound in Great Britain by
Mackays of Chatham PLC, Chatham, Kent

All rights reserved. No part of this book may be reprinted or reproduced or utilized in any form or by any electronic, mechanical, or other means, now known or hereafter invented, including photocopying and recording, or in any information storage or retrieval system, without permission in writing from the publishers.

British Library Cataloguing in Publication Data
Williams, Meg Harris
The chamber of maiden thought: literary origins of
the psychoanalytic model of the mind.
1. Psychoanalysis related to literature. 2. Literature related to psychoanalysis
I. Title   II. Waddell, Margot 1946–
150.195

Library of Congress Cataloging in Publication Data
Williams, Meg Harris, 1951–
The chamber of maiden thought: literary origins of the psychoanalytic model of the mind/Meg Harris Williams and Margot Waddell.
p. cm.
Includes bibliographical references and index
1. English literature – History and criticism   2. Psychoanalysis and literature.   I. Margot, Waddell, *1946–*   II. Title.
820.9′353 – dc20

ISBN 0-415-04364-6
0-415-04365-4 (pbk)

Imperceptibly impelled by the awakening of the thinking principle – within us – we ... get into the Chamber of Maiden-Thought ... intoxicated with the light and the atmosphere, we see nothing but pleasant wonders, and think of delaying there for ever in delight. However among the effects this breathing is father of is that tremendous one of sharpening one's vision into the heart and nature of Man – of convincing one's nerves that the World is full of Misery and Heartbreak, Pain, Sickness and oppression – whereby This Chamber of Maiden-Thought becomes gradually darken'd and at the same time on all sides of it many doors are set open – but all dark – all leading to dark passages – We see not the balance of good and evil. We are in a Mist – *We* are now in that state – We feel 'the burden of the Mystery'.

(Keats, letter to Reynolds, 3 May 1818)

In memory of Martha Harris

CONTENTS

Foreword by Donald Meltzer   ix
Preface   xix
Acknowledgements   xx
Introduction   1

1 SHAKESPEARE: A LOCAL HABITATION AND A NAME   8
2 MILTON: THE MIND'S OWN PLACE   53
3 BLAKE: THE MIND'S EYE   70
4 WORDSWORTH: THE VISIONARY GLEAM   82
5 COLERIDGE: PROGRESSIVE BEING   95
6 KEATS: SOUL-MAKING   109
7 EMILY BRONTË: METAMORPHOSIS OF THE ROMANTIC HERO   126
8 GEORGE ELIOT: THE UNMAPPED COUNTRY   143
9 PARALLEL DIRECTIONS IN PSYCHOANALYSIS   170

Epilogue   184
Notes and references   193
Selected bibliography   205
Name index   209
Subject index   211

FOREWORD

Had psychoanalysis followed the original bent given to it by Freud at the turn of the century, it would have remained a medical sub-speciality of neurology and psychiatry, dedicated to relieving the suffering of neurotic individuals. Its method of cure, conceived in the light of nineteenth-century Germanic medical science, undertook to reach to the 'cause' of the symptoms by bringing into consciousness the repressed events of earlier times, often going back into childhood. Thus it held a neurophysiological model of the disturbance analogous to an inflammation in a vestigial organ like the appendix. It is in no sense a silly model, for it has much truth in it; but it had a very restricted horizon. Once Freud had discovered the transference, in his work with Dora, this method took over the development of the science of psychoanalysis, completely placing in the shadows the massive neurophysiological preconceptions of the 'Project for a Scientific Psychology' which Freud had earlier written for his friend Fliess.

The events of the transference, replacing a patient's realistic observation of the analyst by insistent preconceptions, brought into view the personality, character, way of life, values, aspirations, prejudices, hopes, and fears of the patient. While anxious that psychoanalysis should remain scientific by avoiding embracing any *Weltanschauung*, Freud nevertheless took the lead in broadening the field of observation by focusing interest on the ramifications of the libido in the form of character types, as opposed to the earlier preoccupation with the vicissitudes of the libido in symptom formation. This move was taken up in particular by Karl Abraham in 'A Short Study of the Development of the Libido, viewed in the Light of Mental Disorders', and given a formal dimension as 'organization' of the libido as it moved developmentally from infancy with its oral primacy towards the genitality of mature adulthood.

This broadening of the field of study eventually forced Freud to abandon the most dearly held of his neurophysiological preconceptions: the 'unity of the mind'. In the last decade of his life, and in particular shortly before his death in 1938, he wrote of the evidence that the mind can – and frequently does – split itself, so that the great achievements of men can stand side by side with their follies without apparent conflict. Philosophy would not brook being excluded from the study of the mind: indeed Abraham, and even more definitively Melanie Klein, gave psychoanalysis a distinctly Platonic orientation by discovering that the inner world had its own type of geographic concreteness, and that it was in the transactions of the inner world (manifest in dreams and unconscious phantasy) that the meaning of the outer world derived its origin.

It is over fifty years since Melanie Klein's seminal paper on splitting processes and projective identification established this transformation, and brought 'meaning' into the centre of psychoanalytic study. This naturally focused attention on emotions and on symbol formation as the means by which emotions become available for thought. In earlier days, symbols had been very little differentiated from conventional signs, with the result that thought and language were considered as conjoint, commencing in the pre-conscious where 'thing-representations' were held to be transformed into 'word-representations'. Not only did this take no account of the severe limitations of verbal language, but it greatly reduced understanding of the impact of art and literature to interpretation of its content, its iconography. Even the stirring power of music was believed to be explicable through its programmatic imagery. The alliance with science-as-explanation – exemplified in such works as *Civilization and its Discontents, Moses and Monotheism, The Future of an Illusion* and the paper on Leonardo – alienated the artistic community from psychoanalysis. Correspondingly, this preoccupation with explanation generated an attitude of teaching rather than learning amongst psychoanalysts in relation to the arts, which was a barrier against their own creative response.

FOREWORD

The coming-of-age of psychoanalysis is nowhere better illustrated than in the work of Wilfred Bion, which – for all its obscurity, flirtation with mathematical forms, and refusal to compromise with the limitations of the reader – declares the influence of the arts in promoting psychoanalytical thought and observation. Milton, Shakespeare, Keats, Coleridge, the Old Testament, the Burial Chamber at Ur and the Bhagavadgita are not only Bion's references for exposition but also his sources of inspiration for original thought. Since the present volume is about sources such as these in English literature, it is perhaps necessary to give some precise indication of the position that psychoanalytic thought – its model of the mind – has achieved at present, as a point of reference for the essays that follow.

When Freud in 'Group psychology and the analysis of the Ego' and later in *The Ego and the Id* clarified his shift from a stratified 'topographic' model to a 'structural' model of the mind, consisting of Id, Ego and Superego, he had a problem of defining the status of the Superego. He thought of it as the forms of parental figures 'somehow united' which had been 'introjected into the ego' and subsequently separated off 'by a gradient' to establish an independent function of monitoring the ego's activities. It was Abraham who recognized that, at least in manic-depressive patients, these figures of love-objects were experienced in a concrete way: that they could be destroyed, expelled, reintrojected in a destroyed form. Melanie Klein, listening to children's accounts of the internal space and its lively figures, recognized this concrete inner world and its objects. But she also saw in small children that the maternal figure and its nurturing, protective and pedagogic functions were at least as important as the authority of the paternal figure, and also that the two figures are not, by any means, always 'somehow united'. This internal theatre of phantasy and drama she recognized as the scene represented in the play of children, and the locus of their developmental struggles. In her hands the rather vague concept of narcissism – which in its original form had been a designation of the direction of distribution of the ego towards the body of the subject – became a firmly structural one, describing the way in which the organization of the personality fluctuated. When internal parental figures were dominant, a state of 'object relations' existed; but in contrast to this, infantile parts might unite against these figures to form their own organizations, later called 'gangs' because of their rebellious and delinquent character. Even within the realm of relationships with internal parents, values could fluctuate from egocentric ones (exploiting and potentially being persecuted by parental figures) to trust, love and concern for the welfare of the parents (the 'depressive position'). Melanie Klein saw such mental states as security, optimism, joyousness, and interest in the world, as emanations of a loving relation to internal parents, particularly the mother – a bond rooted in the infantile relation to the feeding breast.

Because Freud thought of the formation of the superego as a consequence of the oedipus complex (its 'heir', contingent upon the relinquishment of erotic yearnings towards the parent of the opposite sex, under the threat of castration) it was natural, given the material he was dealing with, to suppose that the superego would be more harsh than the actual parents. The nearly cannibalistic model of introjection seemed to leave no possibility that the superego might be better in its qualities than the actual parents. This invitation to pessimism was only slightly improved by Abraham pushing introjective processes into earlier phases, since he saw them as dominated by the ambivalence of oral and anal sadism. On the other hand, Melanie Klein's material from small children, while confirming the ubiquity of sadistic impulses, recognized that the first oral stage, although not free of ambivalence, was object-related, not 'auto-erotic'; and that the introjection of a good feeding breast did seem to take place. By recognizing the splitting of the object into good (gratifying) and bad (disappointing, deserting) parts, she could account for the establishment of an idealized breast and mother in the earliest postnatal period.

The concept of splitting-and-idealization thus mitigated the pessimism about the quality of internal objects, while still leaving the problem that their excellence was limited by the qualities of the actual parents. Freud had suggested one way of solving this: namely, by later introjection into the superego of qualities from later loved and admired figures. Melanie Klein added another avenue of improvement (one to which Freud had alluded but not developed): namely, that qualities of harshness and even cruelty in the internal parents could often be seen to be the result of infantile parts of the personality having entered into the parental figures by projective identification, thus contaminating their adult qualities with infantile attitudes and values. Withdrawal of these projections could result in improved parental function of the superego figures, including those qualities Freud had first identified as 'ego-ideal' but later lost sight of – the internal sources of inspiration and aspiration.

To these two sources of hopefulness about the possible evolution of the superego – the assimilation within it of qualities of later admired and loved figures, and the clarifying of it by withdrawal of projections – Melanie Klein added a third factor. In her last writings – the *Narrative of a Child Analysis*, *Envy and Gratitude* and 'Our adult world and its roots in infancy' – she gradually established the concept of the 'combined object' (a term she had introduced in her earlier work with different, more persecutory connotations). In a sense the combined object was the same thing that Freud had located in the material of the Wolf-man, and called 'the primal scene'. Melanie Klein recognized its essential connection with the sexual relation of the internal parents, as a 'powerful' object in its emotional evocativeness; but she also saw in it a quality not clearly visible in the external parents – namely, its mystery and creativity, its essential privacy and perhaps sacredness.

In general, it could be said that psychoanalysts followed Freud's lead in adopting a somewhat cynical attitude towards religion and its history. It is perhaps a tenable view that man has always invented gods, and naturally invented ones that suited him, being no better than himself but more powerful. But that view supposes that religions are invented by adults, rather than evolving in the minds of infants, later to be mythologized. The vision implicit in Melanie Klein's discoveries about infantile mental life is that mental life is essentially religious, and that the growth of the mind is somehow inextricably tied up with the evolution of the relationship between the self and its internal objects. Consequently, death of the mind is entailed by these objects being expelled, dethroned, invaded, corrupted, or fragmented.

What has been described so far could reasonably be claimed to be mainstream history of the psychoanalytic model of the mind, however selective. It is a history which has inevitably been deviated from, lagged behind, and converged upon, by other schools and in other geographical areas. The position by 1960 was that psychoanalysis had become a descriptive science with an artistic method of therapy and research. 'Theories' were now models of the mind – that is, metaphors whose purpose was the description of phenomena; Freud's structural theory of id, ego and superego was seen to operate as self and internal objects; the therapeutic aim had moved from the curing of symptoms to the promotion of personality development; and the pessimistic division of life and death instincts had been replaced by a view of the struggle between narcissistic organizations and object relationships, in which Love and Envy met in combat, struggling free of egocentricity (the paranoid-schizoid position) towards object love (the depressive position). Development of the personality required reintegration of the splitting in the self and clarification of the internal objects by withdrawal of projective identification of infantile parts. It was an enriched frame of reference of clinical observation in a situation where the analyst's counter-transference was as important a function and source of understanding as the analysand's transference. Clinical results were steadily improving, but analyses were getting disquietingly longer and longer.

What follows cannot be claimed as 'history' of the next thirty years in psychoanalytic thought, since it is too soon for key lines of development to have been assimilated within the movement in general. Any account of 'post-Kleinian' ideas at this turbulent point in time must inevitably be a subjective one, all the more since it will be based on the personal application of Bion's ambiguously stated ideas. Yet these ideas and implications in an integrated form are germane to this book and its view of literature and history, so I will proceed with a description of the modern psychoanalytic model in terms of an account of the Vale of Soul-making, which I hope will be seen to parallel the literary ones which follow. My own account – a subjective view of Bion's vision – has its sources of observation in the psychoanalytic situation with adult and child patients and in systematic mother–infant observation by the method developed by Esther Bick and Martha Harris, combined with recent experiences of echographic study of foetal behaviour in non- identical twins.

Long before birth, perhaps as early as fourteen weeks of gestation, the human infant can be said to manifest behaviour and to declare the fundamental qualities of its character. Not only does it relate to objects such as cord, membranes, placenta and twin sibling interior to the womb, but also to its mother's voice and other manifestations of her state of mind and body. Mental life, as distinct from adaptational behaviour, can be seen to have begun, implying the incipience of emotional experiences, primitive symbol formation of the song-and-dance variety, and dream-thoughts. As its ambience loses the ample dimensions of the early months and becomes restrictive, the foetus develops a yearning to recover its freedom and an expectation of another world from which it receives auditory clues. When it is strong enough it struggles to be free and succeeds. This good experience may be blemished by exhaustion, by foetal distress; it may be curtailed by Caesarian section, or if premature, completely distorted into an expulsion. However, where the experience of birth is one of successful escape from restriction, the exterior world impinges with the shock of both panic and of ecstasy. The panic before the first breath is succeeded by the delicious expansion of the lungs; the explosion of noise becomes quickly modulated and delightfully musical; the initial chill is quickly countered; the blinding glare takes wondrous shape. But the mobile limbs have been bound down by a thousand gravitational cords, and the sense of helplessness, of being lost in limitless space, mobilizes the expectation of a saviour, and the mouth seeks it out and finds it. The infant's panicky fragmentation is pulled together by the mother's arms and her voice and smell which are familiar; and the vast space is given a point of origin geometrically by this nipple-in-the-mouth. And when the eyes begin to see the mother's face and breast, and the flesh to feel the chain of desire, her eyes are the sanctuary in which the passionate yearning towards the beauty of this new world can find the reciprocity that makes it bearable.

But the breast has its blemishes, its striae, its wrinkles when emptied; and the face is a landscape over which clouds of anxiety pass and in which storms of pain and indignation gather, sometimes obscured by mists of inattention. From the distrust engendered by these variations the baby must seek its own defence, from a rich variety easily at hand. It can internalize this good object in its full beauty, but finds it takes in also its disappointing form. But that can be expelled as faeces. Once internalized, the beautiful object can afford sleep either in its arms or back inside it. Or the baby can reverse the geometry of space so that its mouth – not the mother's nipple – is the point of origin around which the variety of objects revolve as satellites, ordered by its screams. Or, most enduring of all defences, it can divide itself by variously deploying the attention of its senses so that no single object can exert the full aesthetic impact of consensuality.

When unmodulated by reciprocity, these five lines of defence against the full impact of the chains of desire – that is: introjection, expulsion, projective identification, omnipotent control of objects, and splitting processes – all weaken the passionate contact, whether they are deployed singly or in consortium; all these situations are manifest through dream-thoughts. And it is the moments of passionate contact, in which the baby is able to establish the unique transactions of co-operate projection and introjection with the unconscious reveries of the contemplating mother, that give meaning to the nourishment from the breast. The breast may then nourish the mind with symbolic representations of the baby's emotional experience, and facilitate new dream-thoughts. Eventually it is the establishment of such a thinking head-breast that enables the human child to commence the process of thinking-for-itself – to create its autonomous symbols to enrich its store of received symbols and conventional signs.

This capacity for passionate contact, with its consortium of love for the beauty-of-the-world, hatred of the chains of desire felt in the flesh and on the pulses, and thirst for knowledge of the enigmatic object in its combined form as breast-and-nipple, mother-and-father, fuels the development of the soul: that interior, private core of the personality. At the nucleus of this private core is the mysterious, sacred nuptial chamber of the internal objects, to which they must be allowed periodically to withdraw to repair and restore one another. Against acquiescence in this are deployed all the powerful forces of aversion to emotional attachment and to dependence and submission to the superiority and wisdom of these internal gods. For they are the superior, most evolved segment of the human mind, and their evolution takes place in advance of the self. Artists and poets are (as Shelley said) the 'unacknowledged legislators of the world' because the internal objects are the legislators of the individual

FOREWORD

mind, and this is the artist's field of operation and the focus of his discipline; as Milton wrote, of the relation between the self and God: 'who best/Bear his mild yoke, they serve him best' (Sonnet 19).

Around this core of the personality there develops, in concentric circles of diminishing intimacy, the adaptational carapace of the personality with all its learned devices of casual and contractual relationships, simplified and impoverished in their emotionality, often stimulated by states of excitement engendered by fancy and fear of the group. Every step in development at the core must be worked through from infantile levels, in the context of emotional transference – of which the method of psychoanalysis has no monopoly. Gradually, owing to the mysterious process of aspiration towards the excellence of these evolving internal objects, the adult portion of the personality may emerge and manifest itself in the area of its passionate interests and in the desires of its intimate relationships. Its joyousness takes shape in the work of building the family of private life and contributing to the gradual evolution of the human family. Its opponents, in each individual and abroad in the world, are legion. But fortunately the forces in pursuit of truth are intelligent, and those against it are fundamentally stupid, dependent on negative imitation and perversion of the truth – or the best we can approximate to it: truthfulness of observation and thought.

Donald Meltzer

PREFACE

This book was written in response to the increasing interest in literature amongst psychoanalysts and psychotherapists. Its aim is to help give direction to the present confusing convergence between psychoanalytic and literary and art forms, by providing a historical literary perspective for modern psychoanalytic thinking, instead of a medical-scientific one. The idea is not to deliver any ultimate interpretations of literary works, using psychoanalytic theory as a 'key to all philosophies', but to put the 'post-Kleinian' model of the mind in touch with its origins in the literary tradition. This model is, one hopes, still itself in a healthy state of evolution, so throughout the book we have avoided both psychoanalytic and literary jargon.

In writing this book, therefore, we hope to enable psychoanalytic workers to respond to the seminal influence of literature in exploring symbolic mental processes, and to begin to tap a cultural potential whose wealth and complexity never cease to reward one's awe and amazement – as Bion would say, 'in love, hate and the pursuit of knowledge'.

MHW and MW, 1991

ACKNOWLEDGEMENTS

Margot Waddell would like warmly to thank Gwen Newstead and Sarah Quartey for their unfailing readiness and efficiency in producing typescripts at very short notice.

INTRODUCTION

This book is intended as an introduction neither to English literature nor to psychoanalysis, but to a particular view of the relationship between the two. Our presentation of this relationship depends very much on the reader's sympathy with recent developments in the psychoanalytic view of its own discipline as an aesthetic and imaginative process akin to the experience of literature itself. Literature and psychoanalysis may be seen as different media for exploring the world of the mind, related through congruence and a common drive towards self-knowledge, rather than reductively related in terms of literary phantasy content and psychoanalytic interpretation. It is impossible in a book of this scope to make any attempt at a survey of literary influence amongst psychoanalysts, nor would this necessarily be very revealing; probably only amongst the most recent generation of Kleinian analysts has English literature's influence and status begun to become paramount. It is impossible to do more than sketch the underlying shape of mental action in the work of some of the seminal poetic thinkers in modern English culture (which can be said to start with Shakespeare), highlighting the model of the mind which is being figured implicitly through metaphorical means. Poets and artists have always made their explorations of psychic reality in fictional and metaphorical terms, to overcome the restrictions of the discursive language of their society. In so doing, they have made available symbolic analyses of emotional constellations and thought processes which have guided the philosophy, psychology, and prose fiction of following generations. Again, within the scope of this book, we cannot present comprehensive accounts of writers or their works, but aim rather to open windows on them, to convey the quality and structure of a particular reading experience. We rely on a certain 'willing suspension of disbelief' (in Coleridge's phrase) on the part of our readers, to avoid clogging the text with apologies and explanations. We hope therefore to convey to the reader how psychoanalysis may be seen – not as an interpreter or explainer of literature – but rather, as a true child of literature.

The concreteness of psychic reality has always been dominant and explicit in the poetic consciousness. Shakespeare gave to airy nothing a 'local habitation and a name', and Milton's Satan announced that the mind was neither heaven nor hell, but 'its own place'. It is not a place which can be shaped or furnished by the conscious will; it cannot (as Satan found) make heaven out of hell; rather, it is the place where mysterious powers outside the control of the self can create meaning, in the form of symbols, and expand the horizons of knowledge through inspiration. Plato's realm of Ideas, and God's ineffable effulgence, have found expression through the drama of the inner world. This is the brave new world which overrides cynicism at the end of *The Tempest*, and which lies 'all before' Adam and Eve after their expulsion from Eden. Shakespeare and Milton discovered that the new world is not a place of fixities and definites, of reward and punishment, but a place where the idea of 'the good' consists in the goal of development and the gradual, painful but also joyful, getting of wisdom. It is a place guided by ethical principles rather than by moral codes. Following this, the Romantic poets – after initially hoping to see the new world embodied in the French revolution – turned more emphatically to the inner world, and seized fast hold of its potential as the only real means for mankind's regeneration and progression. Blake called this 'cleansing the doors of perception' towards 'a world of Imagination and vision', for 'all deities reside in the Human Breast'. Keats likewise found that looking with the eye of the mind changed the complexion of the world from a vale of sorrows to a 'Vale of Soul-making', a school for the individual identity. In this vale or school the mind could achieve what Coleridge termed 'organic' fulfilment as opposed to the 'mechanical' form imposed by external forces and social conventions. Coleridge emphasized explicitly the structural importance of symbol formation in promoting the mind's innate 'principle of self-development', and established the getting of wisdom in terms of 'becoming' rather than of 'possessing' knowledge. True wisdom or soul-knowledge was not stored with the accumulations of memory, but altered the very structure of the mind.

The greatest natural talent of the Romantic era, in terms of linguistic facility, was Wordsworth's; so Wordsworth's mental ossification and failure to develop as a poet became a puzzle to the later generation of Romantics, and indeed to ourselves. His vision of the god-like child in mother Nature's arms, eternally encircled by mountain-breast and lake-eyes, had an authentic ring of truth which all recognized, yet which remained a 'visionary gleam' and vanished like a mountain mist as soon as he became established as a 'genius'. Potentially a 'miserable and mighty poet of the human heart', he faded into the 'egotistical sublime' (in Keats's phrases). Coleridge could not deal with the problem, either regarding Wordsworth or its implications for his own relinquishment of poetry, and felt impelled to change his medium of spiritual investigation from poetry to philosophical prose. Only in prose could he formulate the problem of original sin, of the wolf within the fold rather than outside it – that is, of the negative forces of philistinism existing within the mind itself and stunting its development. Poetry's brave new world as seen by Wordsworth and Coleridge made no allowance for childhood's struggle and anxiety over these internal enemies (a type of blindness reflected in their attitude to their own children). The poetic experience, like the childhood experience, when split off into an elevated ideal, lost its grip on reality and became a false heaven rather than a Vale of Soul-making. The wolf in the fold was recognized by Byron, but his excessive ambivalence towards poetry prevented him from tackling it; poetry he regarded as a fury-like pursuing female which would overcome him in the end, yet meanwhile he would seek his revenge on other women (stemming from resentment against his neglectful mother). Keats also regarded his 'demon Poesy' as an ambiguous female figure who might either support or overwhelm his own vulnerable infant-poet identity; but in contrast to Byron, his tenacious grip on his concept of 'the beautiful' enabled him to work through the consequences. Possibly the Rousseauist view of the earlier Romantics was related to an over-romanticization of Milton, as if release from heaven and hell should bring freedom; Milton himself always regarded following the Muse in terms of service, not privilege, and the dutiful using of his God-given talent. The Romantics' attitude to him was a mixture of hero-worship and contempt (as in the case of Blake), or of love and hate (in the case of Keats).

Both Keats and Emily Brontë (herself essentially a poet in prose) recognized implicitly that creative thinking came to an impasse if a line of egotistical, idealizing (meaning self-idealizing) single vision was pursued – if the Wordsworthian infant never confronted the Byronic wolf – and that security was not happiness. The adjective 'Shakespearean' which is often applied to both Keats and Emily Brontë, suggests their revivifying of the Romantic status quo by returning for inspiration to Shakespeare's complex emotionality, by means of negative capability. Keats explored the 'dark passages' associated in his 'Chamber of Maiden Thought' metaphor with 'going on thinking', including the darker side of the Muse in a situation of aesthetic conflict. Emily Brontë in *Wuthering Heights* rewrote the fate of the Byronic hero (descended directly from Milton's Satan) from childhood onwards, in Coleridgean terms of symbol formation. In this way she triumphantly conceived how the mind may be released from its egotistical deadlock and allowed to continue developing. These ultimate poet-philosophers of the Romantic era in different ways confront, rather than romanticize, the love-hate tensions which are necessary to expand the mind; and repel the cynicism, envy and nihilism which continually threaten to close its horizons.

All these poet-philosophers have regarded creative thought as something inseparable from self-knowledge and the soul's search for 'salvation' (though their vision of salvation may differ). And always, creative thinking is distinguished from imitative forms of thinking which are apparent rather than real, or from the type of verbal facility which is a vehicle for lies rather than truth (as seen, for example, in Shakespeare's *Troilus and Cressida*, or Milton's devils' debate in Pandemonium). All forms of pseudo- thought, of which there are a rich variety, stem from the self's omnipotence – the delusion that it knows everything and is in control of its destiny; though the significance of this may vary from infantile self-protectiveness to envious destructiveness. This dichotomy between egotistical omnipotence or grandiosity, and inspired learning from emotional experience under the guidance of internal objects, forms the backbone of the literary model of the mind. There is no dichotomy between thinking and feeling; both contribute to the internal evolution of the mind's ideas through a symbolic medium – for as Coleridge insisted, 'an Idea cannot be conveyed but by a symbol'. The symbolic modes of art and poetry represent true thinking because they focus on these internal relationships or identifications, which govern the soul's progress. Wisdom is achievable only through imagination, which enables the self to see inwards to where this internal drama is taking place – 'things invisible to mortal sight' (as Milton said). The concept of 'the mind', since this era of poetry-as-philosophy, is clearly one which distinguishes it from a *tabula rasa* passively awaiting imprints, or from a mechanical tool or computer like the brain. The mind is (as Keats said) 'the soul's own home', a world of its own where 'the creative creates itself': a place where developments are either taking shape or are being thwarted, by internal as much as external forces. These developments must be organic not mechanical; yet it is a type of organism distinct from vegetable nature, since its health or progression depends on imagination or spiritual vision, and does not unfold automatically or freely as in the Rousseauist ideal. Poets have always been emphatic that it is not they themselves but their Muse (from the realms of internal deities or psychoanalytic 'objects') who presents them with their vision: not as a plan or sketch but fully-formed in the words of poetry itself. The concrete language of the symbol is all-important in the process of conveying the idea. As Blake said: 'I am but the Secretary – the Authors are in Eternity.' The Muse is the symbol-making power, and the relationship with the Muse has to be established each time that inspired poetry is written. The very concept of 'inspiration' refers not to some vague gushing, but to this internal identification. This relationship is the key to imagination's being able to operate, and is usually presented as an integral part of the total poem; in shorter lyrics, it often *is* the poem. So not only is poetry a manifestation of creative thought, but also, its underlying subject is the process of creativity itself. It is not a means of wish-fulfilment or substitute reality, governed by omnipotent phantasy (the delusion of being god-like). On the contrary, it expresses the core of mental life;

and its sources of creativity are internal deities outside the control of the self, yet whose ability to act creatively on behalf of the self depends very much on the quality of the self's receptivity. In this way the poets provide an eternal example of the process by which the mind creates itself, through a dynamic network of psychic tensions – a well that never runs dry. They not only provide brave new worlds for our contemplation, but model the pattern for our participation in remaking our own inner world.

In the novels of George Eliot, the individual's drive towards self-knowledge and the author's concern with the creative process are given a fully social dimension. The nature of the growth of the personality is explored in the context of broader familial, social and historical determinants – the 'world of Circumstances' which Keats described as the school for the identity in his 'Vale of Soul-making'. In addition, the novels offer a bridge between the primarily aesthetic and internal concerns of the poet-philosophers, and the context of everyday life within which the patient–therapist relationship evolves its own genre – as adumbrated in the last chapter of this book.

In George Eliot's work, therefore, are unfolded in minutest detail, those myriad internal and external factors which impinge upon an individual's development – either enabling it to proceed, or holding it in abeyance. The 'unmapped country within' finds its realization through the mother tongue of the imagination and through understanding the landscape of childhood. It becomes structured during the resolution of the tension between processes of projection and of receptivity. Moreover in terms of George Eliot's *oeuvre* as a whole, her representations of these experiences are expressed in decreasingly discursive and more idiosyncratic and symbolic ways. Her 'experiments in life' give a rounded definition to the awareness that our idea of the world and of our self-in-the-world is shaped by imagination through the use of symbols, just as the work of art is the product of a vision which, 'fed by susceptibility to the various minutiae of experience', reproduces and reconstructs this world and these relationships (*Theophrastus Such*). Successive novels describe the developmental shift from a primarily narcissistic organization to an object-related one, founded on a character's genuine emotional experience. As they progress, they each bring into sharper perspective the sense that the quest for meaning and value in life necessitates a move away from religious orthodoxy, political systems and philosophical axioms established as part of a mechanistic worldview. Attention is directed, rather, towards the ethical nature of different states of mind and of emotion. The *experience* of emotion is seen increasingly to diverge from the external *display* of emotion, indicative of narcissism.

Correspondingly, in the context of the psychoanalytic process and of the emotional tensions of transference and countertransference, the therapist and patient become oriented to a world being continually reconstructed by the imagination, 'in fresh and fresh wholes', as George Eliot would say. Each partner has to be 'willing to work and to be wrought upon' by the analytic process.

1
SHAKESPEARE: A LOCAL HABITATION AND A NAME

> O brave new world,
> That has such people in't!
> (*The Tempest*, V.i.184–5)

Miranda's exclamation at the end of *The Tempest* undermines its own apparent irony, by throwing an aura of optimistic wonder over the specimens of common humanity assembled before her, who vary from the weak-minded to the irredeemable. The magician Prospero's appetite has become jaded, but there is hope for the world because his sense of wonder has been released to colonize it and change its complexion. Although this is the end of Shakespeare's play and of his life's *oeuvre*, and the playwright has decided to shed his robe and break his staff, we feel that in a sense every Shakespearean play begins like this: with a collection of characters, perhaps aspects of a single mind, who are none of them much more than 'arrant knaves, crawling between earth and heaven' (as Hamlet describes himself). But when they start to become related to each other in the terms of a dramatic poem, animated by the poetic magic, a veil is stripped away and they become facets of a inner world, revealing the mind in the process of working. This applies even to those elements without poetry in themselves – those who, like Antonio, do not know the difference between their conscience and a chilblain. Yet even the hero in a Shakespeare play, well aware of the 'deity' conscience, is not necessarily particularly virtuous or the 'noblest of them all'. He is the one who – in terms of Keats's 'Chamber of Maiden Thought' metaphor – sees the door standing ajar into the next chamber of thought, and begins to move towards it, impelled perhaps by forces which he would like to resist. This movement draws the other characters, who are realigned around him with the increasing inevitability of a network of psychic tensions. Ultimately this may lead to the threshold of a brave new world, in either tragedy or comedy; or we may find, instead, that more has been learnt about the forces which impede development than those which promote it. Bearing in mind this underlying concern with the struggle toward creative thought and development, this chapter will focus on some crucial aspects of a selection of the plays taken in chronological order.

KING RICHARD II

In *Richard II* (1595), Shakespeare can be seen to portray the violent disintegration of a society which is probably, without being aware of it, ripe for destabilization; the chivalric mode is ready to be exchanged for realpolitik. The unified society, or unified mind, is shown to be really at a crisis point, by the ease with which it splits when a perceptive individual refuses to uphold one of its codes – that is, when Richard dismisses the duel between Mowbray and Bolingbroke. The medieval tapestry of the play's background imagery with its composite emblems, of crown, sun, green land, and tree circulating blood, reminds us continually that the very idea of England the mother-country corresponds to some primitive organism which requires the obedience of each component to maintain its health. As king, Richard is both the most dominant component, and the most dependent on the system. Initially, Gaunt in his famous speech about the 'sceptr'd isle' – 'this other Eden, demi-paradise' – presents in poetic terms the reigning vision of a united mind in a rounded space encompassed by the divine crown. It is a space fertile and magically protected like a fortress:

> This fortress built by Nature for herself
> Against infection and the hand of war,
> This happy breed of men, this little world,
> This precious stone set in the silver sea, . . .
> This blessed plot, this earth, this realm, this England,
> This nurse, this teeming womb of royal kings, . . .
> (II.i.43–51)

The blood-relationships which knit together this organism are repeatedly stressed, and they focus on the king, whose existence and authority depend absolutely upon his obedience to the total worldview. The body of the king is sacred in so far as it reflects the body politic, and his mind is almost adhesively identified with the image of the sceptred isle. Should he fail to uphold this identification, his deathbed will be (as Gaunt warns him) 'no lesser than [his] land'. Land, crown, and mind are one: 'incaged in so small a verge' (l. 101). There is an interlude in which the palace Gardeners describe the principles of the commonwealth, intending to condemn Richard for breaking the rules. However, the naive clarity of their analysis serves instead to expose the defects of the system. For while Gaunt's speech conveys the original poetry of the medieval ideal, the Gardener – unintentionally so all the more effectively – highlights its Machiavellian and (spiritually speaking) uneconomic qualities. Thus the Gardeners' solution to social unrest is to lop off the heads of 'great and growing men' because 'all must be even in our government':

> Superfluous branches
> We lop away, that bearing boughs may live;
> Had he done so, himself had borne the crown...
> (III.iv. 63–5)

Richard has already lopped off the head of Gloucester before the play begins; but this in itself is not his crime against society, for if he had allowed a further murder to take place by means of the duel, that crime would have been expiated, in terms of the chivalric code. This would have been acceptable to all parties. It is not murder as such which the social organism abhors, but breaches in its unifying code of behaviour. This code is what keeps the blood circulating in the tree, and the sun or crown protecting the green island, womb of kings; and probably what stops a steady stream of surreptitious haemorrhages from becoming a bloodbath of civil war (the 'Golgotha' prophesied by Carlisle).

But there are signs that a more complex mentality is ready to emerge. Richard, in his position of privilege as mother England's favourite son, has glimpsed the truth about the surreptitious haemorrhages – their wastage of expensively reared blood (which he is entitled to regard as his own), and also the absurdity and playacting which maintains this code of false art. He deflates the 'honour' of Mowbray and Bolingbroke by dismissing the verbose and pompous chivalric ceremony which supports the social fabric, prologue to the aborted duel:

> Let them lay by their helmets and their spears,
> And both return back to their chairs again.
>
> (I.iii.119–20)

They feel their status as cousins to the crown has been ridiculed and undermined. One of them (Mowbray) accepts his fate as one whom the crown has in a sense entombed alive: symbolized by his tongue 'doubly portcullis'd with my teeth and lips' (l. 167); the other (Bolingbroke) implicitly prophesies a new social order in which he will be instrumental: the 'sun will shine' on other lands than Richard's, and the idea of England – no longer fixed but movable – is 'my mother and my nurse that bears me yet' (l. 307).

The drama then focuses on the split between the political and the poetic, which Richard has initiated without foreseeing the consequences. The inevitable rise of Bolingbroke as political leader is interplayed with the downfall of Richard as the poet-politician king of the old England. Bolingbroke himself is not driven by ambition or even revenge, but by the need to reclaim his dignity. The complexity of the story lies in Richard's internal changes as he sharpens himself against Bolingbroke in an attempt to discover what shape his new identity might take. In undermining the old order he has at the same time undermined himself (as Gaunt prophesied, he was 'possessed to depose himself' – a paradoxical degradation). Originally his personal as well as his political mentality was inextricably linked with his view of himself at the top of the tree, borne by the crown, with a narcissistic faith in its magically protective powers. This had its repercussions in his homosexuality, an integral part of the picture. Having dismissed the 'helmets and spears' of his blood-brothers as childish toys, Richard now has to confront the possibility that his own sceptre and crown are also no longer the expression of a divine poetry but mere toys of office. More than that, the crown in becoming 'hollow', is no longer a protector of England's children but a murderer of those who appeared to be her favourites. The teeming womb of royal kings becomes a death's head as it was for Mowbray (an emotional identification which Richard now has to pursue for himself); it is a cage starving its internal children to death, its infant kings

> All murthered – for within the hollow crown
> That rounds the moral temples of a king
> Keeps Death his court, and there the antic sits
> Scoffing his state and grinning at his pomp,
> Allowing him a little breath, a little scene,
> To monarchise, be fear'd, and kill with looks; . . .
> Infusing him with self and vain conceit,
> As if this flesh which walls about our life
> Were brass impregnable; and humour'd thus,
> Comes at the last, and with a little pin
> Bores through his castle wall, and farewell king!
> (III.ii. 160–70)

Richard bids farewell to a kingship which was a delusory place of nurture for body and mind alike, a castle of false art deflated by a pin-prick. In place of the crown, in the deposition scene he takes up a mirror, as if to consider its potential as a symbolic container for the meaning of his inner world:

> O flatt'ring glass,
> Like to my followers in prosperity,
> Thou dost beguile me. Was this face the face
> That every day under his household roof
> Did keep ten thousand men? Was this the face
> That like the sun did make beholders wink?
> Is this the face which fac'd so many follies,
> That was at last out-fac'd by Bolingbroke?
> A brittle glory shineth in this face . . .
> (IV.i. 279–87)

Bolingbroke quietly observes that this also is an act: 'The shadow of your sorrow hath destroyed the shadow of your face'; yet this speech, together with Bolingbroke's reaction (internalized by Richard as a contrary tension to the Mowbray identification) seems to mark Richard's understanding of his 'brittle' narcissism, a genuine self-recognition. He had imagined himself as some Helen of Troy (the 'face which launched a thousand ships' in Marlowe's *Faustus*), whose innate beauty governed England like the sun, rather than simply retaining power according to the principle of rights of succession stated by Bolingbroke.

Yet in Richard's pageantry there is also genuine poetry, just as there was in Gaunt's vision of the sceptered isle; the poetic strand in both the older and the younger generation contrasts with the rhetorical bombast used by the protagonists of the duel. But the poetry is now being split away from the superficial glamour of political office, a split reflected in the shadow of civil war. The Richard who had the perception to find the duel distasteful, uneconomic and unaesthetic, was not wholly deceived in his sense of some innate privilege in spiritual qualities which would accompany him from the sceptred isle, through the hollow crown and the brittle glass, to his ultimate containing symbol (before the grave itself) – the shadow-world of the prison at the end of the play. Bolingbroke, passively and against his will, finds it his destiny to accept the hollow crown which Richard has (also unwillingly) imposed upon him, together with the illusory glamorous shell of a public identity. Thus in the account of his coronation given by York (who is throughout impressed by such externalities), Bolingbroke is seen as a 'well-dress'd actor', a player-king dependent on popular favour; he is 'painted imagery' for the 'greedy' eyes of the gawping multitude (V.ii. 11–17). The face of a united poetic England will never be seen again. Meanwhile Richard, in prison, is faced with a problem which cannot be solved in this play, since the play's action has consisted in singling it out and defining it: namely, how to construct an artistic or poetic identity which is not a shadow but genuine self-expression, a real drama of the mind:

> I have been studying how I may compare
> This prison where I live unto the world . . .
> My brain I'll prove the female to my soul,
> My soul the father, and these two beget
> A generation of still-breeding thoughts,
> And these same thoughts people this little world . . .
> (V.v. 1–9)

This is Richard's first and only soliloquy, despite the impression of soliloquizing given by the declamations of Flint Castle and the deposition scenes. In it, Shakespeare focuses on the condition of the playwright in his solitary but not lonely prison: 'hammering it out' between contrary poles of the mind ('male' and 'female'), and awaiting inspiration from outside the Chamber of Maiden

Thought, the illumination of a brave new world. The prison doors will shortly open to put an end to Richard's life; but before this there is a curious episode, heralded by music, between the ex-king and the Groom who (unacknowledged by him) used to look after his passionate energies in his previous life (the horse now overtaken by Bolingbroke). When Richard finds he cannot perform his creative act unaided, Shakespeare introduces, as in many another play, the unseen music which so often signifies a divine intervention. But here, the music is not harmonious but awkward and jarring, and it takes Richard a while for the meaning of the symbol to penetrate and bring to him the revelation of his true tragic fault: 'I wasted time, and now doth time waste me' (l. 49). Having done this, he can recognize that this inharmonious, uncourtly music (so different from the days of the sceptered isle) is in fact a sign of 'love': that it carries a quality and a meaning which his previous culture and inheritance had prevented him from hearing:

> Yet blessing on his heart that gives it me,
> For 'tis a sign of love; and love to Richard
> In a strange brooch in this all-hating world.
> (ll. 64–6)

The music 'mads' him, but it is the appearance of madness which accompanies the first steps toward insight, with their initial discordance. Richard is now ready to receive (or imagine) the Groom, who is emotionally if not literally associated with this new music. The Groom in Richard's previous existence was the lowest of his minions, but on the threshold of his new mental existence he represents a Hermes-like spirit of communication with lost or unknown emotional depths (the horse). Richard's renewed contact with the ugly and the humble elements of what was once his kingdom reminds him of a beauty which Helen of Troy never possessed, a 'strange brooch' which could supersede all the jewels in the lost hollow crown – his true sources of poetry in the inner world, had he but world enough and time to pursue them. In *Richard II*, therefore, Shakespeare presents a model of mental destabilization, initiated from within, which undermines the system of basic assumptions that had cemented the fabric of society. These centred on the image of the infant-mind (king) protected by the crown-paradise (mother space): an identification which had rigidified into the superficial beauty of narcissism. Gradually this is broken down as some real emotional contacts are made or remade (including that with the queen), and the play ends at the beginning of a new story of reconstruction.

A MIDSUMMER NIGHT'S DREAM

A Midsummer Night's Dream belongs to the same group of 'lyrical' plays of Shakespeare's early maturity as does *Richard II* (written c. 1595). In a sense it begins where *Richard* ends, and presents the making of a philosopher-ruler by means of inspired dreaming rather than omnipotent patronage. The relationship between Richard and the Groom is developed in that between Theseus (at the head of the mental hierarchy) and Bottom, at the other end. The play was probably an epithalamion for an aristocratic wedding; and while most characters display a passionate zest for role-changing and play-acting, Theseus and Hippolyta stand apart statuesquely, scarcely in the role of protagonists. Yet there is a psychological as well as a social reason for this. In a sense, everything that happens in the moonlit wood (and its extension, the mechanicals' play in Act V) happens within the mind of Theseus, and expresses his symbolic endeavour to think about his forthcoming marriage before its actual consummation. Both Oberon and Bottom are his alter-egos, or serve Theseus (the passive self) the function of internal objects; they present creatively an emotional drama and its resolution, in a way which Theseus is not equipped to do for himself. It has often been observed that the opening of the play has all the classic ingredients of a potential tragedy, which then mysteriously and almost accidentally turns into a comedy (while *Romeo and Juliet* does the opposite). At what point does this happen? The death-sentence on Hermia, showing the incompatibility of mechanical 'law' with enlightened 'reason', not only casts a shadow over the Duke's marriage (a species of curse), but also seems to draw attention to an unspoken shadow within his relationship with Hippolyta. He reminds Hippolyta that he won her 'with the sword, doing thee injuries', but hopes to wed her 'in another key' (I.i. 16–18); yet there is a suggestion that this transposition has not been fully made; and Hippolyta, though silent, clearly identifies with the adolescent Hermia, and is not cheered by

Theseus' 'What cheer, my love?' (l. 122). As Duke of Athens, Theseus is ruler of the sunlit citadel of reason; yet he also is unhappy about the ruling and finds himself (like Richard) ostensibly the voice of authority, yet in reality a prisoner within the deathly restrictions of society's basic assumptions – the 'law' which he is pledged to uphold, and for which he is merely a mechanical instrument. Egeus in classical mythology is the father of Theseus, and so he is in spirit in this play: representing a dangerously unappeased primitive omnipotent god at the back of Theseus' mental heritage, who has to feel in control of the puppets of his creation. For the chains of the law are associated with an omnipotent view of art, in which Egeus' daughter is seen as his artefact, 'a form in wax/By him imprinted' (ll. 49–50), rather than a being with a spirit of her own. Theseus' Athens at the beginning of the play is a place of rigidly hierarchical values liable to clamp down and stifle any potential brave new world: even though, as individuals, all the characters (except Egeus himself) believe they are 'in love', or would like to be. A 'new key' is indeed necessary if the aristocratic marriage is to be a happy and creative one.

The turning-point in this tragic situation occurs when Theseus, having delivered the law's verdict, then turns his back and walks off the stage, sweeping everyone with him apart from the star-crossed lovers who are left to their own devices (I.i. 126). The expected guards do not materialize; instead, the inhabitants of the unconscious mind take over the action of the play (the fairies and workmen) to carry on Theseus' internal investigations for him; it is he, as much as Hermia, who needs time to think. In a romance ballad, Theseus would have fallen asleep under a tree at this point while the other characters danced around him; as it is, the mechanicals agree to meet 'at the Duke's oak' in the wood, to prepare him for his wedding day. Through their unconscious interplay with the fairies, with appropriate malapropisms and poetic reversals of verbal reasoning, new imaginative modes of expression are evolved which unearth and catharsize the lover's anxieties and enrich his appreciation of the opposite sex. In the process, the vestigial false aesthetics of the god who imprints 'forms in wax' is overturned, and a new, dynamic, and revelatory idea of creativity emerges. Bottom recognizes immediately that a play about love, if it is to have any emotional validity, must be rehearsed 'obscenely and courageously' (I.ii. 100), and that 'a lion among ladies is a most dreadful thing; for there is not a more fearful wild-fowl than your lion living' (III. i 30). In his ventures into the female world of Titania's fairy court he sets the pattern for genuine 'courtesy', which involves overcoming 'fearfulness' – that is, not simply feeling like a monster who looks frightful, but also, learning not to be afraid of being bitten or of appearing a fool. The union of Bottom with Titania ('Bottom's Dream') is the core revelation at the heart of Theseus' dream, with Bottom acting on behalf of all the men in the play, and Titania on behalf of the women, both turning the appearance of humiliation into the exaltation of humility:

> So doth the woodbine the sweet honeysuckle
> Gently entwist; the female ivy so
> Enrings the barky fingers of the elm.
> O how I love thee! How I dote on thee!
>
> (IV. i. 41–4)

Titania fell asleep in the midst of the mortal adolescent lovers' quarrels in the wood, and lies at the centre of the stage while these are presented to her as part of *her* dream. Her response to their plight is to exchange her role as the chaste huntress Diana for that of Venus, and to momentarily unite with mortality. She becomes their unconscious guide, even though none save Bottom himself actually see her. Bottom is selected for sexual initiation owing to his innate fine qualities – a 'paramour for a sweet voice', as Quince calls him, an 'angel' despite his ass's head:

> *Titania*: And thy fair virtue's force perforce doth move me
>   On the first view to say, to swear, I love thee.
> *Bottom*: Methinks, mistress, you should have little reason for
>   that. And yet, to say the truth, reason and love keep little
>   company together nowadays. The more the pity that some
>   honest neighbours will not make them friends . . .
> *Titania*: Thou art as wise as thou art beautiful.
>
> (III.i. 135–42)

The union of Bottom with Titania, which on the surface appears inappropriate and impossible, is a model for the 'friendship' of other qualities which seem incompatible – such as reason and love, which Theseus with all his education could not unite. With this going on in the depths of his mind, Theseus will gradually discover a way out of his impasse.

Despite the use of the love-juice, this union is not premeditated by Oberon, but falls out accidentally – that is, according to the mind's internal necessity – and is, he says, 'better than I could devise' (III.ii. 35). For Bottom is in a sense another facet of Oberon himself, coming to heal the rift between the Fairy King and Queen. At a level deeper than the exigencies of plot, the play's pageantry shows us that Titania prefers Bottom to Oberon as a lover, not because she has been tricked, but because of his innate gentility – his freedom from obsession with his own power and status. The vague shadow implicit between Theseus and Hippolyta shows as overt hostility in the night-time, woodland world of their fairy counterparts: 'Ill met by moonlight' (II.i 60). Through Bottom, Oberon woos his queen anew. The stories of both the adolescent lovers and of the fairies' past involvement with the mythological Theseus and Hippolyta in their warring, hunting days, link the sedate aristocrats of daylight Athens with turbulent confused forces in their past history – forces which, in the night-world, are no longer past but still very much present. The quarrel over the mysterious, theatrically non-existent 'changeling child', centred on the question of its 'ownership' (like Egeus with Hermia), turns out to be the expression of a problem of identity which it is feared may dissolve or 'die' when the chaste boundaries between male and female or mortal and immortal are crossed and 'entwist' together. Thus Titania tells of her Indian votaress (her mortal self) who died in childbirth whilst in the very process of laughing at man and mortality:

> Full often hath she gossip'd by my side;
> And sat with me on Neptune's yellow sands,
> Marking th'embarked traders on the flood:
> When we have laugh'd to see the sails conceive
> And grow big-bellied with the wanton wind ...
>
> (II.i 125–9)

Her own sails 'conceive' in the dangerous flood of passion, resulting in death; so she refuses to allow Oberon access to her own 'rich merchandise': 'thy fairy land buys not the child of me'. Then her dream of the mortals' predicament, culminating in her encounter with Bottom as an ass, results in a change in her own attitude to men. The relationships of the mind's internal gods are inextricably entwined with the self's development struggles. To serve the present necessity, Bottom in his new humble status becomes godlike, though he is 'but a man, as other men are' (III.i 42). The model for his 'translation' is that of the high priest donning sacred vestments which elevate him beyond his mortal statue: 'Bless thee, Bottom! Thou art translated', is Quince's awe-inspired cry (III.i. 114); and on awaking from his 'most rare vision', Shakespeare has Bottom echo St Paul's revelation:

> The eye of man hath not heard, the ear of man hath not seen, man's hand is not able to taste, his tongue to conceive, nor his heart to report, what my dream was. I will get Peter Quince to write a ballad of this dream: it shall be called 'Bottom's Dream', because it hath no bottom; and I will sing it in the latter end of a play, before the Duke.
>
> IIV.i. 210–16)

In emotional terms, Bottom's Dream is indeed the subject of the mechanicals' play which is performed before the Duke, extending the experience of the wood into another medium and into the court, and providing the ultimate test for Theseus: namely, whether he will be able to accept and assimilate the symbolic, unconscious work which the inhabitants of his mental dukedom have performed on his behalf.

The proving of Theseus occurs during the struggle which he has to accept the true meaning of the workmen's play with all the woodland experience behind it; he has to use his imagination, and recognize that true reason incorporates what appears to be madness. It is not enough for him simply to have found a way of dismissing Egeus' claims on 'the law'. In this final act, Theseus' struggles for the first time have an aura of heroism, since everybody else has reached a plateau of contentment, and he alone is endeavouring to understand what Bottom is able to convey, and not to sink into superiority or complacency, rejecting the profundity of 'a dream that hath no bottom'. The workmen, according to Philostrate, have 'never labour'd in their minds till now'; and Theseus has to learn that, despite all his worldly experience, he also is a species of novitiate in the progress of his earthly body and mind towards the 'hallow'd house' which they become when blessed by the fairy world, the mind's internal governors. In this sacred place he, too, can aspire to be a workman rather than a ruler. On this stage, any elevating vestments are a sign of service not of personal precedence. Before the play begins, Theseus tries to rationalize his doubts about 'antique fables and fairy toys'; but he ends up, despite his conscious intention, in providing the most famous apologia for the reality of the imagination:

> Lovers and madmen have such seething brains,
> Such shaping fantasies, that apprehend
> More than cool reason ever comprehends.
> The lunatic, the lover and the poet
> Are of imagination all compact: . . .
> And as imagination bodies forth
> The forms of things unknown, the poet's pen
> Turns them to shapes, and gives to airy nothing
> A local habitation and a name.
>
> (V.i. 4–17)

This is his counterpart to Bottom's revelation, and prepares him to accept the play, through which he implicitly acknowledges Bottom's dream as his own. Hippolyta here reinforces the concept of the birth of ideas ('bodied forth'), with her image of how the story of the night 'grows to something of great constancy . . . strange and admirable', differentiating this mental transfiguration from the superficial effect of 'fancy's images' (ll. 23–7). This is the basis for Coleridge's future distinction between imagination and fancy. This new aesthetic of symbol formation, catching the 'shapes' to which imagination gives birth and watching them grow, replaces the omnipotent 'wax imprint' aesthetic of the first act, and enables Theseus to recognize Bottom's play as the true epithalamion for his marriage. Despite being told it is not suitable, he insists, 'I will hear that play', for

> Out of this silence yet I pick'd a welcome . . .
> Love, therefore, and tongue-tied simplicity
> In least speak most, to my capacity.
>
> (ll. 100–5)

He chooses their 'tongue-tied simplicity' not from paternalistic indulgence (disguising hidden sneers) but owing to his unconscious remembrance of Bottom being led 'tongue-tied' to the chamber of the Fairy Queen, and to his genuine perception of a 'welcome' available to his own humble novitiate self in the mysteries of love. Ultimately, this enables him to announce that 'tis almost fairy time' (l. 350): to invite the mind's internal gods to step over the threshold, light his house from the inside and bless his bed, so that 'the issue there create/Ever shall be fortunate' (ll. 391–2). In *A Midsummer Night's Dream*, therefore, Shakespeare demonstrates in what sense a 'dream' constitutes 'work'. A rigid hierarchical model of the mind is set aside, while the mind's workmen pursue the nature of imaginative experience, love and revelation, through various aspects of identification between the self and its objects. Poetic language is revivified by this means, and the self released from its preconceptions and inhibitions, and put back in contact with the fairy world of its internal deities, who are themselves restored to harmony. The ruler becomes a learner and therein finds happiness and the promise of creative conception.

HAMLET

In the 'problem plays' of the middle of his career, such as *Hamlet* (1600–01) and *Troilus and Cressida* (1602), Shakespeare pursues relentlessly the nature of the forces which hinder such 'fortunate issue' – such creative thoughts – emerging from the mind's hallowed house. Egeus in *The Dream* is merely a token caricature of such forces. Shakespeare is bitterly critical of plays and acting during this period; 'playing' becomes a byword for manipulation, rather than for discovery-through-art, or fictions about truth-telling. In *Hamlet*, the very structure of the play seems to expand and crack the neat model of the revenge-tragedy which is its anti-type; in this way a latent, metaphorical drama emerges which makes it in effect a dream-play. *Hamlet* explores the internal frustrations and evasions which the soul encounters in its search for symbolic reciprocity or understanding. Hamlet is throughout plagued by the sense that everyone else wants to write his story, play upon his stops, pluck out the heart of his mystery (III.ii 256–7), before he can envisage who he really is, internally: 'Ere I could make a prologue to my brains,/They had begun the play' (V.ii. 30–1). Before the death of the previous king and the subsequent appearance of 'rottenness' and 'sickness' in the state of Denmark, Hamlet is the ideal Renaissance prince, 'the glass of fashion and the mould of form/Th'observed of all observers' (as Ophelia describes him: III.ii 155–6). His shape seems readymade – to others and perhaps also to himself, until he is faced with the necessity for *becoming* a prince, as opposed to merely *acting* the prince through any of the various 'actions that a man might play' – socially acceptable role-playing. Society's pressure on Hamlet to conform is, however, proportional to its unspoken need for him to do something different and to provide a new model of princeship: as in *Richard II*, there are signs of eruption below the complacent prosperous surface of the status quo. Fortinbras is waiting in the wings with his simplistic solution to internal turmoil, and there are 'more things in heaven and earth' than philosophy ever dreamed of (I.v.174–5). We do not know whether the present instability may prove developmental, or reactionary. Hamlet is the 'expectancy and rose of the fair state', the figure on whom the entire mind of Denmark relies for its continuing fruitful evolution and defence against invasion.

Yet the forces of invasion are not merely external, like hot-headed Fortinbras with his 'list of lawless resolutes', but internal, as embodied in the return of the Ghost. The Ghost presents Hamlet with a dual legacy – an accusation of murder goading to revenge and, more puzzlingly, a strange poetic dream about his relationship with the Queen (his wife – or his mother?), which expresses his infant-like vulnerability when he felt expelled from some idyllic Eden-like afternoon sleep in the garden. Ostensibly describing the poison poured through his ear, the Ghost (on the dream-level) describes his sense of unwelcome knowledge in terms of the infant's pure milk curdling and posseting:

> with sudden vigour it doth posset
> And curd, like eager droppings into milk,
> The thin and wholesome blood. So did it mine,
> And a most instant tetter bark'd about,
> Most lazar-like, with vile and loathsome crust
> All my smooth body.
> (I.v. 68–73)

This is the undigested, indigestible emotional constellation which precipitates *Hamlet* as a dream-play, and which lies behind Hamlet's poignant exclamation: 'O God, I could be bounded in a nutshell, and count myself a king of infinite space – were it not that I have bad dreams' (II.ii. 254–6). He begs the Ghost: 'let me not burst in ignorance' (I.iv. 46). This dream, piercing the nutshell of ignorance, lies behind the ambivalence in Hamlet's relationships with his mother and Ophelia, initiated as much by the dawn of love for Ophelia as by the funeral-coronation-marriage of his parent figures. It lies behind his pacing up and down the lobby for hours on end, reading a sterile and circular diet of 'words, words, words' (II.ii. 192), yet debating the shapes of the clouds and their relation to his sense of identity (III.iii. 366). The turbulent experience which drags Hamlet out of his state of quiescent scholarship at Wittenberg poses problems both deeply philosophical and, as he tells Horatio, 'beyond philosophy'. Searching for a relationship which will express for him the meaning of his revolutionary feelings – a symbolic correspondence – Hamlet feels himself in a condition akin to madness; his 'antic disposition' is both his cover and (for want of a better form) his temporary self-expression. In the soliloquy 'To be or not to be', he makes his closest solitary approach to a solution; it is the beginning of a dream about his own identity which both incorporates and exorcizes the Ghost's disturbed inheritance: 'in that sleep of death what dreams may come'? The embryonic soul which has emerged from the womb or entered upon a weaning process ('shuffled off this mortal coil') 'pauses', disoriented in its new nakedness, for unknown 'dreams to come': dreams which lead eventually to the 'pale cast of thought'. Is this death of a previous state of mind a condition to be desired or not? It is the 'undiscovered country, from whose bourne/ No traveller returns' – the unknown inner world:

> Thus conscience does make cowards of us all,
> And thus the native hue of resolution
> Is sicklied o'er with the pale cast of thought,
> And enterprises of great pitch and moment
> With this regard their currents turn awry
> And lose the name of action.
>
> (III.i. 83–8)

The Ghost's injunction was to 'pursue the act' without 'tainting

[his] mind'; but in the inner world, what constitutes action? 'Thought' is initially experienced as a sickness, while the implications of original sin are digested. All the false actions of an externally supported identity ('enterprises of great pitch and moment') are suspended for a moment, including the frenzy of play-acting which is even now going on behind the scenes. The 'sudden vigour' of the Ghost's curdling blood (in the garden dream) is 'turned awry', while the literal disfigurement of his body ('barked about most lazar-like') is transmuted into the 'pale cast of thought', in a metamorphosis of mental elements. Hamlet seems on the verge of finding a symbol for his emotional predicament, and of glimpsing the undiscovered country of his dream-world.

Yet at this very moment, when Hamlet is at his most vulnerable, Ophelia appears, in her fatal position as emissary of Polonius and Claudius, the two father-figures whom Hamlet justifiably feels to be most instrumental in plucking out the heart of his mystery. He immediately turns to her as a sort of saviour and container in which 'all [his] sins' may be 'remembered' (III.i. 90). But when, instead, she says she comes to *return* 'remembrances' to him (l. 92), he feels betrayed, by someone who is not his idea of Ophelia, but a puppet or vehicle for her father. Ophelia and Gertrude both become painted deceptions in Hamlet's eyes; and he commits himself totally at this point to the false, anti-symbolic action of the Mousetrap, which he has been devising to trap his fathers just as they are attempting to trap him. In both cases, an identical process of false investigation is taking place, which treats the 'mystery' of experience as if it were a riddle or secret to be ferreted out of its hiding place. Hamlet calls this 'catch[ing] the conscience of the king'; Polonius calls it finding 'where truth is hid, though it were hid indeed/Within the centre' (II.ii. 158–9). The lobby is an ambiguous space, not unlike the Ghost's purgatory, with potential to be either a chamber of dreams or a prison for nightmares, a nutshell or a trap. But the inner stage on which the Mousetrap is enacted, is an anti-symbolic space, framed by a misconception about the nature of truth. In it, Hamlet caricatures the figures of his inner world and abuses the external characters most intimately associated with his emotional crisis. Here the rhetoric of revenge is indulged to the full: instigated by the Ghost's 'eternal blazonry' and his threats to 'harrow [Hamlet's] soul' (I.v. 15–21). The manic violence aroused by what he deems (despite Horatio's disapproval) to be the Mousetrap's success, leads Hamlet directly to the Queen's chamber, in which he enacts the phantasy of rooting out and exposing (killing) the interfering father–baby who is forever hiding in the skirts of her arras and manipulating her, to the neglect of Hamlet himself. In his obsession with plucking out the heart of his mother's mystery, he has literally speared 'that great baby ... in swaddling clothes' (as he once called Polonius (II.ii. 378)). The following outburst of disgust at his mother and uncle-father from a standpoint of judgmental sanctimony, hides from himself the knowledge that it is he not Claudius, who has just proved a 'cutpurse of the empire' – the empire of his mother's body, his own mind. But Hamlet's unspoken, unconscious remorse at this spectacle leads to a renewed encounter with the Ghost of his father, this time in soft indoor clothing appropriate for intimacy, without chain mail or leprous disfigurement:

> *Hamlet*: ... a vice of kings,
> A cutpurse of the empire and the rule,
> That from a shelf the precious diadem stole
> And put it in his pocket –
> *Queen*: No more.
> *Hamlet*: A king of shreds and patches –
>   *Enter* GHOST
>   (III.iv. 98–103)

Hamlet in effect summons the Ghost by describing his alter-ego, the 'vice'-like aspect split off into Claudius, such that they are on the verge of integration. Gertrude does not see the Ghost, but she sees the ghost in Hamlet, and for the first time seems to realize that there is more within him than passes show. For one long moment, as the triangle of mother, father and son are held by a mutual gaze, there is another approach towards recognition. But – as is the pattern throughout *Hamlet* – this melts away, as the Queen dismisses Hamlet's vision as 'ecstasy' or madness. Ophelia is the only one who literally believes in Hamlet's madness; and in identifying absolutely with this, she comes closest to containing his 'sins' as he had once requested. Her mad speeches with their poetic *double entendres* ('lord we know what we are, but know not what we may be' (IV.v. 43) intuitively sympathize with his 'bursting in ignorance' in his failure to discover or remember internal parents who could lead him out of his impasse.

After the murder of Polonius it becomes clear to Hamlet that his fate is ultimately sealed, and he has lost the chance to create the new princeship within his own life-span, at least. But like Richard, he has almost at the last moment an unexpected chance to recover meaningfulness, from the confines of the grave itself – the space into which Ophelia is finally to sink with all his sins remembered. In the graveyard scene, the Ghost – or at least, the teasing vengeful aspect of the Ghost – seems to re-emerge in the figure of the Gravedigger. In the ensuing punning match, Hamlet finds his enslavement to sterile rhetoric ('words, words, words') outdone by the peasant who is his master in this field – and in the process, exorcized: 'equivocation will undo us' (V.i. 134). This is symbolized in action by the clods of clay and stray bones – the mind's rubbish – which the Gravedigger unearths and chucks aside, in the process reviewing (or so it seems) the decaying history of the entire court of Denmark. With the rubbish removed, a jewel is uncovered: the skull of Yorick, which is seized upon by Hamlet as a genuine symbol, containing the true meaning of his internal parents:

> Alas, poor Yorick. I knew him, Horatio, a fellow of infinite jest, of most excellent fancy. He hath bore me on his back a thousand times, and now – how abhorred in my imagination it is. My gorge rises at it. Here hung those lips that I have kissed I know not how oft. . . . Now get you to my lady's chamber and tell her, let her paint an inch thick, to this favour she must come. Make her laugh at that.
> (V.i. 178–89)

Like Richard with his inharmonious music, the very ugliness of the skull vitalizes the imagination, and leads Hamlet to an image of the lost father for whom he has been searching – not the Player King, or the armoured Ghost, or the tortuous rhetorician Polonius, or the lecherous, ambitious Claudius, but the 'jester' who once enlivened all those aspects of his father and made the court a place of happiness, of 'infinite jest'. Another interpretation is put on the 'vice of kings', the 'king of shreds and patches'. The jester-father of Hamlet's inner world did not exclude him from his own sources of joy but carried the 7-year-old child on his back, easily sustaining the burden. These are the parents not of wish-fulfilment but of 'imagination', including the necessary emotional grit of 'abhorrence'. Hamlet's imagination puts the flesh back on the skull, which then becomes 'my lady's chamber', the female container for the 'sins' which seem an intolerable burden to his naked self alone; the breast nourishing the infant mind can 'laugh' even at these, instead of vengefully curdling the milk. This is the way the inner world was, before the young prince was sent to prep-school at Wittenberg at the age of 7: returning to find that the possibility of falling in love himself, seemed to have turned his mother into a lust-blinded matron, and his father into a cross between a drunken satyr and a senile policy-monger. So in *Hamlet*, Shakespeare tackles the painful depths and complexity of the soul's search for the mystery of its own identity. In the continual vacillations of both Hamlet and others between regarding this as an awesome mystery and alternatively as a tantalizing riddle to be prised open, Shakespeare shows how integral is the problem of symbol formation (or symbol perception) to the mind's self-knowledge. The cloudy identity of the new prince-to-be, desperately needed by the over-ripe state of Denmark, cannot resolve into its true shape without a clearly established relationship between the self and its internal objects. And Hamlet is frustrated by himself and by others in achieving more than momentary glimpses of this internal foundation.

TROILUS AND CRESSIDA

Troilus and Cressida, Shakespeare's next serious play (discounting *The Merry Wives*), expresses his enraged hostility and contempt for the voyeuristic philistinism which was (perhaps inevitably) excited in relation to the depth and sensitivity of the artistic explorations in *Hamlet*. The play addresses an audience (originally, possibly one of young lawyers at the Inns of Court) which is accused of going to the play as if to a brothel, prompted by an instinct for pornography and ideological wordplay, and hence becoming bawds to their own minds. An armed Prologue announces that he does not come 'in confidence/Of author's pen or actor's voice', and is taking an aggressive stance towards the audience; there is to be no confiding here, as there was in *Hamlet*.

The epilogue is delivered by Pandarus, who speaks explicitly to the audience as to all panders – 'good traders in the flesh', 'brethren and sisters of the hold-door trade'; beneath their 'painted cloths' lie the 'aching bones' of venereal disease. In *Troilus and Cressida* the playwright, armed and angry, offers a specific type of audience-mentality a mirror image of itself: 'do as your pleasures are . . . 'tis but the chance of war' (Prologue 30–1). The pervading linguistic texture of the play is one in which flocks of metaphysical abstractions are generated like flatus by a seething mass of indigestible cookery and bodily malfunctions. The 'stewed phrases' of pornography's language-games revolve in the 'hot digestion of this cormorant war' (II.ii. 6); love is a 'generation of vipers' (III.ii. 129) and the pageant of pride 'bastes' itself in the cooking-pot (II.iii.186). In this context, Greeks and Trojans are not heroic contraries, but blind basic-assumption groupings, in which a sense of status is substituted for a sense of identity. Inevitably, each camp is conditioned to select its most stupid member to be president – manipulated by the decision-makers to wave the banner. Thus the 'elephant Ajax' in the Greek camp has his counterpart in the 'ransack'd queen' Helen, at the pinnacle of Trojan values. The background atmosphere is a farcical mixture of soap opera, sports match (the 'sport' of bed or battle), and election campaign. And Cressida, as she well knows, is expected by everyone to follow the example of Helen – the willing passive monument to the play's equation of woman, the city and art, as fields to be 'toppled', conquered and degraded.

The buzzwords of the Greek camp are: distinction, degree, policy, wisdom, dignity and import. The specialized function of Ulysses (the master-contriver) is to rearrange 'degree' within its disturbed ranks so that mutual subservience can be achieved and the army become an effective fighting machine again:

> Take but degree away, untune that string,
> And hark what discord follows. Each thing melts
> In mere oppugnancy; the bounded waters
> Should lift their bosoms higher than the shores,
> And make a sop of all this solid globe . . .
> (I.iii. 109–13)

To admire this Renaissance soap-box cant as 'Shakespearean' is to fall into the trap of being the type of audience Shakespeare is attacking. The underlying assumption of the play is that the intransigent (female) world whose 'saucy boat ... co-rivals greatness' (in Nestor's words) or lifts its bosom higher than the shore, must be brought to heel: 'distinction ... winnows the light away', as Agamemnon says (l. 28). They voice the perennial anxiety of the fascist or totalitarian mind, that without 'distinction' and 'degree' there must be 'chaos' (l. 125). The present problem of the Greek council is that Achilles, who is their prize tool for maintaining order, has gone 'womanish' and spends his time with his 'masculine whore' Patroclus, making a 'pageant' of the Greek hierarchy and ridiculing it, undermining Ulysses' position as the ruling intellect:

> They call this bed-work, mapp'ry, closet-war
> So that the ram that batters down the wall,
> For the great swing and rudeness of his poise,
> They place before his hand that made the engine,
> Or those that with the fineness of their souls
> By reason guide his execution.
> (I.iii. 205–10)

Ulysses, an extension of the Egeus-mentality, represents the false artist who believes his own 'fineness' or 'reason' manipulates his tools (the 'ram') in a type of sordid 'bed-work' which will batter down the wall of the city of art. The battering-ram Achilles has rebelled, but Ulysses contrives to seduce him by appealing to his sense of fashionability: presuming (correctly) that this is the 'touch of nature' which makes him 'kin' with everybody else in the play. If Achilles is not admired in the eyes of others, there is little point in his rebellion against Ulysses and the principle of order. Ulysses reminds him that

> to have done is to hang
> Quite out of fashion, like a rusty nail
> In monumental mockery ...
> One touch of nature makes the whole world kin –
> That all with one consent praise new-born gauds ...
> (III.iii. 151–76)

He undermines Achilles by insinuating that, through his police-state information service, he is somehow inside his head, in the place where 'thoughts unveil in their dumb cradles':

> There is a mystery, with whom relation
> Durst never meddle, in the soul of state,
> Which hath an operation more divine
> Than breath or pen can give expressure to.
> (ll. 199–203)

The tyranny of the omniscient 'watchful state' is the archetypal anti-artistic stance, subverting the individual's thinking processes and the artist's 'breath or pen', and hijacking the language of creativity – mystery, birth, divinity. In the event, however, all Ulysses' tyrannical psychical manipulations are themselves subverted when the basic-assumption mentality which he has been using, gets beyond his control; and Ajax (the Achilles-substitute) instead of fighting Hector in a duel, is overcome by the pseudo-revelation of their kinship, in the ludicrous episode of 'my sacred aunt' (IV.v. 133). Shakespeare's point is that tyrannical structures based on the enforcement of codes rather than the growth of true value-systems are ultimately not even effective: resulting in the football-hooliganism quality of the last battle, in which the two sides start 'clapper-clawing' and eventually 'swallow' one another (in Thersites' words: V.iv. 1, 34).

In this play, Shakespeare shows how the hooligan gangster mentality is by no means the prerogative of the lower classes but is generated by the highly educated. Thus the Trojan court embodies a sophisticated sub-mentality precisely equivalent to that of the Greek camp, with its own set of buzzwords: value, honour, worth, truth, merit, taste, estimation, right. Their academic debate ('What's aught but as 'tis valued?') focuses on Troilus' narcissistic excitement at his approaching union with Cressida (though this is of course not overtly confessed, since it is a union both clandestine and public). He argues,

> how may I avoid,
> Although my will distaste what it elected,
> The wife I choose? There can be no evasion
> To blench from this and to stand firm by honour.
> We turn not back the silks upon the merchant
> When we have soil'd them, nor the remainder viands
> We do not throw in unrespective sieve
> Because we now are full.
> (II.ii. 66–73)

He has not yet met Cressida; but this speech foreshadows the inevitable history of their abortive love, since it expresses a mentality in which the very idea of love presupposes a 'soiled' object, modelled on the 'ransack'd' Helen. It is a pervading assumption which Cressida has already recognized, despite her cloistered existence observing the world from a 'watch tower'; anticipating Ulysses' words to Achilles, she tells Pandarus 'Things won are done' (I.ii.292). According to the Trojan code here perfectly expressed by Troilus in his institutional maiden speech, the woman is inevitably violated in accepting the man and therefore will inevitably become 'false as Cressida' (as in their strange marriage pact). But this in itself is an excellent opportunity for narcissistic gratification, since it reinforces his own worthiness, that of an 'eternal and fixed soul' which will never betray its code. Troilus' elder brothers are indulgently impressed by his grasp of what it takes to be officer material. Cressida, however, is less easily reassured. During the few minute scraps of dialogue which she has alone with him, she attempts to inject some fear, respect and realism into the concept of love between them. Troilus indeed has expressed to Pandarus his fear of losing 'distinction':

> I fear it much; and I do fear besides
> That I shall lose distinction in my joys, . . .
> (III.ii. 24–5)

He has some sense of the power of love to dissolve his system of codes, but is frightened and repelled by Cressida's voicing the same feeling: her 'fears have eyes', she says, but it is better to acknowledge fear and be led by reason, than to deny its existence: 'Blind fear, that seeing reason leads, finds safer footing than blind reason stumbling without fear. To fear the worst oft cures the worse' (III.ii. 69–71). Troilus is filled with anxiety because she is speaking to a level of deep emotional reality which he recognizes but would prefer to deny, and which suggests that she knows more about love than he supposed, immediately prompting the suspicion – are all women whores, even when they are virgins? (Shakespeare's Cressida is not a widow, like Chaucer's.) Immediately Troilus takes shelter in his code, and praises his own virtue:

> Few words to fair faith: Troilus shall be such to Cressida as what envy can say worse shall be a mock for his truth, and what truth can speak truest, not truer than Troilus.
>
> (ll. 94–7)

In this way he avoids the exploration of uncomfortable feelings – including why he should imagine he is soiling her in the first place, or guilt about the vulnerability of her social position as the daughter of a traitor, or later in the Greek camp where she is given the choice of being 'whore' either to Diomed or to the Greeks 'in general', as Ulysses puts it (IV.v. 21). Although he insists he is a man of chivalry and of 'few words', this is another facet of his identity-shielding code; in fact like Ulysses, he is obsessed with his own rhetoric, and is displeased when Cressida interrupts him before he has finished his 'protestations'. In flight from all emotional reality, Troilus concentrates on writing his posthumous reputation, when 'fame [will] canonize us' and

> 'As true as Troilus' shall crown up the verse
> And sanctify the numbers.
>
> (III.ii. 180–1)

Thus the story of Troilus and Cressida, though it takes up little space in the play as a whole, is at the core of its presentation of false art and of relationships based on status-shuffling and emotional unreality. The link between the abortive lovers, presided over by the Ulysses-mentality, is mirrored in that between play and audience; but it is a vision reflected back by the playwright implying that it is they, not he, who regard the play as soiled goods; and that this rigid, narcissistic attitude to art will eventually lead to the destruction of their own minds.

KING LEAR

The deaths of Richard and of Hamlet are in a sense accidental; they mean that the play has come to an end, rather than that a spiritual struggle has been completed and a brave new world achieved. This is not so in the true or archetypal tragedies such as *King Lear* (1605) or *Antony and Cleopatra*. In these, the deaths of the protagonists represent a genuine catastrophic change in the mental world of the play as a whole; death is a point of metamorphosis, not of closure. *Lear* is perhaps the quintessential expression of a phase in the infant-mind's development: presenting the stages of loss of omnipotence, turbulent disintegration, and ultimate recovery of aesthetic vision, which underpin the mind's capacity to create itself. The struggle in *Lear* is between the thirst for wisdom or self-knowledge ('salvation'), and the temptations of ignorant omnipotence ('damnation'). In Keats's words in his sonnet 'On sitting down to read King Lear once again':

>   once again, the fierce dispute
>   Betwixt damnation and impassioned clay
>   Must I burn through.

Damnation is the 'barren dream' of false or uninspired art; salvation consists in the metamorphosis of 'impassioned clay', burning until it rises phoenix-like from the ashes, living through the emotional crisis and submitting to the structural change which this entails. The great fire of Lear's wrath, and the lesser fire of Gloucester's lust, provide the passionate momentum which carries them through these transformations and is purged in the process. Lear is the archetypal passionate baby who believes he has decided to wean himself from the kingdom of his mother and whose rage is aroused when his omnipotent arrangements for this are not obediently followed: 'Come not between the Dragon and his wrath' (I.i. 122). Instead, he is faced with the unbearable suspicion that she is relieved to be separated from him. Goneril and Regan (who become cruel or bad aspects of the mother) believe that he has 'ever slenderly known himself' (I.i 293) and that his rage is genuinely intolerable: saying 'let us hit together' (l. 303) and, when they finally shut him out of the house, 'wisdom bids fear' (II.iv. 309). Meanwhile the banishment of Cordelia, who offers a 'kind nursery', is considered by the Fool to be 'a blessing' for her, done 'against [Lear's] will' (I.iv. 108). Lear's hundred knights – his mythical powers – melt away, and he prepares to experience the violence of his emotions, in the form of the storm, for the first time turned against himself, uncontained by the mother to whom he is no longer king:

>   you unnatural hags,
>   I will have such revenges on you both
>   That all the world shall – I will do such things,
>   What they are, yet I know not, but they shall be
>   The terrors of the earth. You think I'll weep;

> No, I'll not weep:
> I have full cause of weeping, [*storm heard*], but this heart
> Shall break into a hundred thousand flaws
> Or ere I'll weep. O Fool! I shall go mad.
>
> (II.iv. 280–9)

When this happens, the Fool comes into prominence as Lear's only support: partly because he represents the means of spiritual contact with Cordelia – being her shadowy representative, 'pining away' since she left for France (I.iv. 78), yet clinging to Lear as long as he is needed. Also, the Fool supports Lear's mental struggle by suggesting an avenue out of his egocentricity; he is Lear's real child-soul, the 'little tiny wit' (III.ii. 74) through whom he maintains contact with emotional reality – expressed partly through sensuous awareness of cold, hunger, and the battling of the elements. When Lear asked why the Fool had become so 'full of songs', he explained:

> e'er since thou mad'st thy daughters thy mothers; for when thou gav'st them the rod and putt'st down thine own breeches,
>
> > Then they for sudden joy did weep,
> > And I for sorrow sung,
> > That such a king should play bo-peep,
> > And go the fools among.
>
> (I.iv. 179–85)

The Fool's upsurge of creativity is intimately connected with Lear's newly demoted status in the nursery. Responding to this, Lear's attitude to the Fool changes as the storm progresses, from one of petty paternalistic tyranny (such as, threatening to whip him) to one of solicitude, in line with his acceptance of his own faults as a ruler ('I have ta'en too little care of this'):

> My wits begin to turn.
> Come on, my boy. How dost, my boy? Art cold?
> I am cold myself. Where is this straw, my fellow?
> The art of our necessities is strange,
> And can make vile things precious. Come, your hovel.
> Poor Fool and knave, I have one part in my heart
> That's sorry yet for thee.
>
> (III.ii. 67–73)

The discovery of a maternal aspect within himself – an internal idea of what Cordelia would have done – is inextricable from the coming 'madness' which accompanies his world's disintegration. He must throw off the 'lendings' of a superficial status which have disguised the 'unaccommodated man' within (III.iv. 109) and shielded him from emotional experience.

Halfway through the drama, the function of the Fool is superseded by Edgar as Poor Tom. He is discovered in the 'hovel' (the primitive depths of Lear's mind) by the Fool, who is shocked to see the form which his transmigrating soul is destined to take: 'Come not in here, Nuncle; here's a spirit' (III.iv. 39). Nevertheless Edgar is to become Lear's next 'philosopher' (l. 159), while the original Fool dies, his role completed – 'going to bed at noon' in Platonic sunlight (III.vi. 88).Through Edgar, the struggles of Lear and Gloucester coalesce. Edgar embodies the type of the nascent inspired poet who is drawn into the action against his will, forced to enter in to the emotional states of others: 'Edgar I nothing am' (II.iii. 21). With negative capability, he performs the spiritual services which are required by the mind as a whole: 'I cannot daub it further . . . and yet I must' (IV. i. 51–3); he must carry the story on though his 'heart breaks' (IV.vi. 143). The Fool saw that Lear had to 'go the fools among' and play bo-peep amongst the others in the nursery, no longer uniquely privileged. Edgar sees that Lear is both a child, and a knight on a quest: 'Childe Rowland to the dark tower came' (III.iv. 186). He restores him to the type of folly or madness which precedes spiritual philosophy: just as he will lead eyeless Gloucester, who 'stumbled when [he] saw' (IV.i.19), to 'see feelingly' with inner vision (IV.vi. 150). Edgar, who is the structural hero of the play, draws his inspiration from twin sources or fathers, and becomes for both of them the representative of the brave new world. For Gloucester, Edgar and Edmund represent antithetical aspects of his own mind's potential for being either inspired or omnipotent. His confusion at the beginning of the play as to which of them is the 'bastard' reflects his deep insecurity about his own creativity, and the nature of the 'act of darkness' in which they were conceived. One of his 'sons' (or mental directions) is guided by an internal deity described by Edmund as 'whoremaster man' – offering a 'divine thrusting on' to his social ambition (I.ii. 125–40), a restless, promiscuous attitude to the world which (as Edmund's later attitude to Goneril and Regan shows) is not even motivated by genuine lust. The 'little fire' of genuine lechery – Gloucester's essential spark of life – turns out to have produced Edgar rather than Edmund, not the 'dull, stale, tired bed' Edmund imagines (l. 13). This we learn from the imagery of the meeting on the heath, which in a sense re-enacts the original act of darkness within Gloucester's mind, and restores him to contact with creative internal objects. In this beautiful recognition scene, Gloucester appears at night across the heath with a torch, and the Fool emblemizes his spiritual quest with the comment: 'a little fire in a wild field were like an old lecher's heart' (III.iv. 114). The old lecher is unconsciously searching for the guiding light of his creative 'son' who inhabits the darkness of his mind somewhere – 'lurk, lurk' as Edgar murmurs. Yet he vacillates; and only after Goneril and Regan have 'tied him to the stake' and literally destroyed his vacillating vision, is he able to commit himself to this alternative course, when compromise is impossible: 'They have tied me to the stake, and I must stand the course' (III.vii. 53). Thus the wild and barren heath becomes the womb or cradle of mental fertility for both Lear and Gloucester, a Vale of Soul-making where conception can occur. Once Gloucester's eyes are removed, he returns to the place where he first encountered Poor Tom: unconsciously recognizing him as his son, and seeking out this 'worm' as a substitute for the 'vile jelly' of his own extinguished eyesight:

> I'th' last night's storm I such a fellow saw,
> Which made me think a man a worm. My son
> Came then into my mind; and yet my mind
> Was then scarce friends with him.
>   (IV.i. 32–5)

Gloucester has reached the stage at which interpenetration has become possible between his new and old self; his mind has become 'friends' with the child who will prove father to the man. Dependence on 'the worm' images the mind's acceptance of its embryonic new identity: the process of conception itself. The new idea, Edgar, has mysteriously entered through some unconscious identification, and taken root.

Gloucester's conscious recognition towards the end of the play of the son who has been his spiritual gift, rather than his omnipotent creation, results immediately in the completion of his story – his heart 'bursts smilingly'. His little fire has always been weaker and less stubborn than the great fire of Lear's nature; instead of forging forwards on his spiritual journey towards Dover as does Lear, he has required continual propping up and tying to the stake, by both Edgar and Lear himself – who offers sage advice (of the sort which he could never stomach himself) to this fellow novitiate pilgrim:

> Thou must be patient; we came crying hither:
> Thou know'st the first time that we smell the air
> We wawl and cry.
> (IV.vi. 180–2)

Lear's story has a two-stage resolution: first, reunion with Cordelia; then, parting with Cordelia and handing over to Edgar. The initial reunion represents an idyllic false ending, a sort of return to the womb of adhesive, inseparable emotional security and mutual understanding:

> We two alone will sing like birds i'th' cage . . .
> And take upon's the mystery of things,
> As if we were God's spies: and we'll wear out,
> In a wall'd prison, pacts and sects of great ones
> That ebb and flow by th'moon.
> (V.iii. 9–19)

Lear would like to retreat back into Plato's cave and forever watch the shadows on the wall, secure in his feeling that he is at the heart of the mystery of his mother, and that his good mother Cordelia (his cordial, heart's elixir) would never be so cruel as to wean him and send him out into the world. But this womblike security must be shed – imaged in Cordelia's body becoming 'dead as earth'; and Lear's ultimate heroic effort of imagination, in which he believes he sees the spirit emerging from her lips, enables him finally to relinquish his omnipotent hold on the 'daughter' or creative spirit of his inner world. In *King Lear*, therefore, Shakespeare presents a parable of the false 'lendings' of a delusory infantile omnipotence being stripped to reveal unaccommodated man at the centre of his own internal tempest, the scene of catastrophic change. From this worm-self in its heart of darkness, a new identity is generated, via the language of folly and madness which express the 'blindness' of inner vision and true feeling – 'what we feel, not what we ought to say'. It comes to be embodied in Edgar, whose negative capability subsumes the emotional trauma of his two fathers, while through him they recognize their dependent status and, ultimately, joyously relinquish their previous identities in favour of the spirit of the new world to which they have given birth.

MACBETH

Hamlet follows the frustration of the intelligent and joyous soul's attempt to clamber out of the debris which has been heaped upon it by external and internal forces, and to make a creative relationship based on a truthful understanding of its inner life and godlike figures. In *Macbeth* (1606), Shakespeare analyses a specific problem of perversion, a 'mind diseas'd' (V.iii. 40): a mind which would appear to be of a simpler and perhaps nobler complexion than Hamlet's, save for its dependence on its perverse partner – a Jekyll and Hyde combination. As the background deities – the three witches – indicate, it is the perversion of femininity which is being explored; focusing on Macbeth himself. Initially Macbeth's own feminity is known to exist as the 'milk of human kindness' of which Lady Macbeth feels he has too much (I.v. 17). But the violent and bloody atmosphere of continual civil war which pervades Scotland in the play, is an inhospitable background for femininity's survival. The gentle, noble Macbeth appears to have picked a wife whose 'masculine' nature will compensate for his own feminine one during the periods when he is not actually fighting – when as 'Bellona's bridegroom' he can forget himself (I.ii. 55). We meet Macbeth at a point of transition between the bloody haze of the battlefield, and his domestic life – which can at a stroke be converted into a continuation of that bloody haze. The first words to unite Macbeth, his wife, and the witches in our mind, are those which Lady Macbeth reads from the letter announcing his return as Thane of Cawdor: 'They met me in the day of success'. 'Success' is a crucial concept in the play, and essentially it refers to the type of delusion which is socially countenanced – represented by the murky, red-hazed, smoke-filled atmosphere generated by 'unseaming from the nave to the chops' (I.ii. 22) and being hero-worshipped for it. 'More is thy due than more than all can pay', Duncan tells Macbeth prophetically (I.iv. 21). The witches themselves seem to be precipitated out of this atmosphere, taking on a momentary solidity then dissolving back into the pall of unnatural darkness which hangs over the earth, obscuring its normal complexion:

> Fair is foul, and foul is fair:
> Hover through the fog and filthy air.
> (I.ii. 11–12)

The witch-world of equivocation ('the fiend that lies like truth': V.v. 44) is the opposite of poetic ambiguity; it represents the false clothing of the lie (a consistent metaphor in the play). Macbeth's bloody deeds earn him adulation and the 'borrow'd robes' of new titles (I.iii. 108), thereby confirming the equivalence of success and of false identity. 'Was the hope drunk/Wherein you dress'd yourself?' demands Lady Macbeth (I.vii. 35–6). The ideas of success and of witch-femininity are inseparable; and Macbeth's subservience to their offer of the 'golden round' (I.v. 27) means, as he recognizes soon after the murder, the loss of his 'eternal jewel', his soul (III.i. 60–9). The counter-concept to 'success' in the play is 'growth', though this exists throughout as a shadowy suggestion of that which has been lost, aborted, or made impossible: we see it in the vulnerability of the Macduff home with its unguarded internal children, or in Macbeth's fleeting vision of 'Pity like a naked new-born babe' (I.vii. 21). There is no place in the play for the type of masculinity which is protective of growth; Macduff is no less a 'traitor' in this than Macbeth; while Shakespeare makes clear that the masculinity which is socially esteemed is in reality a type of perverted femininity, a manifestation of the witch-mind.

Lady Macbeth's castle represents the outward feminine aspect of herself, or of herself and Macbeth taken together as a couple. It is taken by Duncan at its surface value as an idyllic haven or 'cradle' for 'temple-haunting martlets', a source of security and nurture for the spirits who cling to its 'jutty, frieze and buttress' (I.vi. 1–6). But in reality the buttresses are those of 'Hell Gate' as in the Porter scene, inhabited by the ravens of revenge:

> The raven himself is hoarse,
> That croaks the fatal entrance of Duncan
> Under my battlements.
> (I.v. 38–41)

Lady Macbeth converts fair into foul with 'unsex me here', making her castle-body into a trap rather than a haven, in a version of the Clytemnaestra legend. As with Iphigeneia, the idea of a murdered child perpetrates the revenge cycle; and though it is here introduced by Lady Macbeth, it touches deep springs of guilt in Macbeth associated with his wartime identity, which make him acquiesce: 'Bring forth men-children only!' he says admiringly after Lady Macbeth's image of infanticide:

> I have given suck, and know
> How tender 'tis to love the babe that milks me:
> I would, while it was smiling in my face,
> Have pluck'd my nipple from his boneless gums,
> And dash'd the brains out, had I so sworn
> As you have done to this.
>
> (I.vii. 54–9)

In this context, Duncan with his white-haired saintly innocence, comes to symbolise the Macbeths' child, who – like the cherub in Macbeth's soliloquy about the new-born babe, or Lady Macbeth's image of 'Heaven' – might 'peep through the blanket of the dark,/To cry, hold, hold!' (I.v. 53–4). The thing which is murdered between them is not the king alone, nor a child alone, but the possibility of creativity itself – Thought, Sleep, and all the inhabitants of mental life: 'Macbeth does murther Sleep – the innocent Sleep' (II.ii. 35). Only after symbolically murdering this child does Macbeth realize the significance of his being king yet having no heirs – a fact which he knew before yet which seemed irrelevant until he became *emotionally* heirless, and imaginatively sterile. The spiritual murder which is demanded by total dedication to the 'golden round', the 'imperial theme', to social mastery, results in the self becoming fearful and terrified of revenge by those internal gods who have now been turned into witches. Soon after the murder, Macbeth's poetic language ceases, and he becomes obsessed with trying to act before he can think: 'be it thought and done', or

> Strange things I have in head, that will to hand,
> Which must be acted, ere they may be scann'd.
>
> (III.iv. 138–9)

In the fearful condition of internal emptiness, the word 'safe' comes to mean 'dead' (III.iv. 24). Macbeth's imagination dries up, and in lieu of symbol formation and thinking, appears a mental space filled or blocked by hallucinations, with a solid faecal actuality:

> the time has been,
> That, when the brains were out, the man would die,
> And there an end; but now, they rise again,
> With twenty mortal murthers on their crowns,
> And push us from our stools.
>
> (III.iv. 77–81)

The hallucinations, like the witches, seem precipitated out of the atmosphere, in a conglomeration of poisons, entrails and deformities, stewed in 'double double' equivocation.[1] Macbeth's obsessive reaction to these hallucinations is to try to erase them, to wipe them from his mind in an authoritarian clean-up operation; instead of 'heirs' which are denied to him, he starts to look for a condition which is 'safe', 'clean', with 'no botches' in it: 'The very firstlings of my heart shall be/The firstlings of my hand' (IV.i. 147–8). This botch-less condition is one in which *everyone* is dead, and he is 'perfect' (III.iv. 20), in complete control of the stool-like evacuations (firstlings) of the omnipotent mind, which are all that is left him now the imaginative inner world has been destroyed. The possibility of living out the future, either through actual heirs or through the spiritual heirs of an imaginative developing mind, has been replaced by the delusion of 'knowing the future' – that is, of controlling the future: a function of the witch-mind and essentially a misconception, a substitute for true thinking.

The play *Macbeth* offers no real alternative to this destroyed state of mind. The ultimate denouement is a circular one rather than an achievement of integration between the split 'Macbeth' and 'Macduff' aspects of femininity. The two families and castles (one heirless, the other initially full of children but made heirless before our eyes in an instant), suggest split aspects of one mind, which finds it impossible to develop or even survive in the prevailing social context, in which to be 'successful' means to be a 'bloody butcher' of the mind's internal contents. There is no catharsis in Macbeth's ultimate defeat; he is simply obliterated by the same primitive mentality that prevailed at the beginning of the play, with its Greek tragedy atmosphere of an eternal revenge cycle in which nothing can come to fruition since it is bound to the past. When Macbeth finally gives himself to Macduff (which is in effect what happens), it is as though the mind of Scotland has made the switch from its wartime to its domestic mentality, and recovered from a species of nervous breakdown; yet we feel that this is a reversible pattern which may yet be endlessly repeated. Nothing in the play's conclusion approaches the depths of recognition which Macbeth in fact achieves in his lonely last soliloquy, encapsulating the meaning of meaninglessness:

> To-morrow, and to-morrow, and to-morrow,
> Creeps in this petty pace from day to day,
> To the last syllable of recorded time;
> And all our yesterdays have lighted fools
> The way to dusty death. Out, out, brief candle!
> Life's but a walking shadow; a poor player,
> That struts and frets his hour upon the stage,
> And then is heard no more: it is a tale
> Told by an idiot, full of sound and fury,
> Signifying nothing.
>
> (V.v. 19–28)

These magnificent lines are inspired by the news of his wife's suicide and by awareness of the grief that is not there; she represents his 'brief candle' as in her sleepwalking – the soul that is but a 'shadow', the pageant of the 'mind diseas'd'. Here, Macbeth paradoxically brings us closer to hope for imagination's rebirth than does the official pageant of Birnam wood marching to restore Nature's order. He has recovered the ability to express the truth about his inner self; the figure of 'pity like a new-born babe' recurs here, in the idiot-infant who wails 'full of sound and fury,/Signifying nothing': the infant who, as throughout the play, symbolizes Macbeth's own creative soul. In the course of *Macbeth*, therefore, the potential new identity or increment in the sense of identity which is represented by the 'babe' image throughout, is suffocated before birth by the pervading witch-mentality, a perversion of femininity. This is applied to Macbeth through his wife, and in succumbing to it, he finds that his capacity to think becomes aborted: poetic language is replaced by hallucinatory forms of fear, denuded of emotional content – the very antithesis of dream-symbols. Instead of revealing meaning to him, these stimulate him to compulsive repetitive murderous actions. This is Shakespeare's analysis of a mind diseased; and as Macbeth's last soliloquy suggests, the very symbolization of this condition is the first step in recovery from it.

THE WINTER'S TALE

The reparative march of Birnam wood in *Macbeth* is a fiction superimposed on the play's real emotional substance. But the concept of 'great creating nature' in *The Winter's Tale* (1611) is a genuine inspirational force, describing the restoration of female fertility goddesses to preside over the mind after its sterile winter of discontent. The romances or dream-plays of the culmination of Shakespeare's career all focus single-mindedly on the mental conditions in which creativity may flourish. Macbeth's diseased mind, his sense of meaninglessness, is transferred to different soil for its regeneration. The winter's tale of the fragile, omnipotent self is a dreary one full of ghosts and graveyards, like that of Mamillius; but the winter's tale of the hibernating, chrysalid self watered by its own tears of repentance, is one of underground growth, closely monitored by deities of the unconscious mind. Leontes says, 'tears shall be my recreation' (III.ii. 240); he places his mind in the lap of 'great creating nature' based in Bohemia (IV.iv. 88). The implications of this dormant, creative winter are imaged in the brilliant sunlight and floral fecundity of the Bohemian sheep-shearing feast which lies at the heart of the play and colours its overall atmosphere. And when Leontes surrenders control over his diseased mind to Paulina, who is as it were the high priestess of this mental landscape, his self-induced sterile winter is transformed into the living soil of re-creation. The growth of Perdita – unknown to him – represents the unconscious development of his own mind during this dark period, and his child-self or lost principle of development and joy; when she returns, she is 'welcome . . . as spring to th'earth' (V.i. 150), and the bringer of inspiration. The underlying myth of Proserpine vibrates through the play – a myth to be used by Milton and Keats, also, as a metaphor for the poetic process. Proserpine–Perdita is snatched away into a dormant period of apparent death; when spring returns, she not only revitalizes the earth, but also restores the earth's goddess, Ceres–Hermione, whose name suggests that of Mnemosyne, the Muse. It transpires that Leontes' muse was not dead, but entombed in stone: that he had destroyed not the internal deity herself, but merely his own access to her. This is the link which Paulina, a combination of conscience and artist, helps him to forge anew.

In the first section of the play, in Leontes' court, we are presented with an idealized myth about Leontes and Polixenes like 'boys eternal', narcissistically identified:

> We were as twinn'd lambs that did frisk i' th' sun,
> And bleat the one at th'other: what we chang'd
> Was innocence for innocence: we knew not
> The doctrine of ill-doing, nor dream'd
> That any did . . .
>
> (I.ii. 67–71)

This idealization disguises an unspoken mutual dislike between the two grown 'lambs', and obliterates from recognition the distress of Mamillius, the real child, at the prospect of the new baby, since he is likewise supposed to be a frisking lamb, 'as like as eggs' to his father (I.ii. 130). Indeed in a sense, the figure of Mamillius on the stage *is* Leontes himself – a concrete projection of his mental age. He disappears (dies) when this period of narcissistic mania comes to an end. Hermione recognizes that the whole picture is one in which she and Polixenes' wife are considered to be the snakes in the grass, instigators of 'offences' ('Your queen and I are devils': I.ii. 82); yet instead of confronting the problems of jealousy of the new baby and envy of her pregnancy, she tries a policy of appeasement (flirting with Polixenes, as if the twin lambs/eggs story were a true one), which has an explosive effect. The moment that she does, finally, make some space for Mamillius to voice his feelings – for he has been 'troubling [her] past enduring ' (II.i. 1–2) – he immediately starts on his expressive 'winter's tale', upon which his alter-ego Leontes enters on cue and sweeps Hermione off to prison. Hermione's trial and imprisonment finally images the true state of Leontes' hatred of her evident manifestation of creativity as she 'swells apace'. At last the wintry state of his mind has achieved appropriate expression for all to see; and now it is possible for Paulina to intervene with 'words medicinal' and become his mentor or means of communication with those cut-off, entombed inhabitants of his inner world. As Hermione tells him in the trial scene: 'My life stands in the level of your dreams', and Leontes replies: 'Your actions are my dreams' (III.ii. 81–2). Everything that happens in the Bohemian section of the play is in a sense his 'dream' about Hermione's inner world, through which she recreates his own. In casting out the baby whom he is unfit to bring up, Leontes is sending it to fitter soil for nourishment. So Hermione becomes the goddess of dreams, and appears to Antigonus in a dream on shipboard, to instruct him in the care of the baby Perdita:

> To me comes a creature,
> Sometimes her head on one side, some another;
> I never saw a vessel of like sorrow,
> So fill'd, and so becoming: in pure white robes,
> Like very sanctity, she did approach
> My cabin where I lay: . . . thrice bow'd before me,
> And, gasping to begin some speech, her eyes
> Became two spouts . . .
>
> (III.iii. 19–26)

The baby has been snatched from its mother with 'the innocent milk in its innocent mouth' (III.ii. 100), yet through this dream of spouting milk from the eyes, the white 'sanctity' of motherhood is transferred to Antigonus, as in Bottom's 'translation'. Antigonus then lays down his courtly identity, which has become a prison to his better self, and metamorphoses into the Good Shepherd – a metamorphosis expressed by his being eaten by a bear. Leontes' court is obsessed by questions of bastardy and inheritance – obsessions of an omnipotent mentality concerned with its own status. Having shed these aspects of himself, the shepherd Antigonus fulfils his feminine potential and adopts the child: 'thou met'st with things dying, I with things new-born' (II.iii. 111–12). The 'fairy gold' which accompanies the infant is only discovered after his decision to father it has been made, and represents Perdita's inner worth – his reward. In the land of milk and honey she becomes the 'queen of curds and cream' (IV.iv. 161). In terms of the overall mental drama of the play, the Shepherd teaches the dreaming Leontes how to be a true father, just as Bottom taught the dreaming Theseus how to be a true lover. Like the Ass, the role of the Shepherd has religious implications. Meanwhile, the superficial aspects of Antigonus – his courtly robes – seem to find their home in the person of Autolycus: 'seest thou not the air of the court in these enfoldings?' (IV.iv. 731). He suggests a gentle parody of the type of artist who is only concerned with the 'nothing' of pageantry, and who sees himself as leading his audience by the nose – 'those moles, blind ones' (l. 837). Yet it is the 'blind ones' – the Shepherd and his son – who ultimately forgive Autolycus his superficiality, and allow him a place in the revised courtly family at the end of the play.

In the final stage of the drama, Leontes confronts those internal figures whom he thought his omnipotence had destroyed. Keats said: 'The Imagination may be compared to Adam's Dream – he awoke and found it Truth.' Now Leontes awakes from his dream, with a revitalized imagination, to find it truth. Paulina's 'poor house', never yet visited by Leontes, appears to contain an entire 'gallery' of works not merely collected but made by Paulina herself, of which Hermione's statue is the culmination ('the stone is mine', she says: V.iii. 58). Paulina's status is that of the artist-craftsman who, in a traditional metaphor for creativity, provides everything except the inspiring breath of life which is engendered by some divine influence. This influence only takes effect when the rest of the family 'awake their faith' (l. 95); then she can summon music, and say to the statue:

> Bequeath to death your numbness; for from him
> Dear life redeems you.
> ... That she is living,
> Were it but told you, should be hooted at
> Like an old tale; but it appears she lives . . .
> (II.102–17)

In *The Winter's Tale*, therefore, Shakespeare answers the question formulated in *Macbeth*: 'Canst thou not minister to a mind diseas'd?' The diseased mind is cured by restoring the internal child to the internal mother, the self to the Muse – a process dependent on both artistry and faith, the inspiring force. This is the 'old tale' which re-writes that of Mamillius: a process of re-creation which is inseparable from the concept of redemption: 'Dear life redeems you'. These internal relationships are outside the self's control, but are facilitated by the artist.

THE TEMPEST

In *The Winter's Tale*, both artist and muse were female figures, while the only truly maternal actions were performed by the male shepherd (owing to his introjection of the spirit of his wife, and ultimately of Hermione). In *The Tempest*'s island of the mind, Prospero figures a more standard male magician figure who on one level appears in control of everything and is almost continuously on stage. Yet on another level – the intimacy of his relations with Miranda, Ariel and Caliban (relationships of love and hate), he is powerless except in the negative sense of power to punish; the poetic or creative developments in the play are the function of poetic spirits whose existence is beyond him. As master of the island's 'full poor cell', he takes over from the witch Sycorax, superseding her in power whilst retaining many of her methods (cramps, threats of imprisonment, etc.). The next drama of supersession occurs when his daughter reaches marriage-ability, which brings all his 'enemies' back to his mind's shore – an action which he recognizes as one of 'divine Providence' just as was his own arrival on the island, twelve years before. In both cases it is his concern for Miranda (like Leontes' Perdita, his poetic spirit) which guides him: 'I have done nothing but in care of thee,/Of thee, my dear one; thee, my daughter, who/Art ignorant of what thou art' (I.ii. 16–18). When Prospero was Duke of Milan, he became trapped in a Faustian self-imprisonment characteristic of the Shakespearean view of false learning; from this he was rescued by violent ejection, along with his infant sense of wonder. Now that Miranda has grown up, it is brought to his notice (by Caliban, who wants to 'people the isle with Calibans' by her (l. 352), that it is time she colonized a new world. Originally she rescued Prospero from mental death in his own library – from sinking with the 'rotten carcass of a butt' which symbolized his state of mind: 'A cherubin/Thou wast, that did preserve me' (ll. 146–53). And she is intimately associated with Caliban, who is in some sense her foster-brother, in terms of language and openness to experience. Like Edgar in *Lear*, she has the ability to follow the true voice of feeling rather than obedience to authority, though this involves 'breaking [her father's] hest' (III.i. 37) – a quality springing from the Caliban aspect of the mind. Indeed Caliban is less an unsatisfactory suitor, than a force within her own mind (as well as Prospero's) which has been reared alongside her; the attempted rape symbolizes the upsurgence of this force in a way which temporarily frightens and repulses her. He is a 'thing of darkness' (as Prospero calls him: V.i. 275) essential to the mind's vitality and continuing poetic existence. Her choice of Ferdinand is not an escape from Caliban but an assimilation – hence Prospero's obsession with virginity before marriage.

Ferdinand, likewise, immediately identifies with the native poetic forces of the island embodied in Caliban and Ariel; his internalization of Caliban is figured in carrying the logs – Caliban's job – and of Ariel, in Ariel's own account of the shipwreck:

> I boarded the king's ship; now on the beak,
> Now in the waist, the deck, in every cabin,
> I flam'd amazement . . .
>   [the mariners] quit the vessel,
> Then all afire with me, the King's son, Ferdinand,
> With hair up-staring, – then like reeds, not hair –
> Was the first man that leap'd . . .
>   (I.ii. 196–214)

The idea of 'flaming amazement' applies both to Ferdinand and to the ship which has in a sense given birth to this Arielized son.[2] Through a mental metamorphosis, Ferdinand is born into a new state of mind which makes him immediately recognize Miranda as a 'wonder' (I.ii. 429), and she reciprocally recognizes the Ferdinand of Ariel's description, which she heard while asleep – that is, dreamed. To her, Ferdinand is a sort of transformed or Arielized Caliban whose lust has been purified rather than tamed. This is the network of intertwined identifications which begins to form the foundation for the 'brave new world' which is, and is not, Prospero's, since it is created not by his omnipotence but by the inner world of his mind as it gradually grows to take on an existence beyond himself. The self-knowledge theme of 'virtue rather than vengeance' (V.i. 28), which would have been central to a Shakespearean tragedy, here becomes secondary to the fascination of the island itself and the ability of its native forces to transform relationships. Ariel embodies those imagining-into, negative-capability exploratory aspects of the imagination which 'tread the ooze of the salt deep', 'run upon the sharp wind of the north' and do 'business in the veins o' th' earth/When it is baked with frost' (I.ii. 252–6). Caliban's nature is a complementary one of receptivity, drawing within himself those 'wonders' which nature seems to pour on him as a result of Ariel's explorations (the Miranda-world). Ariel pours the poetry into the mind's veins, including places beyond the reach of the human eye, and Caliban catches the riches when they 'drop' upon him:

> Be not afeard; the isle is full of noises,
> Sounds and sweet airs, that give delight, and hurt not.
> Sometimes a thousand twangling instruments
> Will hum about mine ears; and sometime voices,
> That, if I then had wak'd after long sleep,
> Will make me sleep again: and then, in dreaming,
> The clouds methought would open, and show riches
> Ready to drop upon me; when I wak'd
> I cried to dream again.
>
> (III.ii. 133–41)

Through this receptive interchange, the 'blessed crown' of the dream-world is realized, like that which Gonzalo sees dropping upon the heads of Ferdinand and Miranda, and which contrasts with the crown of ambition which Antonio sees dropping on Sebastian's. In this the young lovers are following in Prospero's footsteps; it was Caliban who first showed him 'all the qualities of the isle', the dream-world's light and shade: 'fresh springs, brine-pits, barren place and fertile' (I.ii. 334–9). The philistine and cynical aspects of the mind (Antonio and Sebastian) or depressed ones (Alonso) are unable to see these qualities, and regard the island as hostile and deserted, sterile. Ariel provides the haunting music which changes the mind's aspect, yet which is only heard by those with Caliban's faculties. And Caliban is described as a 'moon-calf', a primitive follower of spiritual light, attracted by Ariel's invisible manifestations like an animal to its mother: in Ariel's phrase, 'calf-like, they my lowing follow'd' (IV.i. 179). Miranda, who taught him language and showed him the man in the moon, is an object of his worship, goddess of his mother-space the island (as for Ferdinand). Caliban is easily perverted – following the 'bottle' of Stephano and Trinculo when addled by alcohol – but regains his innate sense of value, dismissing the trumpery of Prospero's garments as 'trash', and ends determined to 'seek for grace' – his natural orientation. Thus Caliban *is* educable, but not by Prospero's omnipotent means (based on fear and denial during this crisis-point in his life); in imprisoning Caliban and separating him from his vision of beauty, he merely invites his perversion. Only the Ariel-faculty of the mind can educate Caliban, which is what happens within Ferdinand.

The intimate identification of the young lovers with these native forces of the island–mind underlies the 'tempest' in which Alonso 'loses' his son, and Prospero (as he says) his daughter (V.i. 152–3). The loss is both desired and abhorred, as always in the catastrophic change from one stage in development to the next. Their worldly destiny is to unite Naples and Milan in a new prosperity. But as always in Shakespeare, the idea of 'prosperity' is ambiguous, as is the idea of the crown of material or spiritual riches. Edmund's banner in *Lear* was: 'I grow, I prosper! ye gods, stand up for bastards!' Sebastian remarks sarcastically on how well they have 'prospered' since their return from Tunis with its 'sweet marriage' (II.i. 70). Yet 'the name of Prosper', when it has been Arielized in Ariel's harpy speech, brings Alonso to the sense of spiritual values which is a turning-point in his depression and ultimately leads to his 'son' being restored and his inner world revitalized:

> Methought the billows spoke, and told me of it;
> The winds did sing it to me; and the thunder,
> That deep and dreadful organ-pipe, pronounc'd
> The name of Prosper; it did bass my trespass,
> Therefore my son i' the ooze is bedded . . .
> (III.iii. 96–100)

Alonso catches Ariel's own sonorous rhythms, 'bassing his trespass'; and through this identification, he confronts the real issue of what constitutes the mind's prosperity. Prospero himself is awed by Ariel's 'grace devouring', the poetic expression beyond his control. Through poetry, one type of loss of a child is replaced by another type – the price of internal prosperity, associated with the relinquishment of a delusory power and authority. Prospero's own crisis occurs before the 'virtue rather than vengeance' speech, which is in a sense a foregone conclusion; it occurs when the idea of Caliban breaks into the 'vanity of [his] Art' during the wedding masque (IV.i. 41), dissipating for ever the stilted quality of its entertainment, the fruit of fancy rather than imagination. Only in the process of its vanishing, does it become a symbolic equivalent to the emotional reality of the marriage he desires to celebrate, and which he knows means the end of his career as Prospero-the-magician:

> The cloud-capp'd tow'rs, the gorgeous palaces,
> The solemn temples, the great globe itself,
> Yea, all which it inherit, shall dissolve,
> And, like this insubstantial pageant faded,
> Leave not a rack behind. We are such stuff
> As dreams are made on; and our little life
> Is rounded with a sleep.
> (IV.i. 151–8)

Like Antony on the point of catastrophic change, 'even with a thought/The rack dislimns' (*Antony and Cleopatra*, IV.xiv. 9–10), and identity seems to 'dissolve'. The cloud-shaped symbol of the self (as in *Hamlet*) means, correspondingly, that the self only has temporary status and then dissolves into the material of which dreams are made, in a continual process of remaking its identities. Yeats similarly defined the poet's task as 'Myself must I re-make' (in 'An Acre of Grass'). This is the equivalent moment to life being breathed into Hermione's statue; but focusing on the artist's sense of disintegration and superfluity. Only in 'losing' his daughter and giving Ariel 'freedom' from the confines of his own technical 'rough magic' (V.i. 50), his artistic vanity, can Prospero give the brave new world the opportunity to create itself; it will not be shaped according to any blueprint of his own.

This recognition is Prospero's internal tempest, resulting in his 'beating mind'; it is not his literal fear of death from Caliban's conspiracy but his awareness that from now on, having given away one 'third' of his life (as he calls Miranda), 'Every third thought shall be my grave' (V.i. 311). The price of the new world of creative thinking, founded on wonder, is the death or dissolution of the self in an insubstantial pageant. The condition of the new world's becoming real, is that it should not be his. In the very process of giving it a habitation and a name, the playwright loses the egotistical solidity of his own identity, which is superseded and subsumed. As Keats was to say: 'A Poet is the most unpoetical of any thing in existence; because he has no Identity – he is continually informing – and filling some other Body.'[3] In *The Tempest*, the omnipotent and the imaginative self coexist. The play presents the 'little world' of the essential Shakespearean mind which Richard II was struggling to cast as drama in Pomfret Castle; and the result of his success is, paradoxically, the slow death which represents the playwright's having to continue living with the insignificant identity of his mere self: 'what strength I have's mine own/Which is most faint'. In the epilogue, therefore, Prospero tries to convey the significance of his role not as commander, but as servant of the imagination, which has an existence beyond himself:

> Gentle breath of yours my sails
> Must fill, or else my project fails . . .

This role demands a new sense of responsibility or awakening of faith on the part of the audience, for whom he can no longer undertake to do everything.

2
MILTON: THE MIND'S OWN PLACE

> The world was all before them, where to choose
> Their place of rest, and Providence their guide...
> *(Paradise Lost*, XII. 646–7)

Milton was revered by subsequent poets to a degree no less than Shakespeare, though in slightly different kind: with a certain ambivalence owing to the dual aspects of Milton's nature as both poet and preacher. As preacher or politician, he tended to stimulate the omnipotent or argumentative side of his poetic descendants; while as poet, he encouraged their capacity to learn from emotional experience, and to overcome the fear of ostracism. Essentially, the heroism of Milton's poetic quest in *Paradise Lost* lies in his disengaging the mind from its dependence on the static poles or non-developmental states of heaven and hell, and internalizing the spirit of religion in the form of a 'paradise within thee, happier far' (XII. 586–7), which could lead the mind ever onwards. Adam and Eve, having metabolized their fall, abandoned their omnipotence, and reinstated humility, find that 'the world is all before them'. In the beginning, their world hangs like a jewel from the neck of heaven:

> And fast by hanging in a golden chain
> This pendent world, in bigness as a star
> Of smallest magnitude close by the moon.

This dependence is disengaged by the emotional storm brought by the burning envy and jealousy of Satan with his 'bursting passion':

> Thither fraught with mischievous revenge,
> Accurst, and in a cursed hour, he hies.
>
> (II. 1051–5)

This stormy disengagement is not a cold Mephistophelean perversion – a conquering and enslavement of the mind – but rather, owing to the passionate quality of the interaction, fights its way through the catastrophic change which brings 'death' into the Garden of Eden. Death becomes a transformation, not an end or imprison- ment: a transition from a state of stasis to one of development.

Blake's famous joke was that Milton was 'a true Poet and of the Devil's party without knowing it';[1] this was at the period when Milton was regarded by the Romantics as a sort of ideologist for the French revolution, as in Wordsworth's sonnet 'Milton! thou should'st be living at this hour'. Certainly God in *Paradise Lost* is merely a mouthpiece for Milton's selfhood, an authoritarian organizer through whom Milton preaches 'the ways of God to men' (I. 26); while Satan is the vehicle for the poetic spirit, at least until the fall of man, when it passes to Adam and Eve. But the 'Devil's party', in the epic, portrays brilliantly the pathetic fragility and uncreativeness of the mind which believes itself to be revolutionary, yet has no concept of anything but omnipotence. If God is omnipotent (the assumption goes), then devils can be omnipotent too, in their own way; hence the building of Pandemonium is a direct imitation of the structure of heaven: 'what can Heav'n show more?' (II. 273). Satan – he who 'durst defy th'Omnipotent to arms' – raises the banner:

> The mind is its own place, and in itself
> Can make a heav'n of hell, a hell of heav'n.
>
> (I. 254–5)

Satan-as-poet makes a statement which he does not yet understand, about the mind as its 'own place'; Satan-as-politician makes a sophistical equivalence which nevertheless indicates the balance and parallelism between heaven and hell. The devils find they are omnipotent-minded, without the power: the power of God's 'red right hand' (II. 174), he 'whom thunder hath made greater' (I. 258). If God is self-sufficient, is his own 'good', why should they not follow his example – the only example they know –

and, in Mammon's words, 'seek/Our own good from ourselves?' (II. 253–4). And in so far as heaven and hell are self-sufficient, they are static; no mental development takes place in them. Belial the 'smooth-tongued' makes a poignant lament for the loss of their 'intellectual being,/Those thoughts that wander through eternity' (II. 147–8), though this is 'vain wisdom all, and false philosophy' (l. 565). Satan alone of all the devils has the complex urge not simply to seek revenge, nor to fall back on delusory consolations, but also to make discoveries: to explore the new world which God is rumoured to have created. While the other devils busy themselves trying to fill the 'vast recess' of hell's empty-mindedness with philosophical discoursing, cultural activities and games, to while away the 'irksome hours' (l. 527), Satan is wading and winging his way through Chaos, fired by insatiable curiosity about heaven's new 'creatures' and tormented by his sense of exclusion:

> O hell! what do mine eyes with grief behold!
> Into our room of bliss thus high advanced
> Creatures of other mold, earth-born perhaps,
> Not Spirits, yet to heav'nly Spirits bright
> Little inferior; whom my thoughts pursue
> With wonder, and could love, so lively shines
> In them divine resemblance...
>
> (IV. 358–64)

At last he has found the power, the means of revenge on the Omnipotent; yet the process of revenge takes on a new complexion owing to the upsurge, despite himself, of his poetic sensibility – 'my thoughts pursue/With wonder, and could love' – which is a function of his being 'Archangel fall'n', not mere devil; retaining an aura of his 'original brightness':

> his form had not yet lost
> All her original brightness ...
>   ... but his face
> Deep scars of thunder had intrench'd ...
>
> (I. 591–601)

The complexity of Satan's reaction will colour the whole process of the fall, in ways which override his omnipotent intentions. Ultimately he will become part of the new world's consciousness, a creative integration of love and hate.

For the Romantic poets, then, Satan was Milton himself: dramatizing the conflict between the selfhood of the politician and preacher, and the creative poet awed by the vision of beauty before him and committed to the exploration of the unknown, invisible world:

> Shine inward, the mind through all her powers
> Irradiate, there plant eyes, that I may say and sing
> Of things invisible to mortal sight.
>
> (III. 52–5)

At key points throughout the long epic journey of *Paradise Lost*, Milton renews through haunting invocations such as these, the relationship with the Muse which he trusts to sustain him in the unfamiliar territory of the mind's 'own place':

> Taught by the Heav'nly Muse to venture down
> The dark descent, and up to reascend, . . .
>
> (ll. 19–20)

In the picture of this relationship which emerges with extraordinary power and clarity in the epic, it is the function of the poet-craftsman to choose the subject, theme, characters, etc; but it is the Muse who 'dictates' the poetic language and 'inspires' his 'unpremeditated verse':

> If answerable style I can obtain
> Of my celestial patroness, who deigns
> Her nightly visitation unimplored,
> And dictates to me slumb'ring, or inspires
> Easy my unpremeditated verse:
> Since first this subject for heroic song
> Pleased me long choosing and beginning late . . .
>
> (IX. 20–6)

Themes may be premeditated and long in choosing, but the symbol which contains their *meaning* appears ready-made, fully formed, presented by the Muse like a dream or in a dream. It is the language of poetry, not its theme, which carries its meaning, and makes the poetry of Milton and Shakespeare infinitely interpretable. Yet this is precisely what Milton, in particular, found disturbing, with his hierarchical view of nature, political polemic, and certainty of moral virtue. It can be said that he wrote

Paradise Regained to set the record straight between himself and his ideal-self, Christ, and to cancel out any blasphemies which might have emerged in *Paradise Lost* outside the confines of his self-control. From earliest days, Milton was fully aware of the emotional strain involved in allowing the poetic side of his nature to achieve fulfilment; and he was in no hurry to become a poet – to pursue what he called 'a manner of living much disregarded, and discountenanc'd'.[2] In the manuscript containing his early poems, there is a draft of a mysterious prose 'letter' (written *c.* 1633) in which he writes with savagery about the 'unprofitable sin of curiosity' which holds him back from the straightforward pursuit of worldly ambition, in a type of self-imprisonment: 'whereby a man cutts himselfe off from all action and becomes the most helplesse, pusilanimous and unweapon'd creature in the world'. At this uncertain point in his career, he was driven onwards only by the thought of his obligation to make use of his God-imposed ability: 'that one talent which is death to hide' – by his sense of duty and virtue, in fact. Long before his physical blindness, he recognized the metaphorical state of blindness and imprisonment from which poetry might germinate: the sense of being 'unweapon'd' and (like Richard II in Pomfret Castle) of being cut off from action. As he wrote much later in the sonnet on his blindness (Sonnet 19): 'They also serve who only stand and wait.'

Milton's first inspired poem – that is, the first poem which he experienced as being written by the Muse rather than by himself – was the 'Ode on the Morning of Christ's Nativity', written spontaneously on Christmas Day 1629, shortly after his twenty-first birthday, as if to mark the beginning of his adult life as a poet:

> Say Heav'nly Muse, shall not thy sacred vein
> Afford a present to the infant God?
>
> (ll. 15–16)

The infant God is the newly born poetic spirit implanted in his mind's 'new' enlightened world' – that infant aspect of his developing soul which the Muse has enlightened:

> It was the winter wild
>   While the Heav'n-born-child
>   All meanly wrapped in the rude manger lies ...
>
> (ll. 30–2)

The local habitation for this new spirit is the 'rude manger' of earthly sense, which is redeemed from its harmful aspects (such as the child-eating Moloch) and guarded by 'bright-harnessed angels... in order serviceable' (l. 244). This poetic guardianship, supplied by the Muse's 'sacred vein', enwraps the 'fancy' or imagination, like the child in the manger, and reorganizes the meaning of the world around it:

> For if such holy song
> Enwrap our fancy long,
>   Time will run back and fetch the age of gold,
> And speckled Vanity
> Will sicken soon and die,
>   And leprous Sin will melt from earthly mold,
> And hell itself will pass away,
> And leave her dolorous mansions to the peering day.
>
> (ll. 133–40)

The infant-poet's first contact with the age of gold, with the bright realities of the Platonic sunlight, is one in which the Muse-mother not only glorifies and irradiates but also protects the mind. Later the Muse is felt to expose him to unbearable realities; but even then, when the story becomes more complicated, the poet's fundamental vision of hell simply passing away and becoming unreal, underlies Milton's ability to undertake the epic journey of *Paradise Lost*. Ultimately this does indeed result in hell passing away from consciousness and a new world opening out. Indeed the genesis of the Muse in Milton's personal consciousness can be traced further back, to some interesting lines which form part of a public address given while he was at university (where only Latin, not English, was permitted). Here Milton 'leaped over the statutes' to hail the 'native language' which he believed to be the proper emotional and educative source for poetry:

> Hail native language, that by sinews weak
> Didst move my first endeavouring tongue to speak
> And mad'st imperfect words with childish trips
> Half unpronounced, slide through my infant lips,
> Driving dumb silence from the portal door,
> Where he had mutely sat two years before... [3]

Through this invocation – a public declaration of a private intent – Milton relates the poetry of mental development which he later hopes to write, to a developmental principle imaged by the two-year-old child learning to speak. The governing factor is 'native language' in the position of Muse or mother. He subverts his own ritualistic role on the occasion as 'Father of Ceremonies' and Latinist orator, in a way which establishes a lifelong antithesis between his patriarchal, omnipotent self and his sensuous, exploratory, learning self. And although he never wrote a theory of poetics, his idea of poetry as more than a discipline but as a vital principle at the very core of the learning process, emerges implicitly from his tractate *Of Education* (1644). In this, he describes his ideal curriculum, which culminates in 'those organic arts' Logic and Rhetoric: 'to which Poetry would be made subsequent, or indeed rather precedent, as being lesse suttle and fine, but more simple, sensuous and passionate'.[4] Poetry for Milton symbolized the vital internal orientation which should infuse any body of knowledge and any intellectual skills; in relation to the getting of wisdom, it was a principle both immanent and transcendent. It is no wonder that Coleridge enthused over this passage defining poetry, since it corresponds so closely to his own particular conception of organic growth.[5] Coleridge makes explicit what is implicitly evoked in the poetic language of Milton's prose. Milton saw the purpose of education as 'to repair the ruins of our first parents by regaining to know God aright';[6] and poetry is the key to this continual process of repairing and regaining – a process to which the idea of a fall, or many falls, is integral.

The first poem in which Milton makes a genuine emotional confrontation with the idea of a 'fall' or 'death' within the poetic experience, is *Lycidas* – the key developmental poem before *Paradise Lost*. *Lycidas* (1637) was written after the death of his mother (though ostensibly about a university acquaintance drowned at sea). The true subject of the poem, however, is the capacity of the internal mother, or Muse, or guardian angel to be resilient in the face of 'death' and overwhelming tides of passion whose very intensity threatens to swamp the poet:

> Yet once more, O ye laurels, and once more
> Ye myrtles brown, with ivy never sere,
> I come to pluck your berries harsh and crude,

> And with forced fingers rude,
> Shatter your leaves before the mellowing year.
> Bitter constraint, and sad occasion dear,
> Compels me to disturb your season due;
> For Lycidas is dead, dead ere his prime,
> Young Lycidas, and hath not left his peer.
> Who would not sing for Lycidas? He knew
> Himself to sing, and build the lofty rhyme.
> He must not float upon his wat'ry bier
> Unwept, and welter to the parching wind,
> Without the meed of some melodious tear.
> (ll. 1–14)

The figure of 'young Lycidas' represents one aspect of the poet, whose identity is divided into a part which seems lost, dead, swamped by whelming and weltering tides of watery grief, and a part which undertakes the task of finding him (the elegist). At the end, the discovery of Lycidas' drowned body corresponds to an internal restoration. To begin with, therefore, the elegist expresses his emotional need through an unconventional, broken sonnet: an invocation which is more of an urgent attack upon the traditional iconography of the Muse. In an image which suggests blinding by tears, the laurels of poetry are torn apart by 'forced fingers rude', and the poet shows that a 'melodious tear' (where 'tear' also means elegy) is impossible in the present state of internal dislocation. During the course of the poem, all the poet's hatred of poetry is laid bare – the sense of degradation and humiliation which accompanies the 'homely slighted shepherd's trade'; the 'thankless Muse'; the vulnerability to the 'blind mouths' that 'scarce themselves know how to hold/A sheephook', and whose 'lean and flashy songs/Grate on their scrannel pipes of wretched straw' (ll. 65, 119–25). These are the false poets, embodying the temptations besetting the true pilgrim poet. Despite their grasping greed, they are unable to use their implements properly to feed their inner selves: 'The hungry sheep look up, and are not fed.' And at the core of the poem's hatred, lies the fear that when it comes to the ultimate breaking point, the Muse (who has not yet become visible) will be insufficient, and unable to withstand the poet's own rage and despair:

> What could the Muse herself that Orpheus bore,
> The Muse herself for her enchanting son
> Whom universal nature did lament,
> When by the rout that made the hideous roar,
> His gory visage down the stream was sent,
> Down the swift Hebrus to the Lesbian shore.
>   (ll. 58–63)

The 'savage clamour' of the 'wild rout' who tore the poet Orpheus to pieces reappears in *Paradise Lost*, again with the reminder of the Muse's insufficiency: 'nor could the Muse defend/Her son' (VII. 32–8). The 'hideous roar' of destructive envy is proportional to the 'enchanting' quality of the poetry, or poetic relationship between the Muse and her son. This is why, in *Paradise Lost*, where Milton feels he is charting very dangerous territory, he is careful to invoke the 'heavenly Muse' who is backed by the knowledge of God, and whom he calls Urania; but even then, lest the name should be mistaken, he guards himself with: 'The meaning, not the name I call' (VII. 5). He recognizes that if this internal object is in some way deficient in quality or strength, he (as the vulnerable voyager within his own poem) will become exposed to the gangsterism of internal basic assumption groups:

> So fail not thou, who thee implores;
> For thou art heav'nly, she an empty dream.
>   (VII. 38–9)

The function of *Lycidas* in Milton's mental development, is to establish a type of Muse within him which can withstand the shattering of the icon (the emotional explosion) and the negative forces of envious omnipotence (the false poets, the gangster 'rout'), then restore the concept of melody or harmony in a way which is not a superficial cover-up but a genuine containing symbol for that original catastrophic 'drowning' experience. This happens during the last movement of the poem, beginning with the lost body of Lycidas returning to view in the eye of the imagination:

> Wash far away, where'er thy bones are hurled,
> Whether beyond the stormy Hebrides,
> Where thou perhaps under the whelming tide
> Visit'st the bottom of the monstrous world;

THE CHAMBER OF MAIDEN THOUGHT

> Or whether thou, to our moist vows denied,
> Sleep'st by the fable of Bellerus old,
> Where the great Vision of the guarded mount
> Looks towards Namancos and Bayona's hold;
> Look homeward, Angel, now, and melt with ruth;
> And, O ye dolphins, waft the hapless youth.
>
> (ll. 155–64)

The language of whelming monstrosity with which the poem began, is picked up but restored to melodiousness, just as the washing seas themselves become a type of cradle for the bones which were 'hurled' to disintegration. They appear to be guarded, in their dreaming sleep ('sleep'st by the fable') by ancient legendary gods of the landscape itself – Bellerus the Celtic god of light (a precursor of Christ), and finally the 'visionary' force of the Archangel Michael who guards St Michael's Mount. The inspired moment of recognition in which the angel seems to turn and 'look homeward' (not outward) in response to the elegist's plea, repairs the broken links between craftsman and infant-soul (elegist and Lycidas), and between Muse and God, who are joined in the figure of the angel. This is the strengthened internal network which enabled Milton to overcome the spiritual paralysis of feeling 'the most helplesse, pusilanimous and unweapon'd creature in the world', and to fly in pursuit of 'things invisible' in *Paradise Lost*.

The fall of man in *Paradise Lost* – the 'ruins of our first parents' – tells in psychological terms the story of a weaning process or conception of a thought, as in *King Lear*. The scene is set, not initially in hell, but in the inner womb-like landscape of a brooding 'spirit':

> O Spirit, that dost prefer
> Before all temples th'upright heart and pure,
> Instruct me, for thou know'st; thou from the first
> Wast present, and with mighty wings outspread
> Dove-like sat'st brooding on the vast abyss
> And mad'st it pregnant:
>
> (I.17–22)

This passage is echoed later in the description of God's creation of the world (VII. 233–7), but without its emotional power.

MILTON: THE MIND'S OWN PLACE

Essentially this 'Spirit' is an attribute of the 'heavenly Muse' whom Milton has just been invoking. The first character to be born from this 'vast abyss' is Satan himself, newly cast out from heaven and

> Hurled headlong flaming from th'ethereal sky
> With hideous ruin and combustion down
> To bottomless perdition, . . .
>
> (I. 45–7)

In terms of Milton's personal evolution (rather than of Christian doctrine), Satan's real predecessor is the Christ-child of the 'Nativity Ode' – the heaven-born child who fell to earth in a cloud of snowflakes. Now he occupies the vast abyss of bottomless perdition, his face scarred by thunder not brushed by flakes, and 'care/Sat on his faded cheek' (ll. 601–2). His scarred face is that of one who has viewed the 'bright-harnessed angels' of the 'Nativity Ode' from the outside. In order to protect man, that 'creature formed of earth', God has 'subjected to his service angel wings . . . to watch and tend/Their earthy charge' (IX. 155–7); God's 'new delight' is 'instead/Of us outcast, exiled' (IV. 105–6). Ultimately the poetic principle is destined to pass from Satan to Adam, when he too incorporates this darker vision. As Keats recognised in *Hyperion*, *Paradise Lost* is about evolution – about successive states of existence, 'born of us and fated to excel us'.[7] By the end of the poem, Satan as a character has become a mere discarded shell of his former heroic self: symbolized by his degenerating first into 'plebeian angel militant' (X. 442) then into serpentine form and being hissed by his fellow serpents in their last political assembly (X. 508). Satan, heaven and hell will pass away; and the Garden of Eden, when empty, will become 'an island salt and bare', the placenta after the 'flood' of birth (XI. 830–5).

Meanwhile, while God stands on the edge of infinity, surveying and ordaining, Satan circles, flies, wades, creeps, and metamorphoses, 'treading the crude consistence' of his new world, swathed in dark flames:

> Forthwith upright he rears from off the pool
> His mighty stature; on each hand the flames
> Driv'n backward slope their pointing spires, and
>   rolled
> In billows, leave i'th' midst a horrid vale.

> Then with expanded wings he steers his flight
> Aloft, incumbent on the dusky air
> That felt unusual weight...
>
> (I. 221-7)

Keats admired the 'affection and yearning of a great Poet' which made Milton put 'vales' in hell, reflecting those of heaven: 'It is a sort of Delphic Abstraction – a beautiful thing made more beautiful by being reflected and put in a mist'.[8] Satan's dark beauty and strenuous sensuous adaptation to the qualities of the mind's wild landscape, with its burning lakes and treacherous ground, express his restless inner conflict, torn by the 'hateful siege of contraries' (IX. 121), as

> full of anguish driv'n,
> The space of seven continued nights he rode
> With darkness...
>
> (IX. 62-4)

Milton strongly evokes spatial tensions to convey Satan's aesthetic conflict at the sight of mankind, as when Satan prophesies a union with them 'so strait, so close', that

> hell shall unfold,
> To entertain you two, her widest gates,
> And send forth all her kings; there will be room,
> Not like these narrow limits, to receive
> Your numerous offspring...
>
> (IV. 376-85)

Such tensions, founded on love and hate of the aesthetic object, indicate the mental realignments which will take place when Satan infiltrates Eden and begins to expand its dimensions. His 'close', ambivalent identification with mankind, projecting and internalizing, takes physical shape in his convolutions as the serpent.

Eden is a classical garden of strictly regulated proportions, without a twig out of place – despite all the references to pruning and tying through which Milton emphasizes his own work ethic. It portrays a quiescent, commensal state of 'unexperienced thought' (IV. 457) and innocent narcissistic reflections between man and woman, mankind and nature; 'mindless the while' (IX. 431), they harmoniously follow the diurnal round. We feel that

Adam and Eve seem destined to remain childless if they should follow the narrator's advice and 'seek to know no more' (IV. 775). 'Evil into the mind of man or god/May come or go, so unapproved', says Adam, 'and leave no spot or blame' (V. 117–18); the father and mother of mankind are waiting for something to initiate the mystery of conception. No spot takes root in Eve's womb so long as she and Adam, in their fleshly natural way, model their intercourse on the lines of the angels – who, bodiless, mix 'easier than air with air ... nor restrained conveyance need/As flesh to mix with flesh, or soul with soul' (VIII. 626–9). But Eve encounters Satan when she is allowed by Adam to set out to discover the meaning of her disturbing dream; and Adam follows, reluctantly. From this point the story splits into a doctrinal and a dream dimension. Even the doctrinal Milton has difficulty in justifying the significance of the Tree in terms of a 'pledge of obedience' (as God puts it (VIII. 325)); his personal doctrine is that Eve falls though the classical temptation of hubris, confusing knowledge with self-glorification and hoping to become 'as gods who all things know' – the desire for omnipotence (IX. 804). This is the story conveyed by the pseudo–logical arguments of Satan, which are swallowed whole by Eve. But the story told by the sensuous imagery of the Muse's language (as opposed to Milton's language of persuasion and self-deception) is a different one. In symbolic terms, Satan becomes the 'restrained conveyance' through which a new idea is transmitted – not from air to air but by a series of extended and compressed perspectives. He eludes the angelic guard by 'gliding obscure', 'wrapped in mist of midnight vapour' or 'involv'd in rising mist', and then himself becomes the 'black mist' which animates the serpent (IX. 75, 158–80). His own angelic essence is 'constrained into a beast, and mixed with bestial slime' as prelapsarian equilibrium swells into symbolic intelligence, and airy nothing finds a local habitation:

> In at his mouth
> The Devil entered, and his brutal sense,
> In heart or head, possessing soon inspired
> With act intelligential, but his sleep
> Disturbed not, waiting close th'approach of morn.
> (ll. 187–91)

This passage is one of the prototypes for negative capability, the poetic condition in which the self is negated so that the imagination can flourish. In Keats's words in his notes on Milton:

> One of the most mysterious of semi-speculations is, one would suppose, that of one Mind's imagining into another. Things may be described by a Man's self in parts so as to make a grand whole which that Man himself would scarcely inform to its excess.[9]

Keats specifically describes the projective, imagining-into aspect of negative capability (the Shakespearean vertex of the poetic mind, as Coleridge saw it),[10] while here, Milton describes the internalizing tension, the being-imagined-into aspect (the Miltonic vertex). As Keats himself said of the serpent passage: 'Whose spirit does not ache at the smothering and confinement – the unwilling stillness – the "waiting close"? Whose head is not dizzy at the possible speculations of Satan in the serpent prison?'[11] The serpent prison suggests Milton's own account, given to his biographer, of awaking in the morning with his head full of lines of poetry, 'waiting to be milk'd'.[12] The period of 'waiting close' is distinct from that of 'contriving' (Satan's word for God's planning the six days of creation (IX. 139)). This serpentine 'inspiring' process is also Milton's 'nightly visitation' by his own 'celestial patroness' (IX. 21), and at the end of the epic, becomes Eve's sense of 'God in dreams': 'For God is also in sleep, and dreams advise' (XII.611).

When the serpent speaks, it will be with 'serpent tongue/ Organic, or impulse of vocal air' (IX. 329–30) – Milton's evocation of the strangeness of being spoken through, which in intention recalls the 'first endeavouring tongue' of 'Hail native language' (though that, inevitably, was far tamer in expression). Satan's first step is to gain Eve's attention. Among the many dumb beasts gambolling around her like potential children, 'duteous' and 'disporting', he becomes singled out by his unusual capacity for speech: his 'gentle dumb expression' fertilized by act intelligential. In aesthetic terms, the serpent becomes a match for her: 'toward Eve' he

> Addressed his way, not with indented wave,
> Prone on the ground, as since, but on his rear,
> Circular base of rising folds, that tow'red
> Fold above fold a surging maze; his head

> Crested aloft, and carbuncle his eyes;
> With burnish'd neck of verdant gold, erect
> Amidst his circling spires, that on the grass
> Floated redundant. Pleasing was his shape
> And lovely, never since of serpent kind
> Lovelier...
>
> (IX. 496–505)

The burnished serpent glows ambiguously through a cloudy haze like the will-o'-the-wisp with its 'wandering fire,/Compact of unctuous vapour, which the night condenses' (language based on Ariel leading Caliban): 'Hovering and blazing with delusive light' he 'misleads th'amazed night-wanderer' (ll. 633–42). Eve, likewise, at the heart of Eden's flora, is in a mist: 'veiled in a cloud of fragrance'. 'Amazed' Eve and 'abstracted' Satan are both night-wanderers veiled in ambiguous spiritual mist, like Keats's Moneta, or Herman Melville's 'mighty, misty monster' the white whale,

> his vast, mild head overhung by a canopy of vapour, engendered by his incommunicable contemplations, and that vapour – as you will sometimes see it – glorified by a rainbow, as if Heaven itself had put its seal upon his thoughts. For, d'ye see, rainbows do not visit the clear air; they only irradiate vapour.[13]

Melville is semi-satiric, just as Milton was disapproving; but neither form of disavowal detracts from the symbol's impact. Melville takes his description of 'the curious involved worming and undulation of the atmosphere over my head' (smoke-rings in his study) from Satan's misty convolutions which disturb the clear air of Eden and make the mind conceive thoughts, just as rainbows irradiate vapour: 'And so, through all the thick mists of the dim doubts in my mind, divine intuitions now and then shoot, enkindling my fog with a heavenly ray.' This is the 'act intelligential' itself, born into a misty mentality of inspired possession, projection and introjection – given a certain aesthetic reciprocity between the self and the symbolic object (Eve and Satan, Melville and the whale). In the 'mist' lies the interweaving of identities and the engendering of new ones. At this point, mental evolution begins: or, in the symbolism of the last two books of *Paradise Lost*, this is where Eden's eternal never-never land is abandoned for time and history.

THE CHAMBER OF MAIDEN THOUGHT

In the last stage of the epic, the archangel Michael (from *Lycidas*) explains to Adam the point of the experience which commenced poetically during the fall. It is a story of evolution which will result in 'a paradise within thee, happier far'; conception and internalization are a single process. The angel's philosophy becomes known to Eve in a dream, and at this point the process of physical expulsion from paradise begins: a catastrophic change suggesting birth or weaning. The tiered terraces of paradise – 'so late their happy seat' – are unwound by the minute massed cherubim descending in a vaporous stream (echoing the entry of the fallen angels into Pandemonium):

> all in bright array
> The Cherubim descended; on the ground
> Gliding meteorous, as ev'ning mist
> Ris'n from a river o'er the marish glides,
> And gathers ground fast at the labourer's heel
> Homeward returning.
> (XII. 627–32)

Satan's prophecy of the gates of hell unfolding and hell's kings going forth, becomes the gates of paradise opening for expulsion, with the fiery cherubim descending the hill of paradise and then in turn merging into the spiritual mist of ethereal connotations which clings to the solidity of the labourer's heel, like the wings of Hermes strapped to the sandal, or the apocalyptic vision at the end of *Lycidas* which is at the last moment attached to the everyday blue-cloaked figure of the elegist. In Coleridge's description of the internal workings of such a symbol: 'the Idea flies homeward to its Parent Mind enriched with a thousand forms'.[14] The thousand forms of angelic associations cling to the labourer's heel, not faintly and diminishing, but 'gathering ground fast', in this image of expulsion which is at the same time a species of homeward journey, enriching the inner world or planting inward eyes of angel vision. The 'hast'ning Angel' literally 'hands' the new world to the children who are our parents, as readers:

> In either hand the hast'ning Angel caught
> Our ling'ring parents, . . .
> Some natural tears they dropped, but wiped them soon;
> The world was all before them, where to choose

> Their place of rest, and Providence their guide;
> They hand in hand, with wand'ring steps and slow,
> Through Eden took their solitary way.
>
> (ll. 637–49)

The new world, the 'paradise within', is a working landscape of ploughed furrows and temperamental mists, rather than the tranquil classic serenity of the original garden. The gardeners have become farmers, developing in an organic line of mental evolution from the heaven-born child, the lost Lycidas, and the fallen Satan. The concrete link of the hands (Adam and Eve are themselves hand in hand) images the continuing spiritual reality of contact with the angelic world through the inner guide of Providence. In this way, Milton the poet establishes a network of internal relationships to guide the working, developing mind when it is its 'own place' rather than a scion of heaven or hell.

3
BLAKE: THE MIND'S EYE

> To see a World in a Grain of Sand
> And a Heaven in a Wild Flower
> Hold Infinity in the palm of your hand
> And Eternity in an hour.
> ('Auguries of Innocence')

In Blake, the concept of God alone, transcendent, and unattainable, is replaced by a Divine Family as guiding deities of the creative mind, responsible for the 'expansion' of inner vision to infinity and eternity, with 'no limits'.[1] He expressed the prototypal fall and redemption of developmental experience with: 'First God Almighty comes with a Thump on the Head. Then Jesus Christ comes with a balm to heal it.'[2] In Blake's image of the creative inner world, which he called Jerusalem, the internal deities are: Jesus (or God-as-Jesus), the female muses or daughters of Beulah (the dream-world) who are agents of Jesus and tend the suffering soul; and the 'little children of Jerusalem', or (as he synonymously terms them) the 'minute particulars' of mental existence – embryonic figments of imagination or intellectual vision, with an innocent potential for experience. Together they comprise the 'Divine Humanity' or the 'Humanity', for 'all deities reside in the Human Breast',[3] yet are quite distinct from the 'selfhood'. The process of coming to knowledge of these internal relationships is the 'building of Jerusalem' – the function of 'every Christian, as much as in him lies',[4] and in particular of the artist. Blake defines his 'task' at the beginning of *Jerusalem*:

> I rest not from my great Task,
> To open the Eternal Worlds, to open the immortal Eyes
> Of Man inwards into the Worlds of Thought, into Eternity
> Ever expanding in the Bosom of God, the Human Imagination.
>
> (pl. 5, 17–20)

To *see* 'infinity' is to *be* 'human', in the Blakean sense:

> If the doors of perception were cleansed every thing would appear to man as it is, infinite.
> For man has closed himself up, till he sees all things thro' narrow chinks of his cavern.[5]

This cleansing of perception is effected by the emotional tensions of a 'marriage of contraries', a phrase in *The Marriage of Heaven and Hell* derived from Satan's 'hateful siege of contraries' in *Paradise Lost*. Milton's poetic struggle becomes Blake's doctrine; these contraries are necessary to make vision expansive and translucent, imaginative – the paradise within. Conversely, if perception is not redeemed through this inner tension, man enters a state of spiritual 'non-entity' or 'error', which Blake in his prophetic books names Ulro, his own version of hell: a condition of self-imprisonment, bounded by meaningless sense-impressions – the walls of the cavern.

Blake's view supersedes both the Christian doctrine of sin and repentance, and rationalist empiricism. Error or non-entity rather than sin comprises the evil to which man is prone, and is only reversible through the spiritual dynamism of contrary passions, which endow him with a complex vision. (In his insistence on rejecting both Christian and classical mythologies, Blake invents a hierarchy of two-, three- and four-fold vision). The complex vision of imagination contrasts with the mechanical conjunctions of memory or the spectrous divisions of reason, like the compasses with which Newton divided the universe. By 'reason' Blake means 'rationalization', a tool of the specious omnipotent selfhood which needs to be abandoned. States in which the selfhood is dominant have a delusory substantiality, though man may in fact be drowning in the waters of materialism, or suffocated by sentimentality – the cancerous 'polypus of soft affections'. Ulro or Chaos appears well-ordered because it is tyrannically regimented, but is in fact 'not organized', since its creative energies are unemployed and useless – those giants which were born free and are everywhere in chains.[6] In their place are the false gods Urizen (tyrannical reason) and Satan, who represents smooth hypocrisy, pseudity, and imitative modes of learning. They are projections of the selfhood, and 'in Selfhood we are nothing, but fade away in morning's breath'.[7] Blake knew that in the realms of imagination, the poet is but a 'Secretary' to his visions; the 'Authors are in Eternity';[8] for 'we who dwell on Earth can do nothing of ourselves; everything is conducted by Spirits, no less than Digestion or Sleep'.[9] These are the conditions for the creation of both true humanity and true art. False art, like humanity, has a delusory coherence. Since Blake's imagination lived and breathed through the visual arts, he extended his descriptions of this false or unreal organisation into terms of an 'opake' or 'excrementitious' covering which is smeared over the true image or symbol, the hypocritical 'covering Cherub' which disguises the living 'line of the Almighty':

> The want of this determinate and bounding form evidences the want of idea in the artist's mind.... Leave out this line, and you leave out life itself; all is chaos again, and the line of the almighty must be drawn out upon it before man or beast can exist.[10]

Blake's use of the word 'idea' suggests it is a substantial presence in the mind not merely a didactic purpose. When the omnipotent selfhood is stripped away, its false 'excrementitious/Husk & Covering into Vacuum evaporat[es], revealing the lineaments of Man'.[11] Blake preferred the translucent properties of watercolour to the building-up nature of oilpainting, possibly owing to this association of the line of truth with an entity which could only be recovered through being uncovered, discarding the smooth husk of fashionable taste, the selfhood's lack of originality. The mind's negative, uncreative condition is a type of superfluous garment of sense-impressions, not a real organized form in itself; as Blake wrote in one of his last verses, to 'the God of This World': 'Truly, my Satan, thou art but a Dunce,/And dost not know the Garment from the Man.'[12]

In the poem 'London', from *Songs of Experience*, we see Blake's aesthetic preoccupation with the bloody and sooty opacities integral to a state of error. The living line of the mind's potential ideas are covered with indefiniteness:

> I wander thro' each charter'd street,
> Near where the charter'd Thames does flow,
> And mark in every face I meet
> Marks of weakness, marks of woe.
>
> In every cry of every Man,
> In every Infant's cry of fear,
> In every voice, in every ban,
> The mind-forg'd manacles I hear.
>
> How the Chimney-sweeper's cry
> Every black'ning Church appalls;
> And the hapless Soldier's sigh
> Runs in blood down Palace walls.
>
> But most thro' midnight streets I hear
> How the youthful Harlot's curse
> Blasts the new born Infant's tear,
> And blights with plagues the Marriage hearse.

The chimney-sweeper's cry, the soldier's sigh, the infant's tear, are voices of the little children of Jerusalem which go unheard because they are immediately converted into opaque coverings: the cry becomes the soot covering the church, the sigh becomes blood on the walls, tears and flowers become syphilitic boils and transform the sensuous vehicle of marriage into a hearse. This state of false art corresponds with the 'charter'd' streets and river of London – where 'charter'd' is the antithesis of 'organized'. The city of anti-Jerusalem is imprisoned by 'mind- forg'd manacles'. It is an image of the cavern of man's selfhood, and its sensuous boundaries are those of vegetable reason, the excrementitious, the opaque, the indefinite. They include sanctimony and moral virtue, which are among the 'self-righteousnesses conglomerating against the divine vision'.[13] All these 'conglomerations' represent the caked-up mind stifled by its own rubbish, like Macbeth's faecal hallucinations. The work-song of those 'at the plow' in *Jerusalem* is to 'labour well the Minute Particulars: attend to the Little-ones', which involves 'pounding to dust' all such 'Indefinites', or melting them in the 'Furnaces of Affliction':

> For Art & Science cannot exist but in minutely organized
>   Particulars,

And not in generalizing Demonstrations of the Rational
Power.
The Infinite alone resides in Definite & Determinate
Identity.

(pl. 55, 51–64)

For Blake, the 'indefinite' is common sense deified: a species of perversity in which the unthinking basic assumptions of the mind are rigidified into moral laws. This rigidity is in antithetical contrast to the definiteness of the 'organized Particulars' or 'little children' of the inner world, which make up the Divine Humanity and contain the infinite in definite and determinate form.

Blake's insistence that the perversity and negativity underlying humanity's false face have to be reversed, not modified, before mental life can begin, prompts the deliberate reversal of labels in *The Marriage of Heaven and Hell*. What the spectrous mind worships by the name of 'Jesus' is in fact Antichrist; the common view of wisdom (i.e. prudence) is really spiritual folly, and vice versa, since 'if the fool would but persist in his folly he would become wise'; corporeal war is really a state of inaction not a state of unbridled passion, and only spiritual war is active. Spiritual war is necessary to mental health, for 'Without Contraries is no progression. Attraction and Repulsion, Reason and Energy, Love and Hate, are necessary to Human Existence.'[14] Founded on Milton's 'siege of contraries', this key feature of the literary model of the mind permanently divorces poetry's sophisticated, exploratory idea of a 'progressive' ethics from the static application of moral or religious codes. In poetry, there are not right or wrong feelings, but real or unreal ones (pseudity), as likewise in psychoanalysis; and the real feelings must be discovered and brought into view if the truth about an experience is to be symbolized and digested into thought. 'Negations are not Contraries; Contraries mutually Exist;/But Negations Exist Not';[15] the positive emotional tension between contraries is the way to lead the mind out of the impasse of the negative state. It appeared to Blake, when translating the lessons of the French revolution and of social injustice into terms of everyman's mental condition, that a species of spiritual murder or obliteration of the truth can be taking place at any time or continuously. 'Sooner murder an infant in its cradle than nurse unacted desires', he wrote provocatively;[16] meaning that desires or passions which achieve no aesthetic organization or fulfilment are, in effect, murdered infants in the world of the mind. Each one is an aspect of truth which has been aborted from fruition, and lies enchained, potentially vengeful. Likewise, tyrannical reasoning means that 'every Minute Particular of Albion [is] degraded and murder'd.'[17] These minute particulars or little children are potential ideas within the individual mind, or ideas presented by poets and artists within the collective or historical mind of mankind – the body of Jerusalem. They emerge with emotional complexity, like Macbeth's 'pity like a new-born babe' or the songs of Lear's Fool, as in Blake's 'Infant Sorrow':

> My mother groan'd! my father wept.
> Into the dangerous world I leapt:
> Helpless, naked, piping loud:
> Like a fiend hid in a cloud.

In Blake's model, there is only one form of real knowing, and that is, imagining what exists in the mind. Imagination is true vision, and is 'surrounded by the daughters of Inspiration', while invention in the form of fable or allegory is associated with the 'daughters of memory' and dominated by the selfhood (a distinction prefiguring Coleridge's between imagination and fancy):

> Allegory & Vision ought to be known as Two Distinct Things, & so called for the Sake of Eternal Life. Plato has made Socrates say that Poets & Prophets do not know or Understand what they write or Utter; this is a most Pernicious Falshood. If they do not, pray is an inferior kind to be call'd Knowing? Plato confutes himself.[18]

The poets 'know' by means of imagination and inspiration; and this foremost means of knowing is to be sharply differentiated from 'inferior kinds' such as backwards-looking memory or tame allegory, which embody the limited or possibly false understanding of the selfhood. The knowledge gained by imagination is made by 'authors in eternity', and on it depends the mind's 'eternal life'. Yet Blake does allow a limited place for allegory in so far as this is 'seldom without some vision', though it is liable to be taken over by the purely mechanical memory or by moral virtues, things which 'do not Exist'. What man does 'of himself' is at best derivative and at worst destructive; only inspiration puts him in contact with the eternal, internal deities who can expand his vision for him. In his 'Vision of the Last Judgment', Blake presents his divine – essentially patriarchal – family of the imagination, with the 'Eternal Births of Intellect' emanating like 'Infants' from the central Sun of Jesus.[19] Intellect and passion are part of the same mental complex: 'The Treasures of Heaven are not Negations of Passion, but Realities of Intellect, from which all the Passions emanate Uncurbed in their Eternal Glory', and men are 'cast out' from heaven only if they have 'no Passions of their own because no Intellect'. Blake's philosophy makes passion not the enemy but the key to the spiritual vision which is the only real knowledge:

> Mental Things are alone Real; what is call'd Corporeal, Nobody knows of its Dwelling Place: it is in Fallacy, and its Existence an Imposture. Where is the Existence out of Mind or Thought? . . . 'What,' it will be Question'd, 'When the Sun rises, do you not see a round disk of fire somewhat like a Guinea?' O no, no, I see an innumerable company of the Heavenly host crying 'Holy, Holy, Holy is the Lord God Almighty.' I question not my Corporeal or Vegetative Eye any more that I would Question a Window concerning a Sight. I look thro' it & not with it.[20]

The eye of the beholder can either reflect the selfhood of its viewer's limitations (to see a guinea, signifying worldly dross), or it can strip away their opacity like a husk, to reveal the rays of organized passion which emanate from the source of mental reality – the heavenly host crying 'Holy, holy, holy'.

Blake's idea of perception makes it inevitable that the story of the mind's recreation or redemption of false vision cannot be a neoplatonic ascent from the sensuous up towards a higher reality. It has to be one of intense looking at and through the sensuous until the veils are stripped away. As Isaiah says in *The Marriage of Heaven and Hell*: 'I saw no God, nor heard any, in a finite organical perception; but my senses discover'd the infinite in every thing.'[21] For Blake it is literally a question of dis-covery, a series of deaths of the selfhood; as he wrote in an autograph album in his later life, he was 'born in London in 1757 and has died several times since'.[22] His repeated condemnation of the 'natural', as perceived by the false 'evidence of the five senses', is not an ascetic doctrine but an attempt to transform the meaning of the sensuous, which would indeed result in an 'improvement of sensual enjoyment'.[23] Looking outwards with a vegetative eye, man's perception is blocked by the impressions which bombard him from the walls of his 'cavern', and he rationalizes them. Looking inwards, sense impressions become irradiated with meaningfulness, and constitute the complex vision which reverses negative 'single vision'. In the prophetic books, Blake experiments with various systems and hierarchies of experience, such as 'threefold' dream-vision and 'fourfold' Edenic revelation; though frequently the mythologies invented (then superseded) in these books have the flavour of what he himself would call allegory rather than vision, contrived by Blake the patriarchal mystic in the spirit of impenetrable didacticism. There is a certain defensiveness in their epic style which is perhaps accounted for by Los's comment: 'I must Create a System or be enslav'd by another Man's.'[24] In wanting to be a system-creator yet rejecting the mythological language of existing culture, Blake tended to construct cryptic codes inviting interpretation by other systems, rather than symbols from which meanings could be drawn infinitely as with the plays of Shakespeare.

Nevertheless, from the prophetic books we glean a general picture of those internal deities, energies or giants whom Blake calls 'fairy hands', engaged in a continual cycle of harrowing, weaving, hammering, and melting; manipulating Time and Space around the 'mundane shell' of the mind's body. The goal is to build the city of art (Golgonooza) in relation to the city of eternal imagination (Jerusalem), and to prevent the mind softening and weakening through materialism, rationalization, and sentimentality. The main agent in all this is Los (=Sol, sun) who ultimately, in *Jerusalem*, forms part of the identity of Jesus. In Blake's personal hell of spiritual non-existence, 'Souls incessant wail, being piteous Passions and Desires/With neither lineament nor form';[25] and the process of redemption consists therefore in building a house for the passions which is truly 'organized' in its 'inward form', to accommodate those outcast children of Jerusalem. In *Milton* (begun 1804) he describes this:

> And every Generated body in its inward form
> Is a garden of delight and a building of magnificence,
> Built by the sons of Los in Bowlahoola and Allamanda, ...
> Some sons of Los surround the Passions with porches of iron
>   and silver
> Creating form and beauty around the dark regions of sorrow,

> Giving to airy nothing a name and a habitation
> Delightful: with bounds to the Infinite putting off the Indefinite
> Into most holy forms of Thought (such is the power of Inspiration),
> They labour incessant, with many tears and afflictions,
> Creating the beautiful House for the piteous sufferer.
>
> (plates 26, 28; *Writings*, pp. 512, 514–5)

Blake's house for the passions, built to replace the prison of the senses, has its dual genesis in Theseus' speech about the imagination and in *Paradise Lost* with its investigation of true and false building systems. Inspiration gives bounds to the infinite – 'holy forms of thought', symbolic containers for the inward form of the passions. In Blake's myth, Milton returns to earth to revise his vision through the existence of Blake, and in the process shows Blake how to avoid becoming a mere 'covering for Satan to do his will' (plates 38, 31). It is a myth which illustrates both Blake's admiration and ambivalence towards Milton. In a 'moment' during the day which 'Satan cannot find' (plates 35, 42) the inspiring forces of the mind enter earthly existence:

> And between every two Moments stands a Daughter of Beulah
> To feed the Sleepers on their Couches with maternal care ...
> Every Time Less than a pulsation of the artery
> Is equal in its period & value to Six Thousand Years,
> For in this Period the Poet's Work is Done, and all the Great
> Events of Time start forth & are conciev'd in such a Period,
> Within a Moment, a Pulsation of the Artery.
>
> (plates 28, 29; *Writings*, p. 516)

Thus the process of redemption may be seen on the vast time scale of the six thousand years of creation, or on the microscopic time scale of a pulsation in an artery. Blake believed that a single 'error', not 'removed', could destroy a soul;[26] but at the same time he believed that a single moment of inspired 'feeding' by the daughters of Beulah (the dream-bringers) could redeem it; in this period the poet's work is done, and the building of Jerusalem.

The last word on Blake's literary contribution to the model of the mind should perhaps be left to one of his most haunting poems, 'The Tyger', written at a time before the visual artistic side of Blake's creativity became paramount. After *Jerusalem* (begun 1804) he wrote little, and concentrated on painting. 'The Tyger' (*Songs of Experience*, 1794) demonstrates symbolically the creative tension between contraries essential to mental life:

> Tyger Tyger, burning bright,
> In the forests of the night;
> What immortal hand or eye,
> Could frame they fearful symmetry?
>
> In what distant deeps or skies,
> Burnt the fire of thine eyes?
> On what wings dare he aspire?
> What the hand, dare seize the fire?

The tiger-light is from from the outset one of those inward lights which in Blake illuminate aspects of eternity, like the uncut diamond image in *Milton* – disguised by duskiness, yet 'open all within' (pl. 28; *Writings*, p. 515) The question at the heart of the poem is whether the poet can tolerate the awesome conjunction between contrary emotions inspired by this light – the 'fearful symmetry' of terror and beauty. The light both summons and repels the poet who feels called upon to 'seize the fire', Prometheus-like, yet is aware such symmetry cannot be 'framed' in the sense of captured or tamed. Gradually, his own feelings become framed in the aesthetic sense – symbolically. In the second stanza, the light in the forest or night-sky becomes specifically a fire in the eyes, burning in 'deeps or skies', in a way which suggests not only the marriage of heaven and hell, but of blue eyes becoming 'deep' and burning.

> And what shoulder, & what art,
> Could twist the sinews of thy heart?
> And when thy heart began to beat,
> What dread hand? and what dread feet?
>
> What the hammer? what the chain,
> In what furnace was thy brain?
> What the anvil? what dread grasp,
> Dare its deadly terrors clasp?

The central stanzas focus on the body of the tiger, and the nature of its framing in the sense of building. These are the labours of Los at his furnaces, hammering at the doors of perception to forge inward vision – the making rather than the inspired receiving aspect of the artist-craftsman. In the process, there is a fusion of identities between creator and created, into which the poet is also drawn through projection and introjection. The 'shoulder' of God becomes that of the tiger; likewise the 'hand' and 'feet'. The beating of the heart (which is conveyed by the poem's quickened rhythm) is primarily the tiger's, but also God's by virtue of its enclosure within that 'shoulder' and 'feet'; and also brings into the identification the poet through his sense of terror. The beats of his heart direct the following series of questions, which culminate in the clinching of the 'grasp-clasp' rhyme in which tiger, God, and poet are united. Meanwhile the pattern of the rhetorical questions 'What dread hand? and what dread feet?', which echoes that of 'On what wings . . . ?', has linked the wings of exploration to the grasp of the tiger, in the poet's journey towards knowledge. The sudden insertion of the abstract word 'terrors' in this section of concrete building references, illuminates how in clasping the image, framing the poem, the poet is himself clasped by terror in the hand of the tiger-god. He feels his own inner world come to life and start beating, as a result of seizing the fire of poetry; he finds his own identity framed by the symbol's fearful symmetry. Thus the doors of perception are cleansed, and start to weep:

> When the stars threw down their spears
> And water'd heaven with their tears:
> Did he smile his work to see?
> Did he who made the Lamb make thee?
>
> Tyger Tyger burning bright,
> In the forests of the night:
> What immortal hand or eye,
> Dare frame thy fearful symmetry?

The first stanza here focuses on the face of the tiger-god: on the eyes (stars) and 'smile'. The mythological reference of 'stars' is to the angelic armies whose rebellion prefigured the fall of man. In 'throwing down', rather than relinquishing their arms, the vigour of piercing rays of light is retained; as these rays transmute into tears, their original spirit continues to shine in them, keeping the link with the 'fire' of the tiger's eyes yet modulating its ferocity. The relationship implicitly figured here between tiger and poet is that of lovers (with a hint of mother and baby in tiger and lamb). 'Did he who made the Lamb make thee?' is a cry of recognition, not a question demanding an answer or even posing an ambiguity. It follows the inevitable progression of the change in quality of the starlight during the recognition-crisis of the poem. Through the 'watering' which dissolves the barriers against vision, a line of intimacy is drawn between eyes and lamb: making the lamb an integral part of the tiger-visage, an emanation from the divine humanity. Finally, in the last stanza (which repeats the first apart from the single key substitution of 'Dare' for 'Could'), the poet recognizes that the fearful symmetry of the tiger is dependent more on emotional capacity than on physical artistry or craftsmanship. Now that the tiger-symbol is made, he discovers that what makes the tiger awesome is the union of contraries: the emotional tension or aesthetic conflict between tiger and lamb, both aspects of God, little children of Jerusalem. This relationship is revealed, rather than crafted by Los with his hammer. Both tiger and Lamb are deities which reside within the human breast. In this poem, which is symbolic rather than didactic like the epics, Blake explores the implications of Milton's 'hateful siege of contraries' – the aesthetic conflict at the heart of the mind's relation to its internal deities. This is the 'golden string' which Blake offers 'to the Christians' in *Jerusalem*, in an image founded on Milton's 'pendent world':

> I give you the end of a golden string:
>   Only wind it into a ball,
> It will lead you in at Heaven's gate,
>   Built in Jerusalem's wall.

(pl. 77)

4
WORDSWORTH: THE VISIONARY GLEAM

> Whither is fled the visionary gleam?
> Where is it now, the glory and the dream?
> ('Ode: Intimations of Immortality
> from Recollections of Early Childhood')

In these lines from the 'Immortality Ode', Wordsworth formulates the sense of loss of vision which he saw as both a personal grief and also as an ubiquitous phenomenon or phrase in the mind's history. In his own 'thought of grief' there is also perhaps a sense of relief, which he proceeds to justify through his account of historical inevitability. Wordsworth and Coleridge both considered the intensity of poetic vision to be an aspect or manifestation of a universal experience of spiritual nourishment, beginning in infancy. Hence Wordsworth's description of the birth of the soul which follows in the ode, with its beautiful evocation of the newborn infant's radiance in its new heavenly home, not naked but clothed in clouds of glory:

> Our birth is but a sleep and a forgetting:
> The Soul that rises with us, our life's Star,
> Hath had elsewhere its setting,
> And cometh from afar:
> Not in entire forgetfulness,
> And not in utter nakedness,
> But trailing clouds of glory do we come
> From God, who is our home:
> Heaven lies about us in our infancy!
> Shades of the prison-house begin to close
> Upon the growing Boy, . . .

Wordsworth's use of the Platonic myth is uncharacteristic and, in this case, seems to invite the encapsulation of what Keats would call 'the Soul's own home' in a distant place, from which it can become separated. The ode (which seems to have been written in sections over a period of two or three years) ends with a reunion which is a consolation rather than a rediscovery of the soul's home:

> Hence, in a season of calm weather,
> Though inland far we be,
> Our Souls have sight of that immortal sea
> Which brought us hither,
> Can in a moment travel thither,
> And see the Children sport upon the shore,
> And hear the mighty waters rolling evermore.

This vision is not a present faculty of the mind but a nostalgic recollection which can only occur in 'a season of calm weather', when mental change and turbulence is not active. Meanwhile, in between these passages, lies the account of 'shades of the prison-house' which, like Blake's cavern, encloses perception in accordance with the 'acting' which life's roles require. The young child is still an 'Eye among the blind' since it still keeps its 'heritage', but soon,

> thy Soul shall have her earthly freight,
> And custom lie upon thee with a weight,
> Heavy as frost, and deep almost as life!

Unlike Blake, however, Wordsworth does not seem to have a conception of internal negative forces against which the mind needs to struggle in a quest to purify its vision. The weight of custom is literally that; in Wordsworth's myth, the soul's imprisonment is an inevitable result of continuing existence. Hence the sentimentality in the central section of the ode (the 'four years' Darling of a pigmy size', etc.) to which Coleridge strongly objected;[1] though Coleridge also was guilty of sentimentalizing childhood. At one moment the child has its visionary eye; the next moment, or next year, this has gone; the child has left one abode and taken residence in another, and the most that can be hoped for is an occasional glimpse in periods of calm weather, to remind it of what was once its spiritual life.

The 'Immortality Ode' was written in 1803–6, in association with and possibly in answer to, Coleridge's ode 'Dejection', in which he formulates his 'shaping spirit of imagination'. It is generally considered to mark the end of Wordsworth's creative career. There is no suggestion in Wordsworth's ode that the visionary eye was ever a *shaping* spirit – a spirit which shapes the developing mind; in Wordsworth, it is a vision which possesses the mind, or is absent from it, leaving the mind open to the encrustation of 'custom'. Correspondingly, the concept of symbol formation which is a cornerstone of Coleridge's aesthetic principles, is absent in Wordsworth's theory of poetry as stated in the prefaces to the *Lyrical Ballads*. Instead of an organic growth culminating in a symbol, Wordsworth speaks in terms of a mixture or balance of flux and permanence: flowing emotions and 'laws' of nature or of human nature, and a 'balancing' of painful emotions with the 'superadded' charms of metre, 'a principal source of the gratification of the Reader'.[2] He does not really have a concept of poetic language (again, as Coleridge objected in the *Biographia*) – regarding it as a mixture of metre and the ordinary language of men. Both poets rejected the triviality of contemporary poetic diction, but Wordsworth (unlike other poets) also ridiculed the concept of 'Sing heavenly Muse' as an outmoded fiction.[3] Insensible of a symbol-making power lying behind his own language (possibly owing to his own technical facility), he saw the poet's job in terms of restoring the equilibrium in which 'pleasure' consists, smoothing the rawness of emotions and controlling the 'fluxes and refluxes' of emotion in such a way as to demonstrate the 'primary laws of our nature',[4] or even the importance of 'good sense'.[5] 'States of excitement' need to be 'tempered' by 'ordinary feeling', and the only artificiality required of verse is that it should produce an 'overbalance of Pleasure'.[6] His most famous definition of poetry is the one containing 'emotion recollected in tranquillity':

> I have said that Poetry is the spontaneous overflow of powerful feelings: it takes its origin from emotion recollected in tranquillity: the emotion is contemplated till by a species of reaction the tranquillity gradually disappears, and an emotion, similar to that which was before the subject of contemplation, is gradually produced, and does itself actually exist in the mind.[7]

Even though Wordsworth modifies the 'tranquillity' by the statement of an emotion actually 'existing' in the mind at the time of composition, the picture is still essentially a recollective one, viewing a past state through a window not unlike the 'season of calm weather' which allows a nostalgic illumination to disperse the shades of the prison-house. Perhaps the nearest Wordsworth's theory comes to an idea of symbol formation is in formulating how 'the passions of men are incorporated with the beautiful and permanent forms of nature',[8] yet even here there is no investigation of what 'incorporated with' might mean; and the context is an idealized view of how rural life becomes a monument to stories of passion. Wordsworth's theory is thus essentially un-Romantic, and though he uses Coleridge's distinction between fancy and imagination (to criticize it) he does not take its implications on board, nor recognize that his own theory is a mixture of the mechanistic and the moral — to stabilize emotional flux by interdigitating aspects of permanence:

> For our continued influxes of feeling are modified and directed by our thoughts, which are indeed the representatives of all our past feelings; and as by contemplating the relation of these general representatives to each other, we discover what is really important to men, so by the repetition and continuance of this act feelings unconnected with important subjects will be nourished, till at length, if we be originally possessed of much organic sensibility, such habits of mind will be produced that by obeying blindly and mechanically the impulses of those habits we shall describe objects and other sentiments of such a nature and in such connection with each other, that the understanding of the being to whom we address ourselves, if he be in a healthful state of association, must necessarily be in some degree enlightened, his taste exalted, and his affections ameliorated.[9]

Wordsworth's idea of the working of an 'organic sensibility' (be this the poet in relation to his objects, or the reader in relation to the poet) is quite different from Coleridge's, and consists essentially in 'obeying blindly and mechanically' when in a 'healthful state of association' whose flux of feelings is ready to be moralized, exalted, ameliorated. Wordsworth's theory of poetry is thus strangely divorced from his poetic practice and does not form part of a vital philosophical tradition, proved on the pulses, as does Coleridge's.

Wordsworth's creative thinking was done in his poetry before

THE CHAMBER OF MAIDEN THOUGHT

the 'Immortality Ode', and this is where we must look for an expression of the mind's sources of nourishment and vision which has itself fertilized the vision of our culture. The *Lyrical Ballads* were published in 1798; after this Wordsworth began to be increasingly preoccupied with *The Prelude*, which he completed in 1805 (though not allowing its publication during his lifetime). The 'Immortality Ode' was written towards the end of this period, and in 1803 he wrote one of his best sonnets, 'On Westminster Bridge'. This sonnet is, like Blake's 'Tyger', a perfect expression of the aesthetic conflict which occurs at a point when the mind takes a leap forward in its apprehension of the rich and awesome potential of its internal deities. 'Westminster Bridge' is also a marriage of contraries, of innocence and experience:

> Earth has not any thing to shew more fair:
> Dull would be be of soul who could pass by
> A sight so touching in its majesty:
> This City now doth like a garment wear
> The beauty of the morning; silent, bare,
> Ships, towers, domes, theatres, and temples lie
> Open unto the fields, and to the sky;
> All bright and glittering in the smokeless air.
> Never did sun more beautifully steep
> In his first splendour valley, rock, or hill;
> Ne'er saw I, never felt, a calm so deep!
> The river glideth at his own sweet will:
> Dear God! the very houses seem asleep;
> And all that mighty heart is lying still!

In Wordsworth's personal religious doctrine at this point, the country is heaven and the city is hell; in the mythology of both Wordsworth and Coleridge, to be brought up in the city is to be a spiritual chimney-sweep, permanently scarred as in Blake's 'London' (a mythology founded on *Paradise Lost*'s 'As one who long in populous city pent', IX. 445). Yet in this sonnet, the city is transformed by the 'garment' of beauty, such that it embodies within it the naked forms of nature – its ships, towers, domes, echoing valley, rock and hill in a way which is a revelation to the poet, who is experiencing what Blake described as 'Did he who made the Lamb make thee?' The city's new garment is not one of Blake's 'opaque coverings' for the truth, but a cleansing of perception through which the city's inner life seems to breathe and emanate – as in 'bright and glittering in the smokeless air'. In effect this is another version of 'trailing clouds of glory'. In the face of this revelation, the poet's own preconceptions are made powerless, and instead, his visionary eye links him to the 'will' of the river which glides powerfully through the whole picture uniting its elements, like Blake's 'line of the Almighty'. It is the only moving object in the picture, the 'mighty heart' which testifies to the awesome reserves of life coiled up within the city, both revealed and veiled by its beauty. The exclamation 'Dear God!' has a tinge not just of wonder but of fear, as the poet realizes the implications of 'that beauty which (as Milton sings)/Hath terror in it' – as Wordsworth describes it in *The Prelude* (XIII. 225–6). The visionary gleam, as he well knew, was 'fostered' from the beginning 'by beauty and by fear' (I . 306). Yet, as in 'The Tyger', the fear of disintegration or destruction is contained or 'framed' by the poem's formal symmetry, which upholds the poet's identity in its network of contrary tensions at the same time as it appears to negate his selfhood or preconceptions. The poet's vision itself wears the garment of beauty which is perhaps more likely to nurture than devour him; his emotional conflict has become symbolized. And unlike the analogous point in the 'Immortality Ode', the sense of 'heaven' does not belong to a distant realm of reality from which the poet is shortly to be cut off; it is present now in the 'calm so deep' which frames the underground tumult. This is not emotion recollected in tranquillity but revelation at the time of writing; its implications point forwards to unknown acts of knowledge between city and river, sun and valley – not backwards to the imprisonment (or is it the relinquishment?) of vision.

Wordsworth's visionary passages in *The Prelude, or, Growth of a Poet's Mind*, embody a vivid perception of tumultuous forces which vitalize dramatically the scene of his inner world. In Book I, Wordsworth describes rowing in a boat as a boy and being frightened by a cliff:

> She was an elfin Pinnace; lustily
> I dipp'd my oars into the silent Lake,
> And, as I rose upon the stroke, my Boat
> Went heaving through the water, like a Swan;
> When from behind the craggy Steep, till then

> The bound of the horizon, a huge Cliff,
> As if with voluntary power instinct,
> Uprear'd its head. I struck, and struck again,
> And, growing still in stature, the huge Cliff
> Rose up between me and the stars, and still,
> With measur'd motion, like a living thing,
> Strode after me.
>
> (I. 401–12)

The boy in his feminine boat (which is both tiny and somehow magical, 'elfin') feels himself a protected, inviolate explorer upon the lake of his mind, ringed by mountains which seem to contain rather than threaten: the function of the 'craggy Steep' at first is to give bounds to his mental horizon, to contain the lake of consciousness. The pattern of rise and fall which ripples the surface of the 'silent lake' is initiated by himself: 'I dipp'd my oars ... I rose upon the stroke'. Suddenly the nature of the horizon which securely bounds his world, changes: the 'craggy Steep' releases the figure of the huge cliff, whose genie-like powers dwarf those of the elfin rower. The movement of the oars is described as if their disturbance of the lake is identical with a feeling of striking against the cliff itself: 'I struck, and struck again'. This action, or feeling-action, seems to animate the cliff further, till 'growing in stature' in response to the boy's fear, it pursues and seems to swallow in its shadow the figure of the boy in the boat. The pursuing cliff becomes the source of a 'darkness' in his mind, which takes the shape of

> huge and mighty Forms that do not live
> Like living men mov'd slowly through the mind
> By day and were the trouble of my dreams.
>
> (I. 424–6)

Now, explicitly, the oar-strokes trouble not water but dreams; the cliff's 'measur'd motion' over the lake becomes 'mov'd slowly through the mind'; though it started 'like a living thing' it has now become part of the world of Platonic forms whose life is not 'like living men'. Through an un-tranquil abstraction, external nature becomes symbolic of the inner world, reflecting the drama between the boy-like self and the giant-like gods of consciousness who at first seem to be evoked by him and are then recognized to have independent life and mysterious power. The giant cliff is a masculine aspect of the feminine goddess-mountain whose arms encircle the scene of the poet's life experiences in a way both secure and frightening, in response to the outgoing quality of his identification with these forces of his inner life. He 'drank the visionary power' from sounds which were 'the ghostly language of the ancient earth' (II. 328): seeing the lines of his own emotional tensions transcribed directly on the face of nature, symbiotically linked with his own boyhood body and present creative mind.

Wordsworth states that both the 'light' and the 'dark' qualities of aesthetic experience contributed to his sense of being one of Nature's 'favour'd Beings' (I. 364). Each visionary experience is founded on a network of dramatic tensions in chiaroscuro which are suddenly lit up by the 'planting' of inward eyes (in Milton's phrase): in Wordsworth's words, these are

> visitings
> Of awful promise, when the light of sense
> Goes out in flashes that have shewn to us
> The invisible world . . . .
> Tumult and peace, the darkness and the light
> Were all like workings of one mind, the features
> Of the same face, blossoms upon one tree,
> Characters of the great Apocalypse,
> The types and symbols of Eternity,
> Of first, and last, and midst, and without end.
> (VI. 533–72)

Tumult and peace, darkness and light, are all necessary to the ability to symbolize – that is, to see – the invisible or eternal world whose 'promise' is 'awful' (awe-ful). And each visionary experience, though transcribed in the past tense, is not a recollection but an enactment which poetry itself makes meaningful: only now becoming part of the growing mind which is fictitiously being traced in memory. We begin to see how the vision of *The Prelude* differs in quality from the nostalgic picture of childhood as the eye among the blind, in the 'Immortality Ode'. Indeed the exploring faculty imaged by the 'boy' in *The Prelude* has more in common with Milton's Satan than with the innocent child of nature which was to become conventional. The clash of qualities and identifications which comprise true aesthetic vision was imaged by Milton in terms of a mist (the distortion of light by water) – beginning with the fallen archangel looking like the sun in mist shorn of its brightness; and the chasms and vapours which so frequently surround visionary experience in *The Prelude* have their origin, or the origin of their meaning, in *Paradise Lost* at the time of the fall, just as much as in the Lake District. The influence of Milton at these points is itself one of those 'huge and mighty Forms' which shape the imagination, an internal deity or poetic object waiting to resonate with the poet. Thus Wordsworth describes an 'ocean' of mist on moonlit Snowdon:

> and from the shore
> At distance not the third part of a mile
> Was a blue chasm; a fracture in the vapour,
> A deep and gloomy breathing-place through which
> Mounted the roars of waters, torrents, streams
> Innumerable, roaring with one voice.
> The universal spectacle throughout
> Was shaped for admiration and delight
> Grand in itself alone, but in that breach
> Through which the homeless voice of waters rose,
> That dark deep thoroughfare had Nature lodg'd
> The Soul, the Imagination of the whole.
> (XIII. 54–65)

Satan entered Eden in the same mists; his complaint 'with what delight could I have walk'd thee round' is echoed in the spectacle 'shaped for admiration and delight'; and his infiltration of Eden's smooth texture is echoed in the 'fracture' or 'breach' in Nature's front which is nevertheless the core of its meaning, a 'dark deep thoroughfare' to its Soul. Paradoxically it is the breach which gives a home to the 'homeless voice' of waters (the innumerable figments of imagination clamouring to be heard, like Blake's minute particulars). This breach in perfection provides a home or 'lodge' for the Imagination which then colours the 'whole', the entire picture, making it in fact a symbol for the poet's own sense of loss or exclusion being ultimately understood and contained. It is Wordsworth's version of Shakespeare's giving to airy nothing (here, vaporous nothing) a local habitation and a name. Imagination is lodged, quite literally, at the heart of nature.

Another of Wordsworth's explorer figures, likewise founded on Milton's Satan, is the sheepdog whose movements of mountain-knowledge seem to trace emotional conflicts and reveal latent lines of imagination embedded in nature's flesh. In Book VIII two separate recollections of sheepdogs seem blended into a single poetic experience: the first taking place on

> a day of exhalations, spread
> Upon the mountains, mists and steam-like fogs
> Redounding everywhere,

when the shepherd and his dog suddenly 'emerge from the silvery vapours':

> Girt round with mists, they stood and look'd about
> From that enclosure small, inhabitants
> Of an aerial Island floating on,
> As seem'd, with that Abode in which they were,
> A little pendent area of grey rocks,
> By the soft wind breath'd forward. With delight
> As bland almost, one Evening I beheld . . .
>
> (VIII. 84–102)

The passage is full of echoes again of Satan's first view of Eden and its inhabitants, a pendent world hanging from heaven by a chain and miraculously wreathed in clouds of glory. This is the first stage in the archetypal Wordsworthian vision; the second stage (vision of another evening of delight) concerns the sheepdog in action, revealing to the observer the inner drama which takes place in the brave new world of that 'aerial Island' which emerges from the mists. The dog,

> with a Man's intelligence
> Advancing, or retreating on his steps,
> Through every pervious strait, to the right or left,
> Thridded away unbaffled; while the Flock
> Fled upwards from the terror of his Bark
> Through rocks and seams of turf with liquid gold
> Irradiate, that deep farewell light by which
> The setting sun proclaims the love he bears
> To mountain regions.
>
> (VIII. 112–19)

Like Milton's convoluting burnished serpent, the dog – an inspired vehicle of intelligence – weaves the sheep into the

THE CHAMBER OF MAIDEN THOUGHT

mountains, in response to the command of the distant shepherd (his god). His tracks follow the mountain's veins, 'rocks and seams' – the inner tensions or routes towards knowledge which lie implicitly in its face, like the breach which allowed the homeless waters a voice. As the waters were 'innumerable' yet spoke with 'one voice', so the massed Flock moves with one accord in a vertical line up towards the sun, as if engendered by the mountain itself: 'Fled upwards from the terror of his Bark'. Both the dog and the flock represent aspects of the poet's mind, responding to some inherent guiding principle which unites both 'terror' and 'unbaffled' persistence in a form of complex artistic tracery. The path towards knowledge which they demarcate is not a straightforward one but an interweaving of tensions (across the mountain), yet still progressing in one direction, upwards. Suddenly, on this foundation, a species of revelation takes place: the weaving tracks are seen to be irradiated by the setting sun, but as though from within the mountain, filling its seams with 'liquid gold/Irradiate' – a line which echoes in language and meaning Milton's plea for inspiration: 'through all her powers the mind/Irradiate, there plant eyes'. The setting sun in his proclamation of love, plants eyes in the mind–mountain–breast: eyes which have always been there but not revealed. Thus is established the serenity of internal deities, in response to the poet's quest for knowledge. This is Wordsworth's presentation of the 'visionary power' from which he 'drank' as a child, from which he now drinks as a poet.

In the face of Wordsworth's inimitable yet archetypal vision of the infant-mind's confident link with its ultimate sources of knowledge, who always seem to respond to the identifications woven by his linguistic magic, it is understandable that Coleridge could write – only half-jokingly – that Wordsworth had 'descended on him, like the ["Know Thyself"] from Heaven; by showing him what poetry was, he made him know, that he himself was no poet.'[10] Coleridge endeavoured to drown his envy through idolization, taking refuge in the self-pitying idea that he 'was no poet'. A myth was invented and maintained between the two of them that Wordsworth (reared in the Lakes) was the poet, and Coleridge (inevitably, reared in the City) was to play the role of observer, supporter, admirer and interpreter to the world. At the end of *The Prelude*, Wordsworth praises Coleridge's 'most loving

Soul! Placed on this earth to love and understand' – that is, to love and understand he, Wordsworth, who has here exemplified 'the discipline/And consummation of the Poet's mind' (XIII. 249–72). Coleridge, in his poem 'To William Wordsworth' (written after hearing Wordsworth recite *The Prelude* to him), envisages him as raised on a pedestal and speaking 'calm and sure/From the dread watch-tower of man's absolute self'; and sees himself as a sort of adoring slave, a 'listening heart':

> The tumult rose and ceased: for Peace is nigh
> Where Wisdom's voice has found a listening heart.

Coleridge's later irritation with Wordsworth must derive partly from this diffident stance adopted to shield himself from confronting his own envy. His criticism of Wordsworth in the *Biographia Literaria*, though apparently rational and coherently argued, seems slightly off-key as though he were not confronting the real issue at the heart of the matter. The myth of poet with his pet-critic was probably detrimental to them both, and must have encouraged the self-idealizing aspect of Wordsworth's character (called by Keats the 'egotistical sublime'). In Book IX of *The Prelude*, Wordsworth substituted the romance of 'Julia and Vaudracour' in the place where he should have analysed his own feelings of guilt about Annette Vallon, illustrating how even *The Prelude* could be used as a false covering over unpalatable truths, not an exploratory mode of writing. Later in the preface to *The Excursion*, Wordsworth compares his epic intentions to Milton's in a way which suggests that his own subject ('the Mind of Man,/My haunt, and the main region of my Song') is a new one, as if he had forgotten or was never totally aware of the nature of his debt to Milton. Wordsworth's growing self-idealization as he retreated into the 'dread watch-tower of man's absolute self' was his own refuge from the conflicts and tensions integral to poetic vitality. Already by the 'Immortality Ode', the 'visionary gleam' has become sentimentalized in recollection and distanced from the visionary experience of *The Prelude*, and poetry is being promoted as a vehicle for consolation rather than for exploration. Coleridge early on recognized that "Tis a strange assertion, that the Essence of Identity lies in *recollective* Consciousness.'[11] Wordsworth never confronted the negative forces arising from within the poet himself, which other poets constantly present as temptations to be overcome. Milton's formulation of the temptation to be a 'petty god', in relation to Samson's recollection of past heroic feats in *Samson Agonistes* (l. 529), would have applied fairly accurately to Wordsworth's internal negativism – which went unacknowledged and so, undefeated. Instead of analysing the 'petty god' within himself as did Milton, Wordsworth accepted the position of god-on-earth offered by Coleridge, as his sanctimonious identity-shield. The moralizing words written later in 'Laodamia' – 'the Gods approve/The depth and not the tumult of the soul' – surely represent his own implicit philosophy of escape from poetry itself after the 'Immortality Ode'. Wordsworth's poetic spirit was not entombed by accumulating years so much as relinquished by inner weakness – by inability to continue with the tumult of the soul in which the life of poetry consists. Indeed, Wordsworth seems to have relinquished it almost as soon as he knew what it was, if we take *The Prelude* to embody present experience rather than past experience. The concept of envy, of internal nihilism, which was so fully explored by Shakespeare and Milton and understood by Blake, is somehow left out of the Wordsworthian model of the mind (and to some extent the Coleridgean), weakening its own ability to continue exploring emotional reality. Keats, who was the least spiteful and egocentric of all the Romantic poets, and a 'three parts' admirer of Wordsworth himself,[12] gave the most virulent condemnation of Wordsworth:

> For the sake of a few fine imaginative or domestic passages, are we to be bullied into a certain Philosophy engendered in the whims of an Egotist – Every man has his speculations, but every man does not brood and peacock over them till he makes a false coinage and deceives himself.[13]

He formulated what perhaps Coleridge did not quite dare to express – the suspicion that Wordsworth with his supreme innate genius had somehow betrayed the cause of the imagination, the continuing life and development of the mind through the poetic spirit. After initially presenting a seminal vision of the mind's sources of spiritual nourishment, he then covered his own identity with a 'false coinage', thereby not only curtailing his own development, but also disappointing succeeding generations who needed to know how their identity could – in Keats's phrase – 'create itself'.

5
COLERIDGE: PROGRESSIVE BEING

> The imagination is the distinguishing characteristic of man as a progressive being.
>
> (Lecture on Literature, 1818)[1]

Coleridge, like Wordsworth, relinquished poetry as a means of mental exploration – the medium through which a 'shaping spirit of imagination' could take over from the self and construct his own mind for him. But while Wordsworth enshrined his past vision and made his earlier self a place of worship by his older self, Coleridge pursued a more rewarding means of assimilating poetic experience. The problem of what 'imagination' is – what makes the mind continue to grow – became the cornerstone of Coleridge's poetic philosophy, always proved upon the pulses of his own imagination. Though feeling himself to be abandoned by 'the poet' (the poet within himself, split off into Wordsworth), his mind seized another mode of working which seemed ugly and cumbersome by comparison with poetic language yet which essentially remained faithful to the poetic spirit. Coleridge was drawn reluctantly into 'delving in the metaphysic depths':

> I was once a Volume of Gold Leaf, rising & riding on every breath of Fancy – but I have beaten myself back into weight & density, now I sink in quicksilver, yea, remain squat and square on the earth amid the hurricane, that makes Oaks and Straws join in one dance.[2]

These 'quicksilver mines' remain Coleridge's image for the mental depths in which it is impossible to escape the tumult of the soul.[3] He felt himself driven into them against his will: 'Sickness and some other and worse afflictions first forced me into downright metaphysics';[4] but in evolving a way of thinking about poetic experience which was based on his own reading and writing of poetry, Coleridge made an invaluable contribution to the bridge between literature and psychology. Probably, part of him (his opium-addict self) would have liked to retire, like Wordsworth; but he was driven onwards by a sense of religious duty like Milton's; as he wrote at the end of his life, 'I have no fear of Dying other than that of being seized with the stolen goods on me – the talents which had been entrusted to me.'[5] And Coleridge's 'talents' for the major part of his career consisted in establishing an experiential philosophy which clearly differentiated the various types of imitative or mechanical learning from organic and imaginative learning in which knowledge is the mind's 'being' and contributes to its growth:

> All knowledge that enlightens and liberalizes, is a form and a means of self-knowledge.... At the best, the several knowledges are in the Mind as in a Lumber-garret: while *Principles* with the Laws, by which they are unfolded into their consequences, when they are once thoroughly mastered, *become the mind itself* and are living and constituent parts of it.[6]

Coleridge's concern was with how the mind acquired 'principles' not information, internal identity not external marks of status, a shaping spirit of imagination rather than a fixed form of fancy. And his immersion in poetry was integral to his approach to these questions; as a species of knowledge which only became real with self-knowledge, it could be said to provide the foundation for Coleridge's model of the mind.

One of the seminal events in Coleridge's own experience was the writing of *The Ancient Mariner* in 1797. In its portrayal of unconscious guilt and remorse it forms an emotional counterpart to Wordsworth's of infant joy, so is also a seminal event in Romantic literature. Later, Coleridge said the classification of 'Fear, Hope, Rage, Shame, & (strongest of all) Remorse, forms . . . the most difficult & at the same time the most interesting Problem of Psychology'.[7] In this poem, the figure of the poet – divided between the personae of Mariner and Wedding Guest – bears little relation to Coleridge's sentimentalized idea of the poet 'rising and riding on every breath of Fancy' (apart from the impetus given by the simple ballad narrative); one suspects that this image of the poet belongs to the realms of wish-fulfilment and idealized security such as those in which he placed the figure of Wordsworth. One side of Coleridge would have liked an indulgent view of inspiration as automatic fancy-riding, but the other side knew that this was not the emotional truth. Even 'Kubla Khan' which has this automatic quality as it mellifluously and effortlessly strings together an aggregation of Romantic hieroglyphs, was described by Coleridge as a 'psychological curiosity' associated with his escapist opium-addiction,[8] not an inspired process of symbol formation. In a poem of inspired self-knowledge like the *Mariner*, the poet does not ride on the breath of fancy but is pursued by 'the Storm-blast, tyrannous and strong'. The voyage of the Mariner is in a sense the dream or internal condition of the Wedding Guest, and is what prevents the Guest from entering the church (like Theseus' 'hallow'd house') to celebrate the 'marriage' of his internal objects. The Mariner instinctively knows 'the man that must hear me', and 'holds' him with his 'glittering eye', until by the end the Guest has internalized the tale and finds he is barred by his spiritual state alone from the bridegroom's door (and perhaps, from the status of bridegroom):

> The Mariner, whose eye is bright,
> Whose beard is age with hoar,
> Is gone: and now the Wedding-Guest
> Turned from the bridegroom's door.
>
> He went like one that hath been stunned,
> And is of sense forlorn . . .
>
> (ll. 618–23)

He is 'stunned' essentially by revelations about himself and his attitude to creativity, the spiritual governors of his inner life. Initially, the bride herself is an alarming figure as she sweeps past and paces into the hall, not so different in her movements from the 'nightmare Life-in-Death' into whom she metamorphoses in the centre of the poem. On her first appearance,

> The bride hath paced into the hall,
> Red as a rose is she;
> Nodding their heads before her goes
> The merry minstrelsy.
>
> (ll. 33–6)

THE CHAMBER OF MAIDEN THOUGHT

Almost immediately her rhythmic pacing turns into that of the Storm-blast, who sweeps the shipful of men before him just as she swept the merry ministrelsy:

> And now the STORM-BLAST came, and he
> Was tyrannous and strong:
> He struck with his o'ertaking wings,
> And chased us south along.
>
> With sloping masts and dipping prow,
> As who pursued with yell and blow
> Still treads the shadow of his foe,
> And forward bends his head,
> The ship drove fast, loud roared the blast,
> And southward aye we fled.
>
> (ll 41–50)

The poet's ship or body is pursued by alarming forces, not yet retributive but raining yells and blows like a child before an adult's temper tantrum. In the sudden wondrous calm which ensues, when 'ice, mast-high, came floating by,/As green as emerald', voices from tumultuous unconscious depths become audible, seeking expression yet speaking a language which is unrecognizable:

> The ice was here, the ice was there,
> The ice was all around:
> It cracked and growled, and roared and howled,
> Like noises in a swound!
>
> (ll. 59–62)

From these primitive heathen growlings (like Wordsworth's cliff, chasms and 'homeless voice of waters'), the Albatross emerges like a 'Christian soul' and seems to contain these infantile tempestuous roarings within a framework of simple piety which steers the sailors through the ice: coming every day for food, play and 'vespers nine'. It perches on the mast, level with the huge icebergs. This representation of an early stage in psychic and poetic development is shattered by the shooting of the Albatross. The Mariner had been unaware of his dependence on the life of the Albatross, and had assumed it was the other way round – a species of infantile misconception about the poetic mother or Muse: in what sense does the bird respond to the 'mariners' hollo' (like an infant's cry) when it is called? Following this misconception, the Storm-blast reappears as the retributive Sun-god, and fixes the boat to the 'painted ocean' by the masthead where the Albatross used to perch:

> All in a hot and copper sky,
> The bloody Sun, at noon,
> Right up above the mast did stand,
> No bigger than the Moon.
>
> Day after day, day after day,
> We stuck, nor breath nor motion;
> As idle as a painted ship
> Upon a painted ocean.
>
> Water, water, everywhere,
> And all the boards did shrink;
> Water, water, everywhere,
> Nor any drop to drink.
>
> (ll. 111–22)

The poet-mariner has cut himself off from his sources of spiritual nourishment, in particular what Wordsworth calls the 'drinking' of the visionary power, owing to his crime of omnipotence. His mind is drained, 'and all the boards did shrink'. He is immobilized within a condition of false poetry, an anti-symbolic universe of artificial 'painting' – painting which replaces or covers life (like Blake's view of error) rather than imagery which springs from inner life and gives a local habitation to the imagination. The effect of this type of (false) poetry was defined by Coleridge: 'Poetry – excites us to artificial feelings – makes us callous to real ones.'[9] Riding on the breath of fancy leads only to the 'wicked whisper' from a 'heart as dry as dust' (ll. 246–7).

The central section of the *Mariner* is a brilliant symbolic expression of this anti-symbolic mental state: the state which bars the mind from witnessing the internal marriage of contraries which constitutes inspiration. Having symbolized this condition, the poet with equal inspiration intuits the remedy, though this involves first of all a confrontation with the 'Nightmare Life-in-Death' which the bride and the Albatross have become in his imagination:

> Her lips were red, her looks were free,
> Her locks were yellow as gold:
> Her skin was white as leprosy,
> The Night-mare LIFE-IN-DEATH was she,
> Who thicks man's blood with cold.
>
> The naked hulk alongside came,
> And the twain were casting dice . . .
>
> (ll. 190–6)

In the game of dice between Death and Life-in-Death, the inhabitants of this spectre-ship or false body of poetry, the latter wins the poet's soul and thereby condemns him to a lifelong struggle with the imagination (which begins to be recounted during the later part of the poem). The ambiguous concept of 'life in death' was, for Coleridge, certainly the most painful of the alternatives, yet also the most fruitful for the soul, and was identified by him with the eternal life of godliness or reason. Thus in an 'epitaph' written for himself he uses the same phrase:

> O, lift one thought in prayer for S.T.C.;
> That he who many a year with toil of breath
> Found death in life, may here find life in death!

In a sense, life in death is the object of the soul's search for development and an essential part of imaginative experience. Immediately after the revelation brought him by the spectre-ship, the Mariner sees the Albatross in another light – as it were spiritualized, in the form of the 'moving Moon' who inhabits realms unreachable by any cross-bow:

> The moving Moon went up the sky,
> And no where did abide:
> Softly she was going up,
> And a star or two beside –
>
> (ll. 263–6)

The moonlight transfigures the water-snakes which he had found so hideous: first outside the ship's shadow (burning 'a still and awful red'), and then within it:

> Within the shadow of the ship
> I watched their rich attire:

> Blue, glossy green, and velvet black,
> They coiled and swam; and every track
> Was a flash of golden fire.
> O happy living things! no tongue
> Their beauty might declare:
> A spring of love gushed from my heart,
> And I blessed them unaware:
>
> (ll. 277–87)

The play of light traces the restored line of identification between the poet and his source of inspiration, the moon who transforms the dry burning shadow into a vital inner world of flashing lights and fountains (Coleridge's characteristic imagery for 'reason'). When the ugly is seen to become beautiful, and the vision of poetry and beauty is restored, the 'naked hulk' aspect of the feminine principle is exorcized – represented by the corpse of the Albatross falling 'like lead into the sea'. The ugliness which had been in the mind of the beholder is lifted when the doors of perception are cleansed. The inspiring force of the moving Moon restores movement to the Mariner's mind, by contrast with the arrow shot from the cross-bow of his ignorant omnipotent self.

This is not the end of the Mariner's story but the beginning; just as the Wedding Guest's assimilation of the dream, and his sense of being turned away from the sacred chamber of his internal objects, may perhaps be the beginning of a future story to be told truthfully rather than omnipotently. Certainly it haunted Coleridge for years, like one of those dreams which he described as the 'very Substances and foot-thick Calamities of my Life',[10] or which Emily Brontë would have described as going 'through and through [one] like wine through water, changing the very colour of [one's] life.'[11] Its symbolic presentation of the drama between inspiration and omnipotence came as a species of revelation, and underlies the whole series of distinctions between true and false (or limited) modes of coming to knowledge, which form the backbone of the essential Coleridgean philosophy. His distinctions between organic and mechanical, wisdom and knowledge, symbol and allegory (or sign-systems), reason and understanding, imagination and fancy, are all founded on this primary revelation of self-knowledge. His own version of the 'organic' philosophy originating in Germany was worked out on the pulses of his Shakespeare criticism, in the context of trying to define the nature of the poetic or imaginative mind which Shakespeare supremely modelled:

> He projected his mind out of his particular being, and felt and made others feel, on subjects in no way connected with himself, except by force of contemplation, and that sublime faculty, by which a great mind becomes that which it meditates on.[12]

The process of self-knowledge is the opposite of egocentric; the mind which 'becomes' its own ideas, does so by projecting itself out of its selfhood, and by imaginatively entering-in is entered into, so grows or 'becomes' an extension of its own being. In this mind-extending process, the poet gives form to 'our own Feelings, that never perhaps were attached by us consciously to our own personal Selves'.[13] Poetry gives form to the unknown which is a latent part of our being, such that we become it, and it becomes us. In analogy with this, Coleridge defined the nature of Shakespeare's works as coming into existence in accordance with a shaping spirit of imagination outside the dominance of the poet's self:

> The form is mechanic when on any given material we impress a pre-determined form, not necessarily arising out of the properties of the material.... The organic form, on the other hand, is innate; it shapes as it develops itself from within, and the fullness of its development is one and the same with the perfection of its outward form. Such is the life, such the form.[14]

Time and again Coleridge reworks the contrast between forms which are 'super-induced' by a static mind, and forms which 'evolve' according to an innate principle of evolution, such that the 'form' of the inspired work of art is a manifestation of the evolving mind itself, and its internal form:

> The difference therefore between Fabrication and Generation becomes clearly indicable/the Form of the latter is ab intra, *evolved*, the other ab extra, *impressed* – the latter is representative always of something not itself,... but the former is representative of its own cause within itself.[15]

We remember Theseus' problems with the 'form in wax' false aesthetics of Egeus. Here as there, the key to the process of internal development which makes the personality of the poem a manifestation of its inner principle of causation, is the operation of imagination. Like Blake, Coleridge sometimes speaks of imagination not as a faculty but as a place, in which the forms of meaning are generated and contained:

> Form is factitious Being, and Thinking is the process, Imagination the Laboratory, in which Thought elaborates Essence into Existence. A Philosopher, i.e. a nominal Philosopher without Imagination, is a *Coiner* – Vanity, the Froth of the molten Mass, is his *Stuff* – and Verbiage the Stamp & Impression.[16]

True thinking is a product of imagination and a form of being (that is, of becoming); in this Coleridge's idea of organic mental growth consists; and as always, it is contrasted with the fake, omnipotent, super-induced version of the merely 'nominal' philosopher with his 'verbiage'. In the famous definition of the *Biographia Literaria* (1817), Coleridge formulates 'fancy' as a 'mode of memory' which has 'no other counters to play with, but only fixities and definites'.[17] Although he sometimes allows a limited usefulness to fancy, he always stresses that it must be kept subordinate as a tool of the imagination, and not worshipped as if it were itself a creative power (which would involve stifling the imagination). Fancy, the 'aggregating' power (as he terms it elsewhere), is not a lower form of imagination (the 'modifying' power), but a different quality altogether. And

> The primary Imagination I hold to be the living power and prime agent of all human perception, and as a repetition in the finite mind of the eternal act of creation in the infinite I AM.[18]

The 'secondary imagination' differs only in 'degree' not in 'kind', and 'dissolves, diffuses, dissipates, in order to re-create'. Imagination is thus the condition of the mind's creating – not only works of art – but itself; it allows the god-like principle of creativity to operate within and to shape its identity.

This brings us to the problem of symbol formation, with which Coleridge was increasingly preoccupied over the years. When the imagination in its laboratory is giving to airy nothing a local habitation and a name, and elaborating 'essence into existence', symbols are being produced. And Coleridge was emphatic that 'An Idea, in the highest sense of that word, cannot be conveyed but by a *symbol*.'[19] Symbols are the concrete evidence of communication between the self and its internal deities who inhabit the realm of ideas – in Coleridge's terminology, the realm of Reason – which he regards as either co-extensive with imagination or (in his later works) as a further realm which nevertheless can only operate through imagination. Symbols are the language of the imagination and the food of the mind, because they carry within them the ideas which are the mind's prerequisite for a condition of continuing growth:

> Every living principle is actuated by an idea; and every idea is living, productive, partaketh of infinity, and (as Bacon has sublimely observed) containeth an endless power of semination.[20]

The *Statesman's Manual,* written at about the same time as the *Biographia*, perhaps contains Coleridge's clearest descriptions of symbolic functioning. As always, he begins by making a differentiation between the real thing and its look-alike – namely, symbols and allegories (sign-systems):

> Now an Allegory is but a translation of abstract notions into a picture-language which is itself nothing but an abstraction from objects of the senses; the principal being more worthless even than its phantom proxy, both alike unsubstantial, and the former shapeless to boot. On the other hand a Symbol ... is characterized by the translucence of the Eternal through and in the Temporal. It always partakes of the Reality which it renders intelligible; and while it enunciates the whole, abides itself as a living part in that Unity, of which it is the representative. The others are but empty echoes which the fancy arbitrarily associates with apparitions of matter.... Alas! for the flocks that are to be led forth to such pastures![21]

The mind which does nothing but fabricate sign-systems (a function of the omnipotent selfhood) and in the 'blindness of self-complacency' is unable to see that they are not symbols but a 'counterfeit product of the mechanical understanding', is condemned to spiritual dehydration like the Mariner when his throat was 'dry as dust', unable to drink the water of faith which 'becomes a well within himself springing up to life everlasting'. A true symbol has its source not in the self but in the fountain of faith or the light of reason, a realm of infinite resource with which the self is organically connected when it incorporates a 'living part' of it into the growing structure of the mind. He wrote in *The*

Friend, in the context of defining the 'method' of the mind's progress, that the object of the 'poetic philosopher Plato' was not to 'establish any particular truth', but to 'open anew a well of springing water . . . by awakening the principle and method of self-development'.[22] For 'all true and living knowledge must proceed from within'.[23] When the inner self makes organic contact with these symbol-producing realms of the mind, then the idea itself becomes known, not in the sense of being owned, but rather, incorporated through this living link of self-development. This is Coleridge's knowledge-as-being, or knowledge-as-becoming. In the same way, the realm of ideas is itself not a 'lumber garret' for filing mechanical codes, but a breeding ground for principles. Contact with a living 'principle' means the 'swallowing-up of self in an object dearer than self, or an idea more vivid':

> At the annunciation of *principles*, of *ideas*, the soul of man wakes and starts up, as an exile in a far distant land at the unexpected sounds of his native language, when after long years of absence, and almost of oblivion, he is suddenly addressed in his own mother tongue.[24]

Principles speak with the 'mother tongue' of the internal mother or poetic muse – the mind's deities, who give birth to ideas,

> that most glorious birth of the God-like within us, which even as the Light, its material symbol, reflects itself from a thousand surfaces, and flies homeward to its Parent Mind enriched with a thousand forms, itself above form and still remaining in its own simplicity and identity![25]

The essential feature of a symbol for Coleridge was thus its organic link with a realm of existence outside the selfhood yet drawn within the mind, being the mind's own 'Parent Mind', with which intimate identification is established, flying back and forth, carrying with it a potential for thousandfold enrichment or endless semination.

Coleridge's conception of a 'symbol' is therefore inseparable from his view of mental growth. The symbol contains the piece of self-knowledge which is organically incorporated as the new part of the mind's structure, retaining its links with its source and hence the potential for future development. The imagination in its laboratory 'gives birth to a system of symbols, harmonious in themselves, and consubstantial with the truths, of which they are the conductors'.[26] The system of symbols resembles Blake's little children of Jerusalem emanating from the eternal mind, but Coleridge is far more emphatic about the principle of progression and about the complexity of the internal identifications on which it is founded. Coleridge wrote: 'we can have no notion of desirable Progression . . . but what supposes a growth of consciousness – or the image of that incommunicable attribute of self-comprehension';[27] the human soul has a 'reflex consciousness of its own continuousness' which allows it to see or imagine mental states beyond its own present condition, hence to grope towards the 'terra incognita of knowledge':

> I do not like that presumptuous Philosophy which in its rage of explanation allows no xyz, no symbol representative of the vast Terra Incognita of Knowledge, for the Facts and Agencies of Mind and matter reserved for future Explorers/ while the ultimate grounds of all must remain inexplicable or Man must cease to be progressive. Our Ignorance with all the intermediates of obscurity is the *condition* of our ever-increasing Knowledge.[28]

A key feature of the progressive mind is the space known only as the Unknown; without this necessary part of an internal landscape, there is no possibility of the organic link (the 'reflex' or 'reflective' consciousness) with the principle of self-development. Coleridge was fascinated by the conditions which had to prevail for the mind to be able to explore its own mystery; and by how these differed from the subjugation of internal structures by the tyranny of the self's fixed ideas and backwards-looking recollective consciousness. He emphasized symbolization rather than verbalization (which he distrusted, despite his own overflowing capacity for it); verbalization is the manipulation of fixed counters, and symbolization (which can include verbal symbolization) the imaginative containment of a living idea. The core of his method of observing the mind was to focus not on 'things only', but on 'the relations of things'.[29] For Coleridge, the very concept of transcendence was a complex one, based not on a ladder of abstraction but on an idea of 'interpenetration':

> The transcendental philosophy demands . . . this one power with its two inherent indestructible yet counteracting forces, and the results or generations to which their inter-penetration gives existence, in the living principle and in the process of our own self-consciousness.[30]

The 'one power' becomes active when a relationship is set up between dialectical forces – perhaps contrary emotions (as in Blake's marriage of contraries), or through the projective–introjective relation between the self and its objects which Coleridge's descriptions frequently foreshadow. He was continually inventing ways of describing this phenomenon of interpenetration, or immanent transcendence: such as, the term 'consubstantial', or the 'prothesis of Inwardness and Outness',[31] or 'the identity of subject and object, subjective and objective' (which he made key critical terms); the 'immanence of ALL in each',[32] or the 'inherence' of the 'empirical I' in 'the absolute I AM'.[33] In this, he felt, lay the crux of the reality of ideas; the *Statesman's Manual* ends with this formulation of the 'highest problem of Philosophy':

> Whether Ideas are regulative only, according to Aristotle and Kant; or likewise CONSTITUTIVE, and one with the power and Life of Nature, according to Plato, and Plotinus ... is the highest *problem* of Philosophy, and not part of its nomenclature.[34]

For Coleridge, with his 'substantial' concept of ideas-in-symbols generating an internal principle of development, there was no question but that ideas could only regulate the mind by being 'constitutive'.

Coleridge's immersion in poetry gave him a conception of the mind as a substantial entity whose internal qualities were like organic fibres linked up by interpenetration. He was interested – perhaps obsessively so – in the relation between mind and body, and in 'psychosomatic' functioning (his own term); he even speculated on the possibility of the soul's prenatal growth:

> One might make a very amusing allegory of an embryo soul up to birth! ... One tiny particle combines with another its like, and, so, lengthens and thickens, and this is, at once, memory and increasing vividness of impression.[35]

Whether pre- or post-natal, he saw the nature of the mind's growth in terms of a continuing transformation from within; the boundaries of the self must be in a potential condition of dissolving to be recreated, under the agency of imagination:

> They and only they can acquire the philosophic imagination, the sacred power of self-intuition, who within themselves can

interpret and understand the symbol, that the wings of the air-sylph are forming within the skin of the caterpillar; those only, who feel in their own spirits the same instinct, which impels the chrysalis of the horned fly to leave room in its involucrum for antennae yet to come. They know and feel, that the *potential* works *in* them, even as the *actual* works on them![36]

This exploration of the mind's terra incognita is a form of spiritual metamorphosis, which occurs when the waters of faith and the energies of reason start to flow; and this only begins when an emotional current of imaginative identification is set up within the mind, and the principle of self-development is activated: 'such is the life, such the form'. Coleridge recognized that the status quo of the human consciousness was in effect a 'negation and voluntary Act of *no*-thinking', but that occasionally development had to occur, whether within the individual or the human race, and that this was the province of 'poetry and religion':

> It is necessary for our limited powers of Consciousness that we should be brought to this negative state, & that should pass into Custom – but likewise necessary that at times we should awake & step forward – this is effected by Poetry & Religion.[37]

Coleridge made the concept of 'the poetic' integral to the quality of an experience – developing hints made by Milton in his tractate *Of Education*, in the passage much admired by Coleridge.[38] Poetry, as a principle of mental action not simply as a verbal discipline, was defined by Coleridge in a way which illuminates it as a touchstone of judgement, a primary criterion of value – the key to the reality or artificiality of a relationship. If an experience or mode of apprehension is poetic – that is, shaped by the imagination – then it is a growth-promoting experience, 'irradiated by the reason' (in one of Coleridge's favourite phrases), leading to 'man as a progressive being'. If not, then it belongs to the sphere of mechanical fancy or un-irradiated understanding dependent on fixities and definites – a sphere of rearrangement, not of growth and transformation: not in itself useless, but liable to be misused and become a 'dead progression'. Poetry awakens the mind from the torpor of its basic assumptions and makes it 'awake and step forward'.

6
KEATS: SOUL-MAKING

> Imperceptibly impelled by the awakening of the thinking principle – within us – we ... get into the Chamber of Maiden-Thought ... intoxicated with the light and the atmosphere, we see nothing but pleasant wonders, and think of delaying there for ever in delight. However among the effects this breathing is father of is that tremendous one of sharpening one's vision into the heart and nature of Man – of convincing one's nerves that the World is full of Misery and Heartbreak, Pain, Sickness and oppression – whereby This Chamber of Maiden-Thought becomes gradually darken'd and at the same time on all sides of it many doors are set open – but all dark – all leading to dark passages – We see not the balance of good and evil. We are in a Mist – *We* are now in that state – We feel 'the burden of the Mystery'.
>
> (letter to Reynolds, 3 May 1818)[1]

Keats's beautiful metaphor of life – that is, the life of the mind – as a 'Mansion of Many Apartments' describes his personal state at the end of his poetic apprenticeship, in the foreshadow of his inspired poetry of 1819. It is a prototypal parable of the infant-soul's explorations in the world of the mind, and also includes Keats's conception of a 'general and gregarious advance of intellect' in cultural history, in which new minds can take advantage of previous endeavours without having to rely totally on their 'individual greatness of Mind' for every step forward in development.[2] In this context, Milton's 'philosophy' (conscious doctrine) is simple by comparison with Wordsworth (whom Keats also regarded as 'a great Poet if not a Philosopher');[3] Keats saw

Wordsworth as having arrived at this point partly by virtue of previous poets, and his 'Genius' as being 'explorative of those dark Passages. Now if we live, and go on thinking, we too shall explore them.'[4] In the event, it was not Wordsworth but Keats who took over the 'grand march of intellect' at this point of poetic Mist and Mystery. He established a relationship with his internal world which enabled him to 'go on thinking'. The Chamber of Maiden Thought is at the heart of the mind's mansion, and all doors open from it. From its original 'infant or thoughtless Chamber', the soul is 'imperceptibly impelled' to the next chamber by innate forces beyond its control, by forces which have strangely 'awakened', on the lines of Coleridge's recognition that 'at times we should awake and step forward', or Ibsen's *When We Dead Awaken*. It is not the 'bright appearance' of Maiden Thought which motivates, though the chamber stands invitingly with its 'wide open door'; rather, it is this innate 'thinking principle'. Indeed, 'we care not to hasten to it, but are at length impelled'. Such is the nature of the poetic principle of self-development, activated by internal forces beyond the self's volition, despite the self's reluctance. Once in the second chamber, the infant soul is 'intoxicated' by the sensuous wonder of its brave new world; yet its very 'breathing' of that new world, incorporating it into the fibres of its own being, 'is father to' the poison of heartbreak and sickness, as an inevitable part of its growing condition. This is the thought-sickness of which Hamlet complained; or in Keats's own words, 'Until we are sick, we understand not.'[5] And eventually, the dark doorways send their emanations into the Chamber of Maiden Thought, so the condition of 'straining at particles of light in the midst of a great darkness' (as Keats puts it later)[6] becomes unavoidable. Now the poetic mind is shrouded in mist, which expresses the knowledge of 'Mystery', at last felt upon the pulses. Keats leaves his extended metaphor at this point, on the threshold of a new chamber of discovery – saying he has not 'arrived' any further.

The initial intoxication of Maiden Thought conveys Keats's own first experience of poetry, which 'swam into his ken' like a 'new planet',[7] and on which he seized with a 'Leviathan' appetite for its emotional food. As he wrote the year before: 'I find that I cannot exist without poetry – without eternal poetry – half the day will not do – the whole of it – I began with a little, but habit has made me a Leviathan.'[8] From the beginning, this passionate need for the immense store of riches which the young Keats sensed were embodied within poetry, co-existed with the daunting fear of 'flattering oneself into the delusion of being a great poet' and thus blaspheming against poetry's god, Apollo, through presumption or hubris – the 'crime' of being a 'Selfdeluder'.[9] And for Keats, writing poetry was the necessary response to reading it; writing constituted the process of digestion of the riches bequeathed by 'great men' such as Shakespeare and Milton who (in Keats's early 'Ode to Apollo') vibrate passions and roll thunders under their god's command. So, Keats wrote, 'I have asked myself so often why I should be a Poet more than other Men, – seeing how great a thing it is.'[10] Keats's world of poetry was inhabited by gods and god-like poets whose identities pressed on his own. His wholehearted and (to superficial appearance) childlike conviction of their reality, was a key factor in his capacity to 'go on thinking' and continually grow out of himself. He paid more than lip-service to these deities within his breast, and this enabled him to override issues which might otherwise have inhibited and would certainly have delayed his poetic quest – such as, the criticism (or praise) of his contemporaries, or his own savage self-criticism. Keats was always conscious of the preciousness of time and the unknown imminence of death (perhaps from the early deaths of his father and mother, and certainly from the death of his beloved brother Tom in December 1818, which was on the horizon from almost the start of Keats's career as a poet). This probably clarified his own aim to be faithful to the 'Genius of Poetry' as an internal principle, and to establish his 'Humbleness' in relation to these internal objects; in contrast with this, deference to the opinions of society or of selfhood was really a type of egotism, or 'Pride'.[11] As he wrote in a rage to his publisher, regarding the 'slipshod Endymion' (whose four thousand lines of blank verse Keats saw as a test of his own capacity to stay the course):

> Had I been nervous about its being a perfect piece, & with that view asked advice, & trembled over every page, it would not have been written; for it is not in my nature to fumble – I will write independently.... The Genius of Poetry must work out its own salvation in a man: It cannot be matured by law & precept, but by sensation and watchfulness in itself – That which is creative must create itself – [12]

Keats never had any doubt about the nature of real ideas as 'constitutive' not merely 'regulative', which Coleridge formulated as the most important problem in philosophy. In the mental orientation in which the creative creates itself, the self's function is to 'sense' and 'watch' the internal manifestations of the Genius of Poetry – the thinking principle, motivated by 'the eternal Being, the Principle of Beauty, – and the Memory of great Men'.[13] The operation of this principle is 'allegorical' – as opposed to 'literal', 'consequitive', or 'by law and precept'; thus,

> they are very shallow people who take everything literal – A Man's life of any worth is a continual allegory – and very few eyes can see the Mystery of his life – a life like the scriptures, figurative –[14]

Keats here uses the term 'allegory' differently from Blake or Coleridge, without its mechanistic connotations; it has the same quality as their 'vision' or 'symbol', as the container for 'mystery'. He makes an equivalent contrast between mechanic and organic qualities when he distinguishes between 'cutting a figure' and 'being figurative' – saying Byron is the former, and Shakespeare the latter.[15] It was in relation to his own strenuous quest to become 'figurative' himself as a poet (to 'be a true Poem', as Milton said), and to conquer the temptation to cut figures, that he furiously insisted he should 'ever consider [people] as debtors to me for verses, not myself to them for admiration'.[16]

'Shakespeare led a life of Allegory; his works are the comments on it.' Inevitably, key figures in the internal drama of the thinking principle's progress, were Shakespeare and Milton (towards whom Keats was more ambivalent, though his admiration was as intense). At the very end of his writing career, Keats wrote that 'Shakespeare and the Paradise Lost every day become greater wonders to me';[17] and though shortly afterwards, when giving up *The Fall of Hyperion*, he was to say that 'life to [Milton] would be death to me',[18] this rejection of his inspiring force was made in the context of suspecting that – as he put it later – the 'continued stretch of his imagination had killed him', and that he refused to 'sing in a cage'.[19] At that point, Milton and the poetic principle were mutually identified and equally hated. Likewise, when Keats was writing the original *Hyperion* during Tom's illness, in the context of both Milton's 'hateful siege of contraries' and Tom's 'identity pressing' on him, he felt: 'I live now in a continual fever

– it must be poisonous to life although I feel well.'[20] But when extricated from the complexities of this tragic context, both Shakespeare and Milton, as creative minds, were seen by Keats as providing not laws and precepts but models for experience: symbolizing through their works the mystery of existence. Keats was determined to internalize their thoughts and their thinking processes:

> I am 'one that gathers Samphire dreadful trade' the Cliff of Poesy Towers above me.... I remember your saying that you had notions of a good Genius presiding over you.... Is it too daring to Fancy Shakespeare this Presider?[21]

Like Wordsworth's pursuing cliff in *The Prelude*, or Coleridge's pursuing forces in *The Ancient Mariner*, the cliff (from *King Lear*) threatens to swallow the tiny figure of the poet. In the same way, Keats half-humorously accused Milton of 'gormandizing' society's limited allowance of 'intellect' owing to the enlargement of his own imagination, so 'leaving the shore pebble all bare'.[22] Yet Keats, instead of shooting the Albatross and denuding his internal world, faces the aesthetic conflict squarely, and derives from the awesome overpoweringness of the object a reciprocal 'good Genius' aspect, presiding over his own development. The aesthetic mentality which Blake had exemplified in 'The Tyger' and Wordsworth in the London of 'Westminster Bridge', was to become characteristically and almost unwaveringly Keats's own mode of experience. In the same context as the Shakespearean cliff, he formulates what will become a consistent principle, and the foundation for his 'Vale of Soul-making' two years later: 'difficulties nerve the Spirit of a Man – they make our Prime Objects a Refuge as well as a Passion'.[23] The Keatsian pattern for creative thought is one of being assimilated into the world of the aesthetic object and then restored to a changed self whose identity has new boundaries. The Grecian Urn, the Nightingale's tree, the bower of Psyche, the vale of Saturn in *Hyperion*, are all symbols of potential new worlds leading outwards from the Chamber of Maiden Thought, each with their governing deities; and in exploring them, the poet each time feels his own boundaries dissolve by means of outward and inward-moving communications, and then re-form. Though the Muse has flown, an aspect of knowledge has been incorporated within the very structure of his mind.

In the context of analysing whether Milton did 'more harm or good' to the world, Keats allegorizes the condition of the 'spiritual Cottager' who is about to be drawn away from his 'mental Cottage of feelings quiet and pleasant – [his] Philosophical Back Garden', towards unknown realms:

> For as the spiritual Cottager knows there are such places as France and Italy and the Andes and the Burning Mountains – so the spiritual Cottager has knowledge of the terra semi incognita of things unearthly; and cannot for his Life, keep in the check rein – [24]

Milton was one of his supreme guides to the terra incognita of things invisible to mortal sight: modelling the process of awakening the thinking principle. In his marginal notes to *Paradise Lost*, Keats writes:

> A poet can seldom have justice done to his imagination – it can scarcely be conceived how Milton's Blindness might here aid the magnitude of his conceptions as a bat in a large gothic vault.[25]

In the process of 'one Mind's imagining into another', the home for conceptions – the spiritual cottage – is magnified like a cathedral in its proportions, as are the conceptions themselves. Earthly obstacles such as blindness are metabolized into spiritual tools, their sensuous implications reversed. Keats internalized this model for expanding the mind, in his own process of metabolizing emotional obstacles by 'etherealizing', 'alchemizing', or 'digesting' (frequent metaphors of his), such that they become developmental aids in the Vale of Soul-making, 'nerving the spirit'. In this way the Chamber of Maiden Thought becomes a Gothic vault. Keats called this searching for 'the principle of beauty in all things', or 'the Beautiful, the poetical in all things';[26] it is the principle which underlies superficial ugliness or fearsomeness and makes 'disagreeables ... evaporate',[27] to reveal the beauty of their spiritual meaning – or as Blake would say, the line of the Almighty. It is in fact the 'thinking principle' of the Maiden Thought model. Keats saw Milton therefore as 'committed to the Extreme':

> Milton in every instance pursues his imagination to the utmost – he is 'sagacious of his Quarry', he sees Beauty on the wing, pounces upon it and gorges it to the producing his essential verse.[28]

This quality of 'extremity' refers to the bat-like sensing of the ultimate boundaries of the mind's chamber in its expanded condition; the idea of Beauty is the quarry and the food which produces in the poet 'essential verse' (in Keats's sense of a 'fellowship with essence').[29] This is what Keats means by his desire for a philosophical mode which will 'widen speculation' and 'ease the Burden of the Mystery'.[30] He is not looking for 'precepts' or 'consequitive reasoning' to keep his imagination or feelings in order; he is looking for a mode which will reveal inherent structure, as well as content:

> The difference of high Sensations with and without knowledge appears to me this – in the latter case we are falling continually ten thousand fathoms deep and being blown up again without wings and with all [the] horror of a bare shouldered Creature – in the former case, our shoulders are fledge, and we go thro' the same air and space without fear.[31]

The 'fledged' poet is not one of modified but of *contained* emotionality, able to divine the meaning and the exploratory or developmental purport of his catastrophic emotional experiences. He can go through the 'same air and space without fear' – a spatial description of symbol formation. Ultimately this culminates in the Vale of Soul-making model of the mind.

In an analogous way, Keats takes two examples of Shakespearean conceits on apparently un-beautiful subjects (the 'barren' trees of winter, and a wounded snail), to show how they become beautiful through the 'intensity of working out conceits' – that is, how they embody an underlying metaphor about Shakespeare's mind in the process of working. He quotes:

> As the snail, whose tender horns being hit,
> Shrinks back into his shelly cave with pain,
> And there all smothered up in shade doth sit,
> Long after fearing to put forth again:
> So at this bloody view her eyes are fled,
> Into the deep dark Cabins of her head.[32]

Like Keats's own dispossessed Saturn later, retired into the shady sadness of a vale where he feels smothered and suffocated, Shakespeare's snail symbolizes the poet's venturing soul which has received a painful blow (in Saturn's case, like Lear's, to his omnipotence), and retires back into the Chamber of Maiden Thought. It is 'his view' but 'her eyes', as if themselves wounded through this identification, retiring bloodied into the cave. Keats comments that Shakespeare like Milton with his 'gormandizing' of intellect 'has left nothing to say about nothing or anything'. Yet again Keats metabolizes this obstacle – the sense of his own snail-like insignificance – and converts it into a feature of self-development under the aegis of Shakespeare as presiding genius (and also of Milton as epic explorer):

> Deep in the shady sadness of a vale
> Far sunken from the healthy breath of morn,
> Far from the fiery noon, and eve's one star,
> Sat grey-haired Saturn, quiet as a stone,
> Still as the silence round about his lair;
> Forest on forest hung about his head
> Like cloud on cloud. No stir of air was there,
> Not so much life as on a summer's day
> Robs not one light seed from the feathered grass,
> But where the dead leaf fell, there did it rest.
> A stream went voiceless by, still deadened more
> By reason of his fallen divinity
> Spreading a shade; the Naiad 'mid her reeds
> Pressed her cold finger closer to her lips.

In these fine opening lines of *Hyperion* (1818), Keats fuses the voices and style of Milton, Shakespeare and Wordsworth. Saturn, as king of the fallen pre-Olympian dynasty, will shortly lament his lost creative powers in terms equivalent to Lear's, having lost his infantile omnipotence: 'Saturn must be King . . . . But cannot I create?/Cannot I form? Cannot I fashion forth/Another world, another universe . . . ?' (I. 125–43). The answer to this question is contained in the original picture in which 'fallen divinity' (the only abstract concept in a concrete picture) itself spreads the shade of its claustrophobic silence and absence of expressive power. The Naiad, a former agent of nature's animism, seals her lips in confirmation of the passage's echo-less resonance ('stone, still, no stir, not so', etc.), whose poetry consists in the ability to express the ugly deprivation of music: 'voiceless, nerveless, listless, realmless'. The extreme sensuousness of the passage conveys mental space and organic suspension, symbolizing the dispossession of Saturn's organizing powers – an enforced passivity and claustrophobia, like Milton's Satan within his serpent prison, expressing the first stage in poetic inspiration. The history of Keats's writing of *Hyperion* is complicated by Tom's death, which Keats associated with the deathly strictures of false art; and the next stage of inspiration by the Muse does not come to fruition here, but only in Keats's later poetry. Nevertheless, before this happens, Keats is aware from his imagining-into the minds of his mentors Shakespeare and Milton, of the potential beauty of this snail-like condition of lost power or lost eyesight. Thus he formulates the 'trembling and delicate snail-horn perception of Beauty' which emerges from 'those innumerable compositions and decompositions which take place between the intellect and its thousand materials'.[33] The snail-poet's pain becomes one of those innumerable, infinitesimal dissolvings of the identity by the imagination (which as Coleridge said, 'dissolves to recreate'), hence a feature of the principle of beauty in all things. In the same way, Keats singled out two passages from *Paradise Lost* as being of a 'very extraordinary beauty': one being Orpheus torn to pieces by the rout, and the other describing Ceres' search for her lost daughter Proserpine, 'which cost Ceres all that pain', after she had been gathered into the cavernous underworld.[34] Yet Proserpine, like the snail, is ready to re-emerge. Both passages are myths about the poetic principle's vulnerability when it becomes separated from its internal deities (Proserpine from Ceres, Orpheus from the Muse) – 'nor could the Muse/Defend her son'. Keats had an unparalleled capacity to internalize the experience of the poetic forebears who formed part of his own internal objects or mental deities; he made their symbolizations his food for thought and 'essential verse', and allowed their experience to structure his own unfledged identity: 'for axioms in philosophy are not axioms until they are proved upon our pulses: we read fine things but never feel them to the full until we have gone the same steps as the Author.'[35] Keats himself 'pounded' and 'gorged' on the quarry of beauty which these poems embodied, and through which he intended to essentialize his own poetic identity.

We see therefore that the beauty–truth equivalent whose most famous expression is contained in the last lines of the 'Ode on a Grecian Urn', runs constantly through all Keats's writings. Keats always regarded a sense of beauty as the first step in recognizing the richness of any potential mind-forming experience; and by 'beauty', as we have seen, he included a range of complex 'sensations' such as pain, ugliness, blindness, etc.: 'I have the same idea of all our Passions as of Love – they are all in their sublime, creative of essential Beauty.'[36] 'The Idea of Beauty' is the hub of all Keats's other critical criteria; such concepts as 'intensity', 'negative capability', 'disinterestedness', 'wise passiveness', 'abstraction', 'fellowship with essence', all radiate outwards from it. 'Essential beauty' – the beauty that is truth – is something which has to be created in the eye of the beholder, 'from his own inwards' as Keats wrote in the context of another characteristic soul-making metaphor, that of the spider spinning its web:

> Memory should not be called knowledge – Many have original Minds who do not think it – they are led away by Custom – Now it appears to me that almost any Man may like the Spider spin from his own inwards his own airy Citadel – the points of leaves and twigs on which the Spider begins her work are few and she fills the Air with a beautiful circuiting: man should be content with as few points to tip with the fine Webb of his Soul and weave a tapestry empyrean –[37]

Keats's idea of creative knowledge, as opposed to mechanical memory or 'consequitive reasoning',[38] is one in which the soul weaves a sort of receiving-net full of fertile crossing-points ('symbols for the spiritual eye'), from which experience can be drawn and radiated back to the centre. The mind – he continues to elaborate – 'receives' like a flower, as well as 'gives' like a bee; and becomes a complex entity with points of contact in both the 'empyrean' vertex and the subsoil, 'mould ethereal':

> Minds would leave each other in contrary directions, traverse each other in Numberless points, and [at] last greet each other at the Journeys end – ... thus by every germ of Spirit sucking the Sap from mould ethereal every human being might become great, and Humanity instead of being a wide heath of Furse and Briars with here and there a remote Oak or Pine, would become a grand democracy of Forest Trees.[39]

Keats, like Blake and Coleridge, saw the possibilities for the collective mind of humanity as modelled on the individual creative mind: both seen in relation to some infinite source of spiritual nurture which Keats described variously in terms of etherealized earth, essential substance, abstracted sensuousness. This is the shaping spirit of imagination, the frame of emotional tensions delicately balanced between giving and receiving, from which 'essential beauty' is evolved – the truth which can make every mind great.

Moreover, the imagining-into faculty is secondary to (perhaps consequent on) the being-imagined-into faculty which (in Coleridge's terms) 'reflects' the mystery of being:

> Several things dovetailed in my mind, & at once it struck me, what quality went to form a Man of Achievement especially in Literature & which Shakespeare possessed so enormously – I mean *Negative Capability*, that is when man is capable of being in uncertainties, Mysteries, doubts, without any irritable reaching after fact & reason – Coleridge, for instance, would let go by a fine isolated verisimilitude caught from the Penetralium of mystery, from being incapable of remaining content with half knowledge. This pursued through Volumes would perhaps take us no further than this, that with a great poet the sense of Beauty overcomes every other consideration, or rather obliterates all consideration.[40]

Keats implicitly regards his own philosophical formulation (made when he was aged 22) as an extension of Coleridge's; yet even he is accused of a sort of premature systemization before the implications of the 'beauty' of the idea he is following have been fully spun out, and the web of mystery established. He probably correctly divined Coleridge's shrinking before the ultimate frightening or 'disagreeable' connotations attendant on the idea of 'Beauty' in the Keatsian sense (of a legacy symbolized in *The Ancient Mariner*), substituting 'reason' at the fountain-head of his value-system. Keats recognised that ultimately, reason – even in its sophisticated Coleridgean sense – would not suffice as the supreme guide to the penetralia of the mystery.[41] For Keats, the 'sense of Beauty' which is elaborated in response to the spidery eye of the beholder weaving in his darkening Chamber of Maiden Thought, is the governing force in the principle of thinking. His criterion of 'Beauty' itself speaks 'volumes', and in its complexity subsumes all other formulations of the poetic principle. Only in response to 'Beauty', can the mind match its tentative explorations to the holding-points of the web of the mystery of its own being, in which it discovers a symbolic congruence. Thus in *The Fall of Hyperion* at the end of his career (two years later), Keats describes the formation of a tapestry empyrean when 'the lofty theme ... hung vast before my mind,/With half-unravelled web' (I. 306–8), as the identity of a poet begins to grow out of that of fanatic and dreamer. When this structural web begins to form, the mind is 'fledged' and set on a course of self-development.

Keats began this process of 'fledging' his mind when he set out on a walking tour of Scotland with his friend Brown in the summer of 1818, determined to 'learn poetry' and to 'harvest' beauty. In the course of the tour he encountered not only the 'countenance or intellectual tone' of the mountains and natural wonders,[42] but also new images for the 'birthplace' of poetry – including Milton's Lycidas guarding Fingal's Cave, and the spirit of Burns in his cottage of degradation, which 'sicklied' Keats's Grecian ideal of beauty on the lines of Hamlet's 'sicklied o'er with the pale cast of thought'.[43] By the end of the tour Keats found himself on the top of Ben Nevis 'blind in mist':

> Here are the craggy Stones beneath my feet;
> Thus much I know, that a poor witless elf
> I tread on them; that all my eye doth meet
> Is mist and Crag – not only on this height
> But in the World of thought and mental might – [44]

In effect, he has walked himself into the position of clouded unknowing which occurs when Maiden Thought becomes darkened, and which enables him to imagine-into the condition of Saturn at the beginning of *Hyperion* (begun on his return from Scotland, all in the context of Tom's illness). Under the strain of this, *Hyperion* collapses and Keats blames Milton and the artistic imagination (as he will a year later when *The Fall of Hyperion* is written under the shadow of his own death). For a period he feels severed from poetry and the Muse: 'Poetry and I have been so distant lately I must make some advances soon or she will cut me entirely.'[45] Yet within a few months, and in the context of falling in love with Fanny Brawne, Keats has regained the adventurous quality of the poetic 'mist' and Socratean 'ignorance', describing himself as 'straining at particles of light in the midst of a great darkness' and 'striving to know [him]self', and suddenly exorcizes the concept of a deathly false art through writing 'La Belle Dame Sans Merci'.[46] The silent Naiad of *Hyperion* becomes the Belle Dame with 'language strange' which is both understood and misunderstood by the infant poet on his 'pacing steed', recognizing a language of love yet not conceding his own powerlessness and inability to possess the object of love, with its magical poetic food of 'honey wild and manna dew'. The knight–poet's 'starv'd lips' and tubercular flush of false poetic roses derives from a misconception which the very telling of his story exorcizes by symbolically containing it within the mind of the questioner in the poem (his alter-ego, the next poet-to-be). The knight's steed and binding flowers evaporate, for in poetry (as Keats writes in a sonnet of the same time) the Muse should be 'bound with garlands of her own'. This is the leap forward which raises Keats from the stalemate of Saturn's hellish vale, and results in his formulation of the world as a 'Vale of Soul-making'. In this, Keats's personal myth of the mind's creativity, he describes how 'intelligences or sparks of the divinity' which occur universally, come to 'acquire identity' and become 'souls' – 'each one personally itself':

> How, but by the medium of a world like this? . . . Do you not see how necessary a World of Pains and troubles is to school an Intelligence and make it a soul? A Place where the heart must feel and suffer in a thousand diverse ways! Not merely is the Heart a Hornbook, It is the Minds Bible, it is the Minds experience, it is the teat from which the Mind or intelligence sucks its identity –[47]

This is Keats's 'system of salvation' or of 'Spirit-creation', which he feels will relieve mankind of its reliance for happiness on a 'seldom-appearing Socrates', by setting its own happiness in evolution. The web is spun 'from its own inwards', and only then can link up with the 'teat' or growth-points through which the ethereal sap flows to build up the mind's identity. And in this process, though Socrates himself cannot help if there is no internally motivated thinking principle, the mind may make use of 'Mediators and Personages' such as those in heathen mythology, who (like Keats's own use of the poet-gods) can mediate between the intelligence and the spirit-world.

Immediately on clarifying this system of spirit-creation, Keats writes the first of his beautiful spring odes, the 'Ode to Psyche'. All the odes (and all Keats's inspired poetry, including the agonizing struggle with *Hyperion* and its later dream-form *The Fall*) are about creativity, but the 'Ode to Psyche' springs directly from his myth of Soul-making, and represents the breakthrough heralded by the 'Belle Dame'; thus it establishes the mental orientation for them all. In it, Keats makes the inspired recognition that a 'heathen goddess' had been 'neglected' and that he is the knight come to rescue her. The goddess of the mind is discovered, not through becoming her lover (as in the 'Belle Dame') but through 'singing' her 'secrets'. As he will write later: 'The Soul is a world of itself and has enough to do in its own home.'[48] In this ode, the curtains are drawn back on the soul's own home, and the source of the thinking principle – the vision of beauty – is revealed.

> O Goddess! Hear these tuneless numbers, wrung
> By sweet enforcement and remembrance dear,
> And pardon that thy secrets should be sung
> Even into thine own soft-conchèd ear.
> Surely I dreamt to-day, or did I see
> The wingèd Psyche with awakened eyes?

The poet's 'awakened eyes' are cleansed doors of perception, marked off from everyday actuality by the initial disorientation of seeming a 'dream'; the sudden revelation complements the agonizing emotional work which lies behind it, 'wrung by sweet enforcement and remembrance dear'. In echoing the opening lines of 'Lycidas', Keats is also reminding the goddess of his own struggle with poetry's destroyed garlands, and making a plea for their restoration. It is implied that this restoration may occur if his 'tuneless numbers' (syllables, rhymes) are heard by this internal deity, who represents *his* soul as well as the Soul. The 'tuneless numbers' begin by representing his own musical or poetic insufficiency (without divine aid), as in 'La Belle Dame''s 'And no birds sing'; but when reflected in the 'ear' of the goddess, they become ambiguous, and foreshadow the suprasensuous music of the 'Grecian Urn''s 'Pipe to the spirit ditties of no tone', or of the negated 'virgin choir' later in this ode. The poet's condensed invocation, with its reminder of his 'tuneless' state, is a condition of 'wandering thoughtlessly' (suggesting both

unfledged, and unreasoning). He sees the lovers' bower, but we
suspect would never have recognized Psyche were it not for his
instant recognition of Cupid: 'The wingèd boy I knew;/But who
wast thou . . . ? His Psyche true!' That is, the love whom he 'knows'
as part of himself, leads him to the essential beauty of the mind,
which though within is also in a sense beyond himself. The mists
of Maiden Thought clear before the light of the non-virgin
goddess whose story (classically taking place in darkness) becomes
illuminated by the poet's own awakened, 'inspired' eyes:

> O latest born and loveliest far
>   Of all Olympus' faded hierarchy!
> Fairer than Phoebe's sapphire-regioned star,
>   Or Vesper, amorous glow-worm of the sky;
> Fairer than these, though temple thou hast none,
>   Nor altar heaped with flowers;
> Nor virgin-choir to make delicious moan
>   Upon the midnight hours –

The 'faded hierarchy' of Olympian Apollo who had been Keats's
god of poetry hitherto, and who had refused to die-into-life
according to the poet's command in *Hyperion*, here transfers all
its sensuous richness to the new goddess or Muse. In herself she
outshines all these attributes, which are delivered as outgrown
negatives; then suddenly the poet realizes what his appropriate
and reciprocal response must be if he is truly to internalize the
vision, and establish Psyche as his soul's deity. His earlier,
doubtful 'Surely I dreamt . . . or did I see . . . ?' becomes
emphatically not dream but vision:

> I see, and sing, by my own eyes inspired.
> So let me be thy choir and make a moan
>   Upon the midnight hours –
> Thy voice, thy lute, thy pipe, thy incense sweet
>   From swingèd censer teeming;
> Thy shrine, thy grove, thy oracle, thy heat
>   Of pale-mouthed prophet dreaming.
>
> Yes, I will be thy priest, and build a fane
>   In some untrodden region of my mind,
> Where branchèd thoughts, new grown with pleasant
>   pain,

> Instead of pines will murmur in the wind:
> Far, far around shall those dark-clustered trees
> Fledge the wild-ridged mountains steep by steep;
> And there by zephyrs, streams, and birds, and bees,
> The moss-lain Druids shall be lulled to sleep;
> And in the midst of this wide quietness
> A rosy sanctuary will I dress
> With the wreathed trellis of a working brain, ...

Once the aesthetic reciprocity is achieved (by the poet echoing the features of worship such that they become a tracing of Psyche's attributes), Psyche truly becomes a symbol for his inner world, whose beauty he can match with numbers which are no longer tuneless, since they are symbiotically linked with their imaginative source – 'With all the gardener Fancy e'er could feign,/Who breeding flowers will never breed the same'. Keats's 'Fancy' is not a mechanical mode but a servant of imagination, breeding poetry's flowers from their fertile and inexhaustible source, and echoing Richard II's words: 'these two beget/A generation of still-breeding thoughts'. The pattern of reciprocation is what links the spider–poet's web with the ethereal mould of his inner world (the shrine in the midst of terra incognita, 'some untrodden region of my mind'); his mind is 'fledged' by branched pine-thoughts. Moreover the branchings will become innumerable once the shrine has been established, as will the figures enclosed within them (zephyrs, streams, etc.) – all intelligences or sparks of identity waiting to become schooled into souls. The ridged, branched mountain-surface is the 'wreathed trellis of a working brain', in which – the poet promises – 'shadowy thought' together with the 'bright torch' of his own reciprocal inner illumination, will always be waiting 'To let the warm Love in!' – to continue the fertilizing of the Chamber of Maiden Thought.

The 'Ode to Psyche' is thus the symbolic presentation of Keats's system of spirit-creation, in which unknown areas of the mind or of the collective mind of humanity can become fertilized and linked in a complex pattern of emotional tensions and identifications, under the aegis of an underlying principle of beauty which will eventually enable each spark of identity to become 'each one personally itself'. The mind feeds and grows by means of this continual process, in which not only itself but also its internal objects (or the idea of Mind itself) shed previous identities and 'hierarchies' which they have outgrown, to be re-born as bright new stars which have retained the essence of their original beauty. Keats became the greatest of the Romantic poets owing not to effortless facility in the display of talent, but to intense work on his internal relations and his determination to see the beauty of truth. For him, 'learning poetry' and 'making the soul' were the same thing. His own beautiful model of the mind therefore subsumes and transcends that of other philosophers of his own – and later – generations.

7
EMILY BRONTË: METAMORPHOSIS OF THE ROMANTIC HERO

One of the most haunting dreams in English literature is that of Lockwood in *Wuthering Heights*, when he first becomes a 'tenant' of Mr Heathcliff and spends the night in the closet-bed of Catherine Earnshaw/Linton. This, with its window on the moor, represents the dream-chamber at the core of the moor-mind governing the interaction of the two houses of Linton and Earnshaw at opposite poles of the mental landscape:

> 'I must stop it, nevertheless!' I muttered, knocking my knuckles through the glass, and stretching an arm out to seize the importunate branch: instead of which, my fingers closed on the fingers of a little, ice-cold hand!
>
> The intense horror of nightmare came over me; I tried to draw back my arm, but the hand clung to it, and a most melancholy voice sobbed, 'Let me in – let me in!'
>
> 'Who are you?' I asked, struggling, meanwhile, to disengage myself.
>
> 'Catherine Linton', it replied shiveringly (why did I think of *Linton*? I had read *Earnshaw* twenty times for Linton), 'I'm come home, I'd lost my way on the moor!'
>
> As it spoke, I discerned, obscurely, a child's face looking through the window – terror made me cruel; and, finding it useless to attempt shaking the creature off, I pulled its wrist on to the broken pane, and rubbed it to and fro till the blood ran down and soaked the bedclothes; still it wailed, 'Let me in!' and maintained its tenacious grip, almost maddening me with fear.[1]

Lockwood is the pubertal mind, or the pubertal aspect of every mind at a certain point of growth, who is 'imperceptibly impelled by the awakening of the thinking principle' (as Keats would say) to leave its quiescent, 'locked' security and grasp the hand of adolescence which makes insistent, tormenting advances. Throughout the novel, the age of twelve or thirteen marks transitions in relationships, generally accompanied by blood. Lockwood's mind has been awakened by his attempting to decipher the 'faded hieroglyphics' of the 'unknown Catherine' – her inner history, which is written in diary notes between the printed lines of the dusty religious volumes left at her bedside. Unwittingly, he has himself invited the spirit which he attempts to keep out ('I must stop it'), and in the very process, establishes a bond sealed in blood and an intimacy beyond his comprehension. He has broken the screen between his established complacency and the world of passionate spirits and internal deities which seem utterly foreign to him, yet at the same time express emotional potential of his own which he has so far found no way of knowing, and which terrifies him. The blood pours from the child's wrist, yet the child is also Lockwood, screaming (as Heathcliff says) as if he were 'having his throat cut'. Like wine flowing through water (as Catherine will express it later), this dream will change the colour of his personality. We know that Lockwood has come to the area to recover from his undignified failure in a 'seaside romance'. Here, however, he is forced to confront the unknown tempest within his mind, as in the island of Shakespeare's play. Catherine's hieroglyphics, together with Heathcliff's anguished cry to the ghost to 'Come in – my heart's darling!', swirl about Lockwood and create the snowstorm which obliterates all the moor's landmarks the next morning – all his previous means of recognition – leaving him in a passive, feverish condition. He is, like Milton, 'cut off' from 'mortal sight'.

Throughout this extraordinary and poetic novel, Lockwood – who represents our primary eye on the story – is almost continually helpless or even (in the final stage of Heathcliff's life) physically absent. This is not because he is incapable of understanding the passion, but because he represents the dreaming self who is in a sense merely a spectator in relation to the extraordinary events of his own mind, like Theseus or the poet–visionary in the 'Ode to Psyche'. Heathcliff has his generic origins in the traditional Romantic hero; Lockwood represents the opposite vertex, the anti-hero or Blakean 'contrary', who is emotionally necessary to transform melodrama into passion. The structural keys to Emily Brontë's inspired revision of the progress of the Romantic hero in *Wuthering Heights* are: the tension between Lockwood the dreamer and Heathcliff the protagonist, and the development of the Romantic story over two generations, which gives the original emotional explosions the chance to repeat themselves with a difference. By the end, both generations of moorland lovers are incorporated within Lockwood's dream-consciousness; and we see that, despite his passivity, his receptivity has been instrumental in reforming the alignments of his internal gods and in allowing them to achieve creative union. This orientation gave Emily Brontë negative capability: the means of letting the story write itself, rather than having to conform to a standard Romantic or Gothic pattern, or to one of her own omnipotence and self-idealization. She put herself in the position of learning through the experience of writing-the-dream, following out the thinking principle thus activated. This creative evolution then becomes the essential subject of the novel, focusing on Heathcliff's struggle to regain knowledge of Catherine (his 'soul' as he calls her), via his relationship with the younger generation. In effect the story of *Wuthering Heights* tells how the internal contacts established in Lockwood's dream eventually result in symbol formation and aesthetic reorientation within the mind's moorland geography, like Keats's spider building its tapestry empyrean from a few 'twigs' of contact.

All the Romantic poets were concerned with the post-revolutionary implications of internal revolution, of catastrophic change within the self as a model for society's regeneration. Poetry was not merely *about* change, but the *means* of change. Shelley in his brilliant *Defence of Poetry*, written shortly before his death, saw poets as the 'unacknowledged legislators of the world'.[2] Often in his own poetry, however, he had attempted to apply his idea of a new world literally, in a propagandist idealized manner. Thus the 'new world of man' prophesied in his *Prometheus Unbound* is one in which the mind is an 'ocean/Of clear emotion' and language a 'perpetual Orphic song' (IV. 96–7, 415); Prometheus himself (as Forethought) is – as Shelley says in the preface – a version of Satan without his badness, an idealized hero who talks to Asia (Imagination) in the words of Lear to Cordelia:

> we will sit and talk of time and change,
> As the world ebbs and flows, ourselves unchanged . . .
> . . . and make
> Strange combinations out of common things,
> Like human babes in their brief innocence.
> (III. iii. 23–33)

Shelley's reformed world stops short of the essential final catastrophe in *Lear*, and strives to perpetuate the 'innocent babe' vision of happiness, uncontaminated by life's stain on the 'white radiance of eternity',[3] or by the 'pestilence-stricken multitudes' of the 'Ode to the West Wind'. Shelley's vision is one of purgation rather than of assimilation and metamorphosis. Byron's relationship with poetry was also basically an omnipotent one, though later in *Don Juan* this becomes a complex, tongue-in-cheek type of omnipotence, a battle of wits between the poet and the words of the poem which threaten to take over on their own; thus he tells his Muse, 'Thou shalt not write, in short, but what I choose' (I. 206). Byron's self-idealizing side produced the fashionable 'Byronic' hero such as Childe Harold or Manfred, who like Heathcliff has a tortured relationship with the ghost of Astarte – 'I loved her, and destroyed her!' (II. ii. 117). In this stereotypal Byronic pattern, the poet destroys the woman/spirit of poetry and is then destroyed himself. It is a pattern which Emily Brontë de-romanticizes and transcends, and which Byron himself considered self-indulgent and unreal by comparison with the *idea* of poetry or of 'Mind' which beset him in his dreams or meditations. As he wrote in a journal:

> I awoke from a dream! – well! and have not others dreamed? – Such a dream! – but she did not overtake me. I wish the dead would rest, however. Ugh! how my blood chilled, – and I could not wake – and – and – heigho! . . . And am I to be shaken by shadows?[4]

The dream itself (as well as perhaps its content) is 'she', a pursuing female fury who chills his blood and is more substantial than any shadow. Byron was throughout his life tormented by his inability to lay the ghost of the spirit of poetry or beauty which was continually threatening to 'overtake' him; he claimed it had made him a 'martyr' yet, as with Hamlet, failed to contain his identity and make the ultimate transformation from dream to symbolic reality. His fashionable image was a projection into society, for which he had the utmost contempt; but his journals (known to Emily Brontë) express his awareness of this deficiency in his capacity for symbol making: saying that the 'mainspring of Mind' has an 'innate tendency to Good' but is 'at present a sad jar of atoms'. The existence of mind is an elusive mystery, uncapturable, yet more real in dreams than when awake:

> Attend for the moment to the action of Mind. It is in perpetual activity... independent of body: in dreams for instance incoherently and madly, I grant you, but it still is *Mind*, and much more Mind than when we are awake.[5]

Or as he puts it ironically in *Don Juan*:

> 'To be, or not to be?' – ere I decide,
> I should be glad to know that which *is being*...
> For me, I sometimes think that life is death...
>   (IX. 16)

Emily Brontë, through Heathcliff, makes an intimate identification with the problem of non-being profoundly felt by Byron. Heathcliff's mind, when Lockwood first encounters him, is also a sad jar of atoms, containing only a 'collection of memoranda' of the dead Catherine, and unable to make contact with her ghost or spirit. The reason he is not sleeping in the dream-chamber himself (always regarded as his own) is that he is unable to dream; tantalizing hallucinatory expectations of Catherine (like those of Macbeth) continually jerk his consciousness: 'I must open my lids to see. And so I opened and closed them a hundred times a night – to be always disappointed!' He is 'mocked' by the 'resemblance' of Catherine in every concrete physical shape, including his own face: 'The entire world is a dreadful collection of memoranda that she did exist, and that I have lost her!'[6] She 'mocks' him with her deathly, unspiritual existence, her mental unreality; she can play no part in his own mind. Her ghost does not appear to him as it did to the inexperienced Lockwood: 'it gave me no sign of being, but the wind and snow whirled wildly through'.[7] This mental emptiness, the inability to dream or see symbolically, is called by Heathcliff 'the abyss', and he regards it as her vengeful form of tormenting him. As he pleaded (or cursed) on the 'great occasion' (as Nelly calls it) of their final meeting: 'Is it not sufficient for your infernal selfishness, that while you are at peace, I shall writhe in the torments of hell?'[8] And immediately after her death:

> Catherine Earnshaw, may you not rest as long as I am living! . . . Be with me always – take any form – drive me mad! Only *do* not leave me in this abyss, where I cannot find you! Oh God! It is unutterable! I *cannot* live without my life! I *cannot* live without my soul![9]

Catherine is his 'life', his 'soul', the key to his own mind's reality and self-knowledge, his mystery; yet she is form-less, hence he finds his own condition 'unutterable'. He is prepared for her to 'take any form', but not for the abyss of non-existence represented by these pseudo-resemblances, the collection of memoranda, the jar of atoms; these are unreal forms, mental rubbish, not symbolic conveyors of meaning. This is the state of emotional deadlock which Lockwood begins to unlock when, like Heathcliff himself forty years earlier, he brings a fresh perspective to the moor–mind. Through the new vertex provided by Lockwood with his naive misunderstandings yet persistent curiosity and ability to endure humiliation, Emily Brontë pursues the Byronic dream beyond its impasse – the mindless revenge cycle. The concept of a 'love for life' which Lockwood believes should be possible in this 'heavenly' country is finally his reward[10] – not as his personal possession, but as the new governing idea of his dream-world.

During the two-generation traversings and explosive encounters across the moor–mind which were originally set in motion by Heathcliff's arrival, a picture of the mind's history is built up, showing its characteristic qualities seeking different modes of expression and alliances: gradually spinning the web of its mystery. Initially the two houses of Linton and Earnshaw co-exist in quiescent non-communication: monuments to a decaying, non-developing state of mind. Into this, old Earnshaw imports the child Heathcliff, who is in one sense the ultimate outsider ('Where did he come from, the little dark thing?' wonders Nelly at the end of the narrative); yet in another sense embodies an obscure, primitive and vital aspect of the Earnshaw mind which has not as yet been born into recognition. Earnshaw discovers him at Liverpool, gateway to the vast unknown spaces of the Atlantic, and incorporates him within his greatcoat. The unwrapping of the child from the coat is described as if it were a form of giving birth, to an offspring of strange and ambiguous potential. 'See here, wife', he cries, amidst 'laughing and groaning' and other imagery of labour: 'I was never so beaten with anything in my life; but you must e'en take it as a gift of God, though it's as dark almost as if it came from the devil.'[11] Like all the Romantic heroes, Heathcliff is descended from Milton's Satan; but only Emily Brontë's has the same unsentimental, Miltonic quality of 'archangel ruin'd', of a chiaroscuro which defies moral categorizations. Earnshaw's ultimate creative effort is to produce Heathcliff – he can do no more; after this he subsides into the fragile egotism (the need to be 'master' or 'queen') which is equally characteristic of the Earnshaw mind, always threatening to destroy from within its fiery spark of creativity. So in his death-scene, he praises Cathy for being quiet, and asks, 'Why canst thou not always be a good lass, Cathy?', to which she pointedly replies, 'Why cannot you always be a good man, father?'[12] His vulnerable authoritarianism reappears in Hindley's egocentricity, the need to be obeyed or 'loved by everyone' (as Catherine puts it). When Hindley's delicate wife dies (who represents his own musical soul, crushed by Heathcliff's arrival in the family), Hindley feels he is no longer 'master' of his house or destiny, and succumbs immediately to degradation. Similarly when Catherine during her pregnancy feels she is no longer queen over both Edgar and Heathcliff, she succumbs to 'brainfever' as at the time of Heathcliff's disappearance. When Catherine reaches puberty, she recognizes that the childhood adhesive relationship between herself and Heathcliff has reached a stalemate: 'You might be dumb or a baby, for all you say to amuse me', she tells him;[13] and this has a deeper cause than Heathcliff's stunted education. Her mastery over him has resulted in his becoming a sort of pet, like the Linton lap-dog or false baby which runs as a theme through the novel, on both sides of the moor: contrasting with the dogs of passion which assail Lockwood on his first entry to the Heights, or the second Catherine on hers. In her attempt to cross over into adolescence, Catherine separates herself from Heathcliff, even though this results in an internal split which in a sense denatures her and makes her a perpetual emotional invalid, whose fragile happiness in the Linton 'heaven' is dependent upon her will never being crossed. In the banishment scene, Heathcliff is listening unobserved behind the settle, while the baby Hareton lies asleep in front of Catherine and Nelly. We realize Catherine is unconsciously aware of Heathcliff's presence, and of the moment of his departure; and that her conversation and attempt to report her 'dreams' about marriage and its consequences to Nelly, are inspired by this knowledge. She needs not merely to convey her feelings to him, but to awaken in herself an awareness of the new world beyond childhood, though this is a world which she only glimpses prophetically, and knows she will never truly enter. (In her delirium during her pregnancy, she says all those years since Heathcliff's departure have been 'a blank', an 'abyss';[14] hence in Lockwood's dream she appears as a child, though under her married name – sign of an illusory maturity.) Only when she feels Heathcliff's physical absence, can she formulate to Nelly her 'feeling' of his symbolic significance:

> I cannot express it, but surely you and everybody have a notion that there is or should be, an existence of yours beyond you.... If all else perished, and *he* remained, I should still continue to be; and if all remained, and he were annihilated, the universe would turn to a mighty stranger.[15]

In expressing her preoccupation with an 'existence beyond herself', Catherine is concerned not only with Heathcliff as a person but also with the Heathcliff element within them all and its ambiguous potential for creation or destruction, a gift from God or the devil. The presence of the sleeping Hareton throughout this poetic tableau, to whom Nelly sings a gruesome lullaby about children crying and mothers lying 'beneath the mould', suggests Catherine is trying to find a voice for the generalized Earnshaw baby or part of the personality whose spiritual needs are smothered or deadened by conventional society – 'dumb or a baby' like Heathcliff himself. As the three headstones on the moor at the end of the story will show, Catherine's creativity requires both Edgar and Heathcliff – indeed the three are interdependent; for her, they are the 'foliage' and the 'rocks beneath' the landscape of her mind,[16] a marriage of heaven and hell, whose integration seems an impossible achievement within one generation or one stage of mental development. At the deepest level, Emily Brontë draws on the archetypal patterns of development symbolized by Milton and Shakespeare – in particular *Paradise Lost* and *Lear* – in order to transcend the Romantic egotistical deadlock. Thus Catherine mentions two dreams to Nelly: the first is about her being expelled from heaven by the angels (the first stage in *Paradise Lost*); and the context of the sleeping Hareton and the recumbent Heathcliff suggests that her second, unspoken dream (to which Nelly refuses to listen) is probably about the implications of a pregnancy from her forthcoming marriage: an 'existence beyond her' which she prophesies will have a quality of catastrophe, at least regarding her own continued existence (the second state in *Paradise Lost*, the price of the 'paradise within'). In the same way, the death of the old omnipotent Lear results from inspired contact with the new growing self which emerges from within him. Both Hareton and Catherine are dreaming of a mother beneath the mould, and during the second half of the novel Catherine's operations are indeed all ghostly; she works most effectively and creatively through her agents on earth – Edgar, Heathcliff and her daughter Catherine – who are all in their own ways engaged in a search for knowledge of her spirit, to internalize its creative quality within their own minds, which it turns out are intimately related. Their mutual search, driven by love and hate of each other, eventually fulfils Catherine's idea of an existence beyond herself: shedding her own selfhood, and guiding the Earnshaw mind–baby through the dream-window from childhood to adulthood.

Catherine works by means of spiritual emanations from beneath the peat-mould, in contact with the primitive volcanic foundations of creativity associated by her with Heathcliff. Simultaneously, above ground, Edgar and Heathcliff evolve unusual, unpremeditated relationships with the second generation of the moor–mind – Cathy, Hareton and Linton – who are all in a sense her offspring. The idea of 'conception' is revised, as with the meetings on the stormy heath in *Lear*. During a period of what Heathcliff calls 'moral teething',[17] the mind's negativity is confronted and exorcized through a series of false sentimental romances – delusions about creativity, in which everyone is implicated. Linton Heathcliff becomes as it were the dead end of this misconception; yet if he were merely cast aside, excluded, he would return with a vengeance in the age-old pattern. Instead, the negative knowledge which he embodies has to be incorporated and understood, by someone strong enough not to be destroyed by it. Heathcliff instinctively recognizes that the second Catherine (who is also the second 18-year-old Linton girl whom he seizes) has the innate capacity to do this. He finds her, like Isabella, repulsive (saying he would 'rather be hugged by a snake') yet at a deep level, beyond the operation of reason or will-power, sees her as a child of his own who can lead him out of his spiritual impasse; when he comes after Edgar's death to 'fetch Catherine home', he explains that he 'wants [his] children about [him]' – expressing an emotional need deeper than his intended irony'.[18] Like Gloucester, he needs to place the true and false fruits of conception in juxtaposition, in order to develop his relationship with the first Catherine's spirit. It therefore devolves upon the second Cathy to detoxify the spiritual death embodied in Heathcliff's son. She becomes his wife–mother and, nursing him in the dream-chamber at the Heights, takes within herself the emotional poison which is ending his life: but in a spirit of responsibility, not masochism (unlike the first generation). When she emerges from this dream-experience, Heathcliff demands insistently to know how she feels, and she replies, 'I feel like death.'[19] Through her identification with Linton, she comes to understand death from the inside, so that she is reinforced against its destructive implications; the experience of this deathly marriage frees not imprisons her. Thus on hearing of her father's approaching death, she realizes that she can escape from Heathcliff's tyranny via the window in the dream-chamber which had been her mother's – emphasizing that she is never really Heathcliff's prisoner, except when it coincides with her own spiritual necessity. Her escape images a sort of rebirth from the womb of the mother whom she never knew in the external world, and whom she has found again internally, clinching her Earnshaw identity. Through re-traversing their forebears' emotional conflicts in this field of concrete mental reality, the second generation learn to achieve resilience without loss of spirit. Their inner fire makes Cathy 'elastic as steel', and Hareton 'tough as tempered steel', revising the brittle and egotistical emotionality of their parents.[20] The key to Cathy's resilience is her internalization of a concept of love between her father and mother which has been conveyed to her by Edgar; she can survive the smashing of their portraits and the burning of her books because their inner meaning is 'printed on her heart'. The key to Hareton's resilience is his love for Heathcliff, whom he regards as his true father, because he can recognize Heathcliff's love for him beneath its superficial veneer of degradation and revenge. Hareton's nobility is earned, not inherited, so has the strength of genuine growth based on inner principles of judgement. Their relationship was cemented at the time when Heathcliff 'accidentally' rescued Hareton as a baby from his father who had 'accidentally' dropped him down the stairs. Thus the resilience of the second generation of lovers is founded on their ability to distinguish true from false parenting qualities, to discover the jewel of emotional reality despite the dross. This internal linkage, in both of them, is in turn derived from the spirit of the first Catherine as it passes through the minds of her two lovers. For Edgar, his daughter is a 'living hope at [his] side';[21] she will enable him to rewrite internally the fragile happiness of his actual marriage, not as escapist fantasy but as an imaginative reality to feed the mind of their child. Had he died immediately after his wife, as he wished, their mutual love would have been shadowed by delusion; it becomes real owing to his own mental work in endowing Cathy not with privilege and status, but with emotional and educational richness (represented by her library, pony, etc.). He, too, earns his internal idea of Catherine as a deity of the mind; and is able to die when he perceives Cathy's achievement of internalization – her part as a living link in his web of love. On his death-bed he says: 'I am going to her, and you, darling child, shall come to us', fixing his 'radiant' gaze on this governing spirit which he clearly perceives through her features.[22]

Heathcliff's emotional transformation in response to Catherine's spirit, now embodied in the development of the second generation, is both more turbulent and complex than Edgar's; and with the help of the Lockwood perspective, it expands the moor–mind's structure into another dimension. As the relationship between Cathy and Hareton develops under Heathcliff's eye, against his omnipotent will yet according to his imaginative need, Heathcliff 'turns [his] mind out' (as he puts it) to his observers (Nelly, Lockwood, ourselves), in a series of Shakespearean semi-soliloquies which fully express the mind's predicament, torn between the abyss of revenge and the substantial spirit of love. Unlike Edgar, who was sustained throughout by a 'living hope', Heathcliff has been tormented by 'the spectre of a hope' – an empty spectre, with a 'spectre's caprice' (as in the vacuum after Lockwood's dream), not a spiritual ghost such as that seen by Lockwood. At the time Lockwood arrives on the scene, Heathcliff is at the summit of his worldly power, apparently with all his machinations to avenge himself on 'persons belonging to [Catherine]' fully under control: he has 'paid Hindley back', distorted Hareton's education, subdued Cathy's defiance, made them hate each other, taken possession of the houses of Linton and Earnshaw, and usurped their status in the neighbourhood. Yet as his reaction to Lockwood's dream showed, this omnipotent domination is directly proportional to the extent of the spiritual vacuum within him; in possessing Catherine's belongings, or treating her children as belongings, he loses contact with Catherine's spirit: 'Do not leave me in this abyss, where I cannot find you.' His soliloquies during the second half of the novel clarify his internal war between omnipotence and creativity. He begins by relating to Nelly his attempted desecration of Catherine's grave, eighteen years earlier, and how his violent activity of scraping and hammering at the coffin was arrested by his sudden conviction of Catherine's spiritual presence:

> As certainly as you perceive the approach to some substantial body in the dark, though it cannot be discerned, so certainly I felt that Cathy was there, not under me, but on the earth. A sudden sense of relief flowed, from my heart, through every limb. I relinquished my labour of agony, and turned consoled at once, unspeakably consoled. Her presence was with me; it remained while I re-filled the grave, and led me home.[23]

In these lines echoing the 150th Psalm, Heathcliff expresses his awareness of a live and (paradoxical though it may seem) substantial spirit, substantial enough to displace his delusory mechanical activity of 'delving', 'cracking' and 'wrenching' at the outworks of the coffin. This episode contains in microcosm the entire drama of the next eighteen years, covered by the 'twenty years' in which the wailing child–ghost of Catherine Linton tells Lockwood she has been a 'waif', trying to 'get in' and 'come home'. Heathcliff's own dream of Catherine leading him home, could have told him that his plan of revenge – to get 'levers and mattocks' to demolish the two houses[24] – would be as false and destructive of his own inner world as was the misconception implied in breaking open her coffin. But he is not yet able to assimilate this knowledge, which has to be earned, as with Edgar, through interaction with the younger generation. On that occasion, when he reached the Heights, he tried again to possess literally the object of his desire, in hallucinatory visual terms, but finds he is barred from the image he seeks: 'I could *almost* see her, and yet I could not! She showed herself as she often was in life, a devil to me! And since then, sometimes more and sometimes less, I've been the sport of that intolerable torture!'[25] Heathcliff says he feels 'beaten out' of their childhood bedroom, Lockwood's dream-chamber – the one room in the house which has the significance of encouraging symbolic formations; he finds that this mental space is one which he does not possess emotionally, despite his ownership of everything else. For years he is surrounded by meaningless resemblances to Catherine – her dead eyes imaged in Hindley's or degraded through Hareton; even the paving-stones reflect her non-existence through the ever-accumulating 'collection of memoranda' which show only that she has become 'a devil to him' – the antithesis of a Muse or soul. Only when he comes to accept the living continuation of her spirit through the eyes and love of Cathy and Hareton, the beauty through the ugliness which he attaches to each of them individually – can he attain his personal 'heaven' and die, and the ghost's spirit 'come home'. Heathcliff calls this expansion of his imagination by Catherine 'a strange way of killing, to beguile me with the spectre of a hope, through eighteen years!'[26]

Coleridge, in the *Biographia Literaria*, makes a distinction between two types of 'men of genius' which illuminates the philosophical implications of Heathcliff's struggle at this point; together with Milton and Shakespeare it serves as a model for Emily Brontë's own transformation of the Byronic Romantic hero. In line with his dichotomies of organic versus mechanical form, and imagination versus fancy, Coleridge differentiates between the 'creative and self-sufficing power of absolute genius' and a more authoritarian or omnipotent type of mentality which he terms 'commanding genius'. Men of true or absolute genius exist 'between thought and reality, as it were in an *intermundium* of which their own living spirit supplies the substance, and their imagination the every-varying form'. They are the symbol-makers, the receivers of ideas; for as he says elsewhere in the *Biographia*, 'an Idea, in the highest sense of that word, cannot be conveyed but by a symbol'. The men of commanding genius, in contrast,

> must impress their preconceptions on the world without, in order to present them back to their own view with the satisfying degree of clearness, distinctness, and individuality. These in tranquil times are formed to exhibit a perfect poem in palace, or temple, or landscape-garden; or a tale of romance. . . . But alas! in times of tumult they are the men destined to come forth as the shaping spirit of ruin.[27]

Instead of seeing symbolically, commanding genius imposes preconceptions, and insists that the world – or the world of its own mind – conform to them, rather than allowing ideas to modify the mind. Coleridge acknowledges that commanding genius may be a type of artistry, at least in times of peace, when it can construct a 'perfect poem' or 'landscape-garden'; but in 'times of tumult', its fragility shows all too readily. Depending on prevailing circumstances, it may result in good works, in external prosperity; but it is never truly creative, never the conveyor of ideas 'in the highest sense of the word'. *Wuthering Heights* is of course, as its title indicates, about times of mental tumult, points of catastrophic change; in Blake's terms it is about 'spiritual war' as distinct from 'corporeal war' (which is a time of regimentation not of tumult). These are the times when the distinction between absolute and commanding genius shows starkly as a choice between the 'shaping spirit of imagination' or the 'shaping spirit of ruin'. Heathcliff's mind has the potential for both types of genius, and when – in his mental agony– he advertises for a 'tenant', a new mental vertex to release his spiritual deadlock, he is poised on the knife-edge between them. Superficially, he appears to have committed his energies totally to vengeful commanding genius; but it takes only a single dream-movement on Lockwood's part (one 'moment' in Blake's terms) to uncover the latent creativity of the moor–mind, waiting for the moment to make the ultimate reversals and linkages which will transform its landscape. Lockwood's receptive presence during the final year of Heathcliff's story is both the catalysing agent and the new perspective which allows the mind to learn from experience, and to accept that the creative must create itself. The total symbolism of the novel at this point images Emily Brontë's own mind when she finally made the 'final bound' from her Gondal daydreaming to the imaginative reality of *Wuthering Heights*.[28]

During the final stages of the evolution of absolute genius, Lockwood is indeed absent from the moor, as always during the main events which have to be relayed to him at one remove, as if a dream. Meanwhile, Heathcliff in a sense internalizes the Lockwood vertex, wondering how he can 'supply [his] loss in this desolation'.[29] Heathcliff's new way of seeing Catherine begins with the pressure of Hareton's identity upon him; despite his efforts to triumph over Hareton and see him as a descendant of Hindley, he cannot help seeing Catherine in him 'every day more'. Lockwood, on the verge of departure, records Heathcliff's consequent insight that he may 'thwart himself' and fail to fulfil his revenge.[30] The next stage is when Hareton comes to symbolize Heathcliff's own youthful, developing self – the progressive aspect of his own mind, which commanding genius had tried to distort. This occurs at the moment when Hareton and Cathy, reading a book, 'lift their eyes together to encounter Mr Heathcliff', and he suddenly recognizes their identity with the living eyes of Catherine Earnshaw, not in the already obvious external resemblance (the sort of thing which merely 'mocks' his loss), but in the living spirit which their *united* vision – their love – conveys to him.[31] This awakens a new mode of vision in Heathcliff; as he explains to Nelly (who explains to Lockwood): 'Five minutes ago, Hareton seemed a personification of my youth, not a human being'; he adds that he cannot even 'try to describe the thousand forms of past associations, and ideas he awakens, or embodies'.[32] Despite himself, Heathcliff's mind begins to re-live its history in a day which offers hope for development: via the internalization rather than the possession of the spirit of Catherine. Like Gloucester, he is learning to 'see feelingly'. For Heathcliff, Hareton is beginning to become a 'symbol' in the Coleridgean sense, showing 'the translucence of the Eternal through and in the Temporal': the god-like within him 'flying homeward to its Parent Mind enriched with a thousand forms'. Hareton (in combination with the second Catherine) is seen to contain the first Catherine – the moor's goddess or parent mind, the muse – and thereby Heathcliff: not the old Heathcliff who had been ostracized and banished, but the new Romantic hero who is born from the old like a snake shedding its skin. At last, Heathcliff is able to re-enter the dream-chamber and die, attaining his 'heaven'.[33] He describes himself as 'swallowed in the anticipation' of the fulfilment of the 'one universal idea ... [which] has devoured my existence'.[34] The 'idea' has been conveyed by his new ability to see symbolically, and changes the structure of his mind irrevocably, as with Lear's final transition. The window of the dream-chamber swinging open, leaving his dead body soaked with rain, indicates the passage of his soul through the place where Lockwood had first encountered Catherine trying to 'come in', and where the second Catherine was guided by innate knowledge to escape Heathcliff's commanding genius. The soaking of the body, which will be reinforced by Hareton's 'streaming' tears, begins the process of dissolution alongside those of Catherine and Edgar in the peat-mould. The idea of Catherine has become real to the satanic Heathcliff, as it did to the saintly Edgar: in both cases owing to their emotional involvement with her children; and she, correspondingly, has succeeded in establishing an 'existence beyond herself'.

What we see in the final phases of *Wuthering Heights* is an electric interchange of significance between the characters as they realign themselves into a system of symbols, all interdependent, and (in Coleridge's phrase) 'consubstantial' with the truths which they conduct. The second generation lovers inhabit the earth's surface, the first generation the soil and air; their memory continually replenishing the moor-mind's life through decay and metamorphosis. Each mental space depends logically on that adjoining. Lockwood – the naive, curious, pubertal mind – is both the instigator and the recipient of a vision of beauty (a 'love for life') from which he is excluded on one level, yet included on another, since it has established relationships within his own dream-world which have revolutionized his own capacity for experience in the future. '*They* are afraid of nothing', he grumbles, skulking in hot satanic envy as he watches the lovers through the window after the collapse of his own omnipotent 'fairy tale': 'Together they would brave satan and all his legions.'[35] Lockwood recognizes the inevitability of future tumult, in the form of coming 'autumn storms' which will batter the church roof, and of satan's legions. But he now has a new conception of how such tumult may be weathered and converted into the principle of self-development. The love of Cathy and Hareton has been weathered in its making, through their quarrels in which they battled with the internal inheritance of the previous generation; forged in the Vale of Soul-making, there is hope that it may continue to foster absolute genius in future times of tumult, without recourse to the tyranny of commanding genius. Lockwood grumbles at the relinquishment of his own false romance; but his acceptance of this, and his appreciation of the beauty of the three headstones set in the moor like a new altar, indicate his assimilation of the two generations of internal deities within his own moor–mind as a symbolic system to govern his own development. Olympus' faded hierarchy gives birth to Psyche; the mind's internal objects are not static authorities but developing deities in themselves which supersede one another. Emily Brontë's moor is also a Vale of Soul-making, and through her reworking of the Romantic hero, overcoming her own omnipotence, she pays her obeisances like Keats to the gods of the mind. As Chaucer said, 'For every wight which that to Rome went/Halt nat o path, or alway o manere.'[36]

8
GEORGE ELIOT: THE UNMAPPED COUNTRY

> Here undoubtedly lies the chief poetic energy: – in the force of imagination that pierces or exalts the solid fact ...
>
> (*Daniel Deronda*)[1]

George Eliot's novels can be described as successive attempts to image and contain the truth about emotional experiences, and to participate in the drama of psychic development. This fundamental goal directed the workings and reworkings of similar conflicts and preoccupations in each of her 'experiments in life',[2] though they belonged by her own account, to 'successive mental phases',[3] and as such represented rather different models of the mind.

Her central commitment never wavered: it was to find a basis for meaning in human affairs. Meaning lay in the truth of feeling, however much in conflict that position might be with the implications of the rationalist psychologies, methodologies, and social theories to which her intellectual side demanded an important, if partial, assent. The attitude she describes on reading Darwin's *Origin of Species* on the eve of its publication in 1859, remained essentially unchanged, although the respective weighting she gave to the different emphases varied considerably as her novel writing developed.

> We have been reading Darwin's Book on 'Origin of Species' just now: it makes an epoch, as the expression of his thorough adhesion after long years of study, to the Doctrine of Development ... the book is ill-written and sadly wanting in illustrative facts.... This will prevent [it] from becoming popular

... but it will have a great effect in the scientific world, causing a thorough and open discussion of a question about which people have hitherto felt timid. So the world gets on step by step towards brave clearness and honesty! But to me the Development theory and all other explanations of processes by which things came to be, produce a feeble impression compared with the mystery that lies under the processes.[4]

These comments are suggestive of the continual dilemma of her position. She was attracted to the type of scientific explanation of which Darwin's book was an expression. The implication was that the mind of man was not an exception to nature's other works but that, like everything else, it had received a determinate character. Yet she was also persuaded of that inexplicable 'current' in the mind 'into which all thought and feeling were apt, sooner or later to flow . . .'[5] which lay in a quite different kind of development – in the mysterious processes of the growth of the mind.

Lacking a framework for an intellectual understanding of psychic mechanisms in any significantly different way from that described by the mechanical philosophy of the Associationists, the mid-Victorians laboured under precisely those limitations which J.S. Mill describes as having alienated Coleridge: 'the apparent insufficiency of the theory to account for the mind's activity'.[6] In the *Biographia Literaria*, Coleridge records his objection to that 'subordination of final to efficient causes in the human being, which flows of necessity from the assumption, that the will and, with the will all acts of thought and attention are parts and products of this blind mechanism, instead of being distinct powers, the function of which it is to control, determine, and modify the phantasmal chaos of association'.[7]

The mid-century version of the Romantic movement's attempts to come to terms with science, was expressed in Tennyson's *In Memoriam*. It is the problem of mechanism which appalls him: 'The stars,' she whispers, 'blindly run.'[8] Tennyson, as A.N. Whitehead points out, stands in this poem as the perfect example of the distraction of thought, whereby 'a scientific realism, based on mechanism, is conjoined with an unwavering belief in the world of men and the higher animals as being composed of self-determining organisms'.[9] In prose writing it was George Eliot who confronted these opposing visions of the world

– both of them commanding assent by appeals to ultimate intuitions from which there seemed no escape. For in her work, as in that of many of her contemporaries, the values incorporated in the philosophy of the Romantics stood in uneasy juxtaposition with the implications of a rationalist philosophy.

The novels embody her engagement with the nature of development. What is meant by 'development', however, undergoes a fundamental change from the early stories, *Scenes from Clerical Life*, to the last great novel, *Daniel Deronda* – a change which has significant aesthetic implications. The overall *oeuvre* explicitly describes, and implicitly expresses, the evolving of the creative mind: the process of self-creation. Explicitly, both in authorial statements in the novels, and in numerous letters and journal entries, George Eliot monitors her successive phases – describing the shifts in the conception of her art which indicate developmental processes which are also becoming evident in the fabric of the novels. In 1848, she writes, 'Artistic power seems to me to resemble dramatic power – to be an intuitive perception of the varied states of which the human mind is susceptible, with ability to give them out anew in intensified expression.'[10] In 1857 she writes, 'my stories always grow out of my psychological conception of the dramatis personae'.[11] In 1866 she describes her struggle 'to make certain ideas thoroughly incarnate, as if they had revealed themselves to me first in the flesh and not in the spirit'.[12] In her final works she is more explicitly concerned with the 'force of imagination that pierces or exalts the solid fact'.[13]

The present concern is with the internal evidence of the books: with the shift from the ideas of the intellectual, consciously struggling to 'reconcile the philosophy of Locke and Kant',[14] to the Ideas which embody the 'shaping spirit of Imagination' – for Coleridge the essence of the self-creative process. The shift occurs through the gradual relinquishing of the tendency to impose morality on character and action, and the evolution, rather, of the capacity to allow 'the force of imagination' its freedom. This changing emphasis from knowing 'about' things to knowledge 'from experience' characterizes George Eliot's own development. Her difficulty was in letting the thinker be shaped by the thought rather than the other way round – in letting go of the omnipotent manipulation of meaning and allowing meaning to emerge through the symbolic structure of the work itself. In *The Mill on the Floss* she writes,

> All people of broad, strong sense, have an instinctive repugnance to the men of maxims; because such people early discern that the mysterious complexity of our life is not to be embraced by maxims, and that to lace ourselves up in formulas of that sort is to repress all the divine promptings and inspirations that spring from growing insight and sympathy. And the man of maxims is the popular representative of the minds that are guided in their moral judgement solely by general rules, thinking that these will lead them to justice by a ready-made patent method, without the trouble of exerting patience, discrimination, impartiality – without any care to assure themselves whether they have the insight that comes from a hardly-earned estimate of temptation, or from a life vivid and intense enough to have created a wide fellow-feeling with all that is human.[15]

This passage makes explicit George Eliot's conception of the different sorts of knowledge: knowledge that was in the service of evading or mastering experience, in contrast to knowledge of the kind that constitutes the growth of the mind, rooted in the capacity to undergo and to understand emotional experiences. The implicit development of the novels as a whole, and their mixed achievement, offer evidence of the author's evolving mind and her uneven capacity to hold on to the distinction between true and false modes of coming-to-knowledge. The difference can be couched in Coleridge's terms of that which is super-induced by a static mind and that which is evolved from the mind's own growth.[16] It is the difference between an egotistical fabrication of representative sign-systems, and a generative process whereby meaning is evolved in the process of self-creation. Author, character, and reader may then alike 'think' and 'grow' as the 'axioms' are 'proved on our pulses'.[17]

George Eliot's early aspiration to reconcile the philosophies of Locke and Kant may perhaps merely reflect a youthful idealism, not unlike that of the 'theoretic' Dorothea, or even of Maggie Tulliver, who yearned for some unlearned secret of existence, 'something that would link together the wonderful impressions of this mysterious life. . . . '[18] But the artistic implications were more interesting and serious. In the Lockean world, the movement of atoms was considered the only reality. Meaning did not inhere in the processes; the individual fell back upon emotion with the fundamental acknowledgement that it was independent of reality. This inevitably invited sentimentalism – pseudo-emotion, stemming from the stirring of excitations that simulate feeling; the display of emotional states when emotion does not inhere in the object. The Romantics sought to transform reality – to show that it had no meaningful existence apart from the emotional apprehension of it, and to establish the metaphoric reciprocity of the mind of man and the world of nature. In George Eliot, it is where the object does not in itself naturally carry emotion that her writing falls into sentimentalism and that nostalgia and sententiousness obtrude – a tendency which characterizes the early novels far more seriously than the later ones. And it is where, later on, she projects herself out of selfhood and into a symbolic relationship with her object which transcends past experience, that her writing acquires the greatest force. For in her work, as in that of the Romantics, sentimentalism is its occasional failure and not its characteristic.

In the later writing a shift is evident towards what might be thought of as a more Kantian notion: of imagination irradiating perception; of the mind as an *active* co-operator in all sensation; of the two-fold co-operation of object and subject as *indispensable* to all knowledge. For George Eliot, 'emotion links itself with particulars, and only in a faint and secondary manner with abstractions'.[19] Her greatest writing occurs when the specificity of the subject is transcended – when subject and object become one in symbolic form, the symbol not being a cipher but with its ideal meaning complete within.

The threads of the fabric of the novels are woven with extraordinary complexity – internal and external factors being inextricable. The present emphasis will be on the development of character. But as to medium, a schematic formulation may briefly be offered of the development from one novel to the next, tracing the shift from plot as containing structure, in which characters function rather in Aristotle's sense of the word 'character' – as a moral quantity (the direction in which the agent exerts force), to plot as internal drama for the sake of which the external action unfolds. *Adam Bede* represents a relatively coherent world view, where morality is tightly linked to rank and expectations of behaviour associated with that; where character relates to moral type in a classically Aristotelean way – an imitation not of persons but of action – involving issues of appropriateness and narrative verisimilitude. The world of *Adam Bede*, as of the other early novels, is the provincial Warwickshire of George Eliot's childhood, infused with familiarity, reminiscence, nostalgia, certainty. Although, as with the other stories that are set a quarter or half a century in the past, there are significant elements of social change and cultural transition, the underlying morality nevertheless inheres in what still remains predominantly a 'knowable community'. There is a sense in which the people in the story figure as moral quantities, conforming to a prescribed pattern. This is a more coherent, bounded world, local, recognizable in its splits, contrasts, and polarizations (symbolized by the geography – Loamshire and Stonyshire) than that of the next novel, *The Mill on the Floss*. Here, despite the frequent explicit references to the world of the Greek tragedians, we already find Maggie having to carry meaning beyond that required by the generalization. Yet still the classic allusions and invocation of fate as the final arbiter fits the moral scheme firmly within the scientific world view, which, despite misgivings, George Eliot's intellectual self so firmly espoused at the time. It brings to mind A.N. Whitehead's comment about the Greek tragedians being the pilgrim fathers of the scientific imagination.[20] (Fate in Greek tragedy becomes the Order of Nature in modern thought.) For George Eliot, at this stage, morality was a comparatively simple matter: 'Consequences are unpitying. Our deeds carry their terrible consequences, quite apart from any fluctuations that went before – consequences that are hardly ever confined to ourselves.'[21]

At the far end of the continuum lies the predominant emphasis of *Daniel Deronda*, a different kind of writing, of the sort described by Wordsworth as where 'the feeling therein developed gives importance to the action and situation, and not the action and situation to the feeling.'[22] Browning clearly meant something similar when he said, 'My stress lay on the incidents in the development of a soul; little else is worth study.'[23]

The finest characterizations allow insight into the evolution of the mind's structure: its modification in the process of taking in or internalizing a piece of self-knowledge, and its slow decline in the failure to do so. This kind of knowledge often involved relinquishing what had previously felt to be 'known', and approaching the vast 'Terra Incognita of Knowledge'.[24] Some such process may have been occurring when George Eliot, twice, unexpectedly departed from the large-scale novel which she was working on and turned to a much shorter story before proceeding – in both instances she was weighed down with intense personal suffering. Each of the shorter works was in total contrast to what had seemed the main preoccupation at the time. Each, though in wholly different ways, is concerned with the creative process. The earlier, *The Lifted Veil* (1859) is 'about' it, the later *Silas Marner* (1861) offers the experience of it. Inseparable from this, each also centrally concerns itself with aspects of the mind's development, again in wholly contrasting ways. Briefly examining the two affords insight into the creative and emotional problems posed at the time in the context of the respective longer novels, *The Mill on the Floss* (1860) and *Romola* (1863). It also affords a way of focusing some of the issues which are spread much more discursively across the larger works – though eventually coming together in the relationship between Deronda and Gwendolen Harleth in *Daniel Deronda*.

These two stories, *The Lifted Veil* and *Silas Marner* illuminate George Eliot's struggles with her deeper insights – how high she erects the barriers of, respectively, moral purpose and of learning, as defences against engaging with psychic realities of another order, which are expressed in these 'interruptions', and for which she had available neither intellectual framework nor artistic convention.

In 1859, in the early months of her work on *The Mill on the Floss* – shortly after the successful reception of *Adam Bede* – George Eliot broke off her train of thought to write the curious story, *The Lifted Veil*. It was so at odds with the basic tenor and character of her earlier work, that her publisher, Blackwood, was reluctant to bring it out. We know that it contained ideas which George Eliot found important from her comments to Blackwood fourteen years later, when, after revising his view of the book, he requested to publish it. Though declining his offer, she says 'I care for the idea which it embodies and which justifies its *painfulness*.... There are many things in it which I would willingly say over again, and I shall never put them in any other form. But we must wait a little.'[25]

The story was written in a state of emotional turbulence. Not only was she troubled by the failure to remain incognito – feeling the burden of 'eyes all round',[26] but she was 'weary and ailing and thinking of a sister who is slowly dying'.[27] Her sister Chrissey, now mortally ill with consumption, had finally written to her after a long rift in the relationship. 'It has ploughed up my heart.'[28]

What was it about *The Lifted Veil*, which could not be incorporated into the creative process of the larger novel – intended to be 'a sort of companion picture [to *Adam Bede*] of provincial life',[29] and which necessitated George Eliot breaking off her larger project to write? The answers may be two-fold and inextricably related: it is about the nature of psychic development and about the creative process. The story expresses an unassimilable reality: the profound disjunction between what, at the time, she took to be an appropriate expression for her moral aesthetic ('If Art does not enlarge men's sympathies, it does nothing morally')[30] and her disturbing insight into the nature of psychic processes, particularly, one assumes, her own. In *The Lifted Veil*, she was addressing a set of issues which had to remain temporarily separate – a troubling area which informs her subsequent novels and which was finally, and uneasily, realized in *Daniel Deronda*. It seems to have been becoming clear, though perhaps not wholly consciously, that development of the kind which interested her did not reside in investigating the vicissitudes of the human spirit in a world of inexorable, natural law, but in a struggle of a different order, intimately related to external reality, but also, in some strange sense, independent of it – 'the mystery that lies under the processes'.

After a serious illness, the central character of the story, Latimer, acquires a prescience of the future and a superadded consciousness of the present – a kind of clairvoyance whereby he can see 'behind the veil' of day-to-day reality and concealment into 'the sordid narrow room' of others' souls. The only mind that remains hidden to him is that of the woman whom he had first seen in a vision and whom he believes himself to love – Bertha, his brother's fiancee, a 'Water Nixie', a 'pale, fatal-eyed woman', fascinating in her opacity and unavailability (foreshadowing the much richer delineations of Rosamond Vincy and Gwendolen), and whose existence is primarily constituted by others' projections onto her.

What characterizes Latimer is his wretched, self-pitying alienation, his egotism and the unremittingly horrible nature of what he sees. He calls his morbid self-preoccupation, a 'fatal solitude of the soul', an imprisonment within the confines of a mawkish sensibility, unrelieved by any hope, beauty or finer feeling. By drawing on the phenomena of clairvoyance and prescience, George Eliot explores projective processes of a fundamentally narcissistic kind, founded in intrusive curiosity about others, averse to self-knowledge and therefore putting development into abeyance. This is in sharp contrast to a penetrative sensibility for the sake of understanding, which has no place in this story.

Latimer's mother died when he was young. He remembers, in particular, her loving care when he was temporarily afflicted with blindness. As a child he recovers, but after her death, and utterly bereft of her encircling arms, he becomes psychically blind. The external holding, which might have offered him an internal container to enable him to make sense of his experience, is gone. In its absence, he exemplifies the death of the thinking capacity which could help him forge links with the rest of the world. Lacking, metaphorically, a 'veil', or boundary between inner and outer, he is described as experiencing reality as a sensuous bombardment of his overwrought sensibility. Without the internal capacity to render meaningful these fragmentary elements of experience, he confuses what belongs to himself with what belongs to others.

These are adumbrations of aspects of mental suffering that are developed much more fully in later novels. But at this point, and related, perhaps, to her own suffering, George Eliot seems to have been undergoing some kind of crisis of creativity, apparently lodged in the complex relationship between the coming-to-know of internal and external worlds, and the dangers of intrusive projection into character and plot, or of manipulation of an omnipotent kind, when the author finds herself personally too close to the material. The unevenness of *The Mill on the Floss*, in particular, exemplifies the difficulty.

Through Latimer's failings she is drawing attention, in negative terms, to an important aspect of creative imagination. For he is quite incapable of piercing or exalting the solid fact. He demonstrates the fallacy that you could 'know' the world and write

THE CHAMBER OF MAIDEN THOUGHT

creatively about it, either by means of this kind of intrusive process or through accuracy of representation, if not inspired from internal sources, rooted in the writer's self-knowledge. It was the Fallacy, as Whitehead would put it, 'of Misplaced Concreteness'. Latimer's false creativity mistakes poetic genius for what is, really, a two-dimensional reproduction of accurate correspondences – an issue surely related to George Eliot's early aesthetic as to the moral importance of detailed observation reproducing the minutiae of her characters' lives. Fortunately, she never relinquished her extraordinary capacity to observe, but its main strength was yet to be realized in an ability to express the minutiae of the outer states as informed by the inner, projecting emotive knowledge into objective forms – the essence of imagination. She describes the process in one of her final essays: 'having a keen interest in the natural history of my inward self, I pursue this plan I have mentioned of using my observation as a clue or lantern by which I detect small herbage or lurking life . . . '.[31]

Without that inner experience the artist falls prey to the false Muse, false inspiration, the green-eyed serpent woman, whose mind was, in fact, but a 'blank prosaic wall' (like the 'blank unreflecting surface' of Rosamond's mind, or of Keats's Lamia). It was not until later that George Eliot treated these insights on a much broader canvas, establishing in *Daniel Deronda* a congruence between the development of an authentic art and culture, and the true growth of the personality. By contrast, *The Lifted Veil* describes and embodies the emptiness and corruption of art, if not genuinely informed by the inner world. It is this realization of the hard internal work that has to be done before anything can really be understood that measures the distance between a scientific worldview, concerned with *explaining* 'reality' and adapting to it, and a set of inexhaustible *descriptions* of the myriad phenomena of human relations in the artistic expression of it.

In *The Lifted Veil*. George Eliot is posing, in embryonic and schematic form the preoccupation which finally found sustained creative expression in *Daniel Deronda* – the problem of self-knowledge and its relationship with the creative process. In this early story she offers the dual implication that it is unbearable to confront the chaos of inner experience, or face bare reality, without the capacity to transform it into something meaningful, and intolerable to settle for the two-dimensionality of the alternative. For adhering to the surfaces and mores of the phenomenal world affords only an illusory protection against this painful inner experience. The phenomenal world has no intrinsic meaning, and therefore no sustaining quality. Here she was adumbrating a conception of truthful and fraudulent experience which she was later to develop as being based not so much in moral precepts, in terms of standards of behaviour, but in ethical principles underlying behaviour – aspects of character embedded in the avoiding or confronting of the truth about oneself, inextricably related to the creative process and therefore at the heart of the mind's potential to grow. The connection between the two has to be made in order to be thought about and for change to occur. Latimer was unable to do so.

George Eliot describes in a letter the particular 'phase' she was in when writing *The Mill on the Floss*:

> at present my mind works with the most freedom and the keenest sense of poetry in my remotest past, and there are many strata to be worked through before I can begin to use *artistically* any material I may gather in the present.[32]

The distinction between the two modes of knowing is again caught, in essence, in the contrast between *Romola* and the story which 'thrust itself between me and the other book I was meditating. It is *Silas Marner, the Weaver of Raveloe*.'[33] Of all the novels *Romola* epitomizes the shift from 'picture to diagram'.[34] The author's learned historical and political preoccupations are imposed and the characters move across the pages scarcely incarnate, draining the vitality of the action. While amassing the historical details of the novel, however, and in a state of deep depression, indeed near despair, George Eliot describes something coming '*across* my other plans by a sudden inspiration' – a story, 'which has unfolded itself from the merest millet-seed of thought'.[35] It turned out to be in complete contrast to *Romola*. With a kind of mythic quality, it offers itself as a beautifully simple, but rich, symbolic expression of some of George Eliot's deepest thought – an embodiment of the processes of the generation and degeneration of the mind; a distillation of the much more discursive expressions of similar ideas in the longer novels, finding equivalents in her writing only in the later works –

occasionally in *Felix Holt*, more extensively in *Middlemarch* and finally, and most comprehensively, in *Daniel Deronda*.

With *Silas Marner*, as with *The Lifted Veil* the theme forced itself upon George Eliot. Far from the sense that she is imposing preconceptions and insisting that the world of the story conform to them, she demonstrates, for the first time, an extended capacity to write as a symbol-maker rather than as an exerciser of authoritarian and omnipotent authorial control. It is the story which most nearly fulfils her aspiration to make 'matter and form an inseparable truthfulness'.[36] The content is inseparable from the internal processes of the author in the writing of it, but, unlike *The Lifted Veil*, the processes seem fully metabolized and transformed symbolically rather than remaining an uneasy expression of unexalted ideas. It seems to have sprung fully formed from her mind, with none of the laborious working out which weighs so insistently on the longer novels.

It reads as a parable of self-creation. She describes it to Blackwood as having come to her first of all quite suddenly, suggested by a childhood recollection of seeing a linen weaver with a bag on his back. This description was amplified by Blackwood in a letter to his wife: '"Silas Marner" sprang from her childish recollection of a man with a stoop, and expression of face that led her to think that he was an alien from his fellows.'[37] George Eliot felt that the story lent itself to poetry rather than to prose fiction and doubted that anyone would be interested 'since William Wordsworth is dead'.[38] The epigraph (slightly altered) is a quotation from Wordsworth's 'Michael':

> A child more than all other gifts
> That earth can offer to declining man,
> Brings hope with it, and forward-looking thoughts.

In essence the tale embodies the evolution of the mind from a two-dimensional, adhesive existence, dependent on empty structures – initially the narrow and ignorant constructions of a religious sect (ironically located in Lantern Yard), subsequently the crock of gold, which, when gone, left Marner 'groping in the darkness'. He had no internal resources, or endo-skeleton to sustain his successive losses.

The story was written swiftly and apparently impulsively, out of the author's turbulent feeling – her sense of alienation, of identification with an experience of being cut off from the roots of her being, physically weak, depressed, living in a dreary furnished London house, and mourning the loss of the country. The familiar bulwarks of intensive intellectual activity as a defence against depressive anxiety suddenly gave way with the eruption of this inspired story. The idea which prompted it seemed to belong to those aspects of experience which are alien – the darker and less comprehensible regions of the mind.

Silas Marner manifests clear elements of her youthful passion (and lasting reverence) for Wordsworth. Reading him for the first time on her twentieth birthday George Eliot had commented, 'I have never before met with so many of my own feelings, expressed just as I could <wish> like them.'[39] And yet, although clearly belonging to a Wordsworthian tradition, neither the associated weaknesses of the sentimentality which elsewhere attaches to her treatment of childhood, for example, nor the nostalgia which at times stultifies 'emotion recollected in tranquillity', nor the idealization and sermonizing which so often impinge, have any place. Here nature is not sentimentalized. The natural settings, in terms of detail and atmosphere, are at one with the meaning of the tale. Before such calm external beauty the presence of a vague fear is more distinctly felt 'like a raven flapping its slow wing across the sunny air'.[40] The story does not suffer from the excessive personal immediacy, almost intrusiveness of the author into her main character, which had marred the treatment of Maggie with elements of self-idealization and self-pity, but comes near to the creative distancing which typifies her much later treatment of Gwendolen. In *Silas Marner* George Eliot demonstrates the capacity to be at one with, and yet separate from, her central character; to describe the logical necessity of the inner development of a prior reality.

For Marner, regeneration comes not from without but from an inner reality – the child Eppie, born of sorrow. In the aftermath of one of his cataleptic fits, he discovers her already inside his hearth/heart. That evening marks the birth of Marner's soul and the death of Godfrey Cass's. The latter definitely shuts off 'that hidden life which lies, like a dark bystreet, behind the goodly ornamented facade . . . '.[41] He denies the Dunsey part of himself, and as Tito was to do in *Romola* and Bulstrode in *Middlemarch*, begins a life premissed on falsehood. In this shorter story the specious and self-deceiving justifications for action sow the seeds of disreputable conduct. Lies become the poison of the mind, which withers and dies for want of truthful experiences. Meanwhile, by contrast, the confines of Marner's world, which had previously been reduced to the 'unquestioning activity of a spinning insect', were re-opened. He had worked, 'from pure impulse, without reflection.... Thought was arrested by utter bewilderment, now its old narrow pathway was closed....'[42] Marner's face and body shrank and bent themselves into a mechanical relation with the objects of his life – part of the loom which had no meaning standing apart. Later, when his gold is stolen, Marner's thoughts 'were baffled by a blank like that which meets a plodding ant when the earth has broken away on its homeward path'.[43] In this state of mind, 'that habit of looking towards the money and grasping it with a sense of fulfilled effort made a loam that was deep enough for the seeds of desire ... '.[44] Lacking the inner resources to make sense of his experience Marner had no symbolic representation for his suffering. Eppie's arrival provided the impulse to regeneration, the awakening of 'the thinking principle' towards a fully-dimensional capacity slowly to recover the continuity of his existence. In the containing company of the motherly and attentive Dolly Winthrop he began to remember, to reflect on, and try to make sense of, the nature of his losses, and to trace more meaningful threads back to his early life. The dual processes of the different kinds of learning are sparingly described: 'As the child's mind was growing into knowledge, his mind was growing into memory: as her life unfolded, his soul, long stupefied in a cold narrow prison, was unfolding too, and trembling gradually into full consciousness.'[45]

Through the experience of 'finding' Eppie, Marner, buried alive for fifteen years, was able to rejoin the human race. She brought his inner being into relation with the world outside:

> the little child had come to link him once more with the whole world. There was love between him and the child that blent them into one, and there was love between the child and the world – from men and women with parental looks and tones, to the red lady-birds and the round pebbles.[46]

The gold coins to which he had clung turned into the golden hair and golden experience of the birth of the principle of growth –

fostering his parental qualities, long held in abeyance, and awakening him to the beauty of the world. For Eppie is the pure gold of the mind's capacity to develop; she represents the birth of the new idea; the internal object or presiding deity – carrying the spirit of the Romantics, or of Bunyan, or Shakespeare.

> Marner took her on his lap, trembling with an emotion mysterious to himself, of something unknown dawning on his life. Thought and feeling were so confused within him, that if he had tried to give them utterance, he could only have said that the child was come instead of the gold – that the gold had turned into the child.[47]

Out of George Eliot's despair was born a child/story which created that which it meditated upon. The tale carries an immediacy of identification of thought and feeling, form and content – the operation of imagination which indeed 'pierces or exalts the solid fact'. The Wordsworthian 'recollection in tranquillity' and what George Eliot later called 'the stored residues of passion'[48] coalesce. It is a parable of the nature of development, of a vision of the world – a sustained poetic expression of the essence of some of the longer novels. George Eliot was to achieve a similar coalescence in particular characterizations and aspects of the later works, but never with such assurance, or so spare an economy of words, and of action that were uniquely representative of the deeper meanings of her thought. One such meaning was the ethical centrality, in art and life, of richness and poverty of imagination, as distinct from moral notions of good and evil. The distinction was one that she had been reaching after as an idea in *The Lifted Veil* but in *Silas Marner* it takes its place, in parable form, at the heart of the matter.

The story was the first clear expression of her capacity to embrace the darker side of human nature as genuinely residing within, and not occurring as a consequence of external experience; the first explicit intimation of the Epigraph of *Daniel Deronda*: 'Let thy chief terror be of thine own soul...'. Previously, like Wordsworth, she had tended to see the corrupting and constraining forces on the personality – the 'shades of the prison-house' – as impinging from without, with varying impact depending on the individual disposition. In *The Mill on the Floss*, in particular, she tries to reconcile flowing emotions with the 'laws' of nature and of human nature – a mixture of the mechanistic and the moral – and in so doing ends by manipulating the action rather than allowing it to evolve. The shift in her mode of thinking from that earlier novel to this short story is distinctive. It was not until the last novel *Daniel Deronda*, however, when the mapping moves within, that George Eliot realizes, on a much broader scale, the ideas she was raising in *The Lifted Veil* and the meanings implicit in *Silas Marner*. This final drama emerges from the internal conflicts of the characters, rather than from an externally imposed moral or ideological position of a kind which masks the true nature of the irreconcilable and inexplicable forces. It has an end but no 'ending'.

In *The Mill on the Floss* the moral imperative of her aesthetic doctrine encouraged in George Eliot sentiments more akin to the conservative and priggish side of Wordsworth, 'moralising, exhorting and ameliorating the associative connectiveness of human existence'.[49] In *Silas Marner* it is evident that in tension with this, and gradually replacing it in her later writing, was a different 'vision' of the life of the mind, based essentially in the Romantics' notion of imagination as 'shaping' experience. The non-Wordsworthian 'tumult of the soul' determines the action and the creative energy resides in the hidden pathways of relationship, in the inspired observation of the nature of 'the invisible thoroughfares'[50] of human interaction, which in part characterizes the development of *Middlemarch* but finds its extended expression in *Daniel Deronda*.

The scintillating quality of *Silas Marner* is the realization of experience which has been fully 'lived' internally, freeing the author, it seems, to engage much more forcefully with aspects of psychic and creative processes hitherto held somewhat in abeyance. In the large-scale novels which follow, it becomes clear in the action and the characterization – for example of Tito, Mrs Transome, Bulstrode, Rosamond, Lydgate, that the growth or decay of the mind, and the nature of development or of degeneration, depend on the capacity to recognize and metabolize those aspects of experience which originate, not from external pressures alone but from aspects of character – internal demons mobilized or dispelled by life's experience. The successive and massive disillusionments of, for example, Dorothea's 'epochs' shake her emotional stability and threaten her with internal catastrophe which temporarily arrests her capacity to function. Her despairing sense of internal fragmentation as she begins to change, is dramatically expressed in the description of the chaos of the external surroundings during her honeymoon in Rome. She had been becoming more and more aware with a certain terror, that her mind was continually sliding into inward fits of anger and repulsion or else into forlorn weariness. 'That new, real future which was replacing the imaginary drew its material from the endless minutiae, by which her view . . . was gradually changing with the secret motion of a watch-hand from what it had been in her maiden dream.'[51] Her ability to undergo, and survive, the serial and painful experiences whereby she is dislodged from her mental preconceptions, thereafter constitutes her mind's capacity to grow. Unlike Lydgate, she learns from her experience. Each new trauma eventually constitutes a form of baptism or rebirth, though never obliterating the epoch when a motive is born or an expectation dies. It is the 'unhistoric acts' of the 'Finale' of *Middlemarch* rather than the 'epic life' of the 'Prelude' which describes the evolution of the internal life of the novel. Disappointing though the ending must, in some sense, inevitably be in any work in which, as George Eliot says, 'there is any merit of development', it none the less represents an internal shift of great importance. The developmental process lies not in historic acts but in the coming-to-have a truer vision of the world and of the self-in-the-world, aided, indeed initiated, by a capacity to learn from experience rather to adapt to the structures of social conformity. It involves seeing self and life as they are – stripped of grandiosity, of emotionalism, of self-righteousness, and of the impulse subjectively to defend against psychic pain by being someone one isn't. This is in contrast to becoming someone one is, by drawing on projection of a rather different kind – the projection, that is, of parts of oneself into the life and minds of others for the purpose of sympathy and communication – a true attention to 'what is apart from oneself'.

After much has been said about the nature of development in the novels, its essential mystery remains – as it always must. Yet the last novel not only centres, as never before, on the internal development of a character, but throws a different kind of light on George Eliot's conception of the nature of the process whereby internal changes come about. That process is lodged, as ever, in relationship – that between Gwendolen Harleth and Daniel Deronda – but this time in a type of relationship which is unique in the novels. The source of trouble for critics may lie in the fact that it is much more akin to the nature of the transference relationship than anything else.

In the course of the novel Gwendolen emerges from a two-dimensional sylph girl, encased within an adhesively dependent, narcissistic existence – in which all the essentials to mental growth are held in abeyance – to a fully dimensional, courageous woman; one who has confronted and survived the 'terror of her own soul'. Of compelling interest is the scintillating characterization which is swept along by the force of the inner logic of her reality. George Eliot seems hardly to be leading Gwendolen, but following her; not reviving memories of what has been known or felt, but undergoing, with fine precision, the moment-by-moment, perilously-poised crises and possibilities of Gwendolen's consciousness.

The action evolves in accordance with the mind's internal condition – the emphasis being ultimately on the nature of the structuring of inner space rather than outer. The symbolic patterning of these inner states (the dead face and fleeing figure, the gambling, the horse-riding, the diamonds) is highly condensed, quite unlike the predominantly narrative and representative 'signs' in *The Mill on the Floss* (for example, the river). The author emerges from the tangled web of social and individual interrelations of the world of *Middlemarch*, prepared, it seems finally, to work through some of the ideas which had been adumbrated in *The Lifted Veil*, distilled in *Silas Marner*, and partially elaborated in *Middlemarch*.

Daniel Deronda is about the generative process. It focuses on the particularities of the development of an individual mind, and on the generalities of the spiritual future of the Jewish nation – the growth of a culture which embodied 'religion, law and moral life, [which] mingled as the stream of blood in the heart'.[52] The central instrument, or vehicle, for these very different, yet fundamentally related, developmental processes is Daniel Deronda himself. The growth of the individual personality and large-scale creative endeavour coalesce.

In this final 'mental phase' George Eliot moves confidently outside the structures of naturalistic explanation, outside the known relationships of provincial communities and the conventions of the contemporary novel, and into a world where those fatal meshes are 'woven within more closely than without'. The book moves into the theatre of the mind. The leitmotifs of art, drama and music constantly bring into confrontation false and true culture – the projective roles of assumed identity and emotional display, in contrast to the authentic creative experience. The familiar associative mapping takes place with sets of mental associations which have in consciousness the status of external fact, 'the solidity of objects'.[53] Gwendolen, as with other, though paler, characterizations before her, is at first busy with her own social drama, 'as little penetrated by a feeling of wider relations as if it had been a puppet-show'.[54] She has to suffer the pain of being dislodged from her narcissistic supremacy. The process comes to embody aspects of inner reality which take on a different dimension and order of intensity from before. 'The iridescence of her character – the play of various, nay contrary tendencies'[55] are evident from the first. George Eliot's next comment makes the nature of the forthcoming drama absolutely clear: 'Macbeth's rhetoric about the impossibility of being many opposite things in the same moment, referred to the clumsy necessities of action and not to the subtler possibilities of feeling. We cannot speak a loyal word and be meanly silent, we cannot kill and not kill in the same moment; but a moment is wide enough for the loyal and mean desire, for the outlash of a murderous thought and the sharp backward stroke of repentance.'[56]

Early in the first book, George Eliot refers to Gwendolen's infelonious murder of her sister's canary, which she had strangled when its shrill singing had interrupted her own. She was not, we are told, remorseless, but she liked 'to make her penances easy'. At this stage, when self-idealization holds sway, her murderous and sadistic impulses, together with her self-hatred and terror of intimacy – whether sexual or emotional – have to be dominated and controlled, locked behind the panels of her mind, relegated, like Rex's occasional vicious tendencies, to the 'outer courts and little-visited chambers' of the mind.[57] She is only occasionally in touch with them in experiences external to herself, most dramatically evident in the episode of the dead face and figure fleeing with outstretched arms in the mysterious picture behind the panel. This image describes both Gwendolen's inner dynamics – the contrary tendencies of her mental struggle, in both committing wrong and fleeing from it – and the subsequent events of the story. Hitherto her narcissistic supremacy had been main-tained by a resolute splitting between different parts of her personality and denial of extensive inner regions. Confronted with this inner reality when the panel flies open, she is struck with terror, 'like a statue into which a soul of Fear had entered'.[58] When the figure had first been revealed, she had insisted that the panel be permanently closed and that *she* guard the key – an indigestible experience, at this stage, which had to be locked away. Those aspects of her psyche had to be rigidly controlled, along with most of her external relationships. At this time, 'she had no permanent consciousness of other fetters'[59] than those offered by this limiting social existence. She is appalled by the untamed parts of herself which force their presence upon her when the social roles which she usually inhabits, believing them to *be* herself, are not available.

George Eliot presents a brilliant portrait of the infantile aspects of an adolescent state of mind, characterized by splitting and projective identification. Gwendolen's consciousness was cut off from the rest of the world which represented 'the vastness in which she seemed an exile'.[60] Impelled by her 'inborn energy of egoistic desire', she denied anything that was unpleasant. She

> knew nothing of such inward strife. . . . How could she believe in sorrow? If it attacked her, she felt the force to crush it, to defy it, or run away from it, as she had done already. Anything seemed more possible than that she could go on bearing miseries, great or small.[61]

Depressive concern is foreign to her nature at this point. Enthralled by her own beauty and capacity to captivate and control, she would simply overcome sorrow. Yet the control was not as perfect as she would have wished. Into the fabric of her normal life other experiences would occasionally intrude, of a different order which 'seemed like a brief remembered madness'. When alone she would at times suffer a feeling of uncontrollable insignificance, of profound alienation when unprotected by the illusion of her supremacy.

The description of her relationships in terms of tyranny and submission gives a foretaste of the sado-masochistic bond which comes to predominate in her involvement with Grandcourt. The emotional tyranny extends to the sway she holds over her mother. Mrs Davilow, childlike in her own way, is a woman with the life gone out of her, submissive to Gwendolen's dominating personality, weak, and quite unable to digest her own mental pain such that she might help her daughter separate from her adhesive relationship to her and begin to grow up. In the absence of maternal strength it is a different kind of dependent relationship which enables Gwendolen to begin that process.

As the book proceeds, Gwendolen suffers a series of narcissistic blows which she attempts to 'manage' by recourse to her old exoskeletal props: 'proud concealment, trust in new excitements that would make life go by without much thinking; trust in some deed of reparation to nullify her self-blame . . . trust in the hardening effect of use and want that would make her indifferent to her miseries'.[62] But the defensive structure is weakening and the murderous impulses, hinted at in the killing of the canary, take on more obsessive and horrifying dimensions as unconscious guilt is confirmed by the conscious awareness of having done wrong – in breaking her promise to Mrs Glasher by agreeing to marry Grandcourt. 'Side by side with the dread of her husband had grown the self-dread which urged her to flee from the pursuing images wrought by her pent-up impulse.'[63] The flash of self-knowledge, of her inner truth, suffered by Gwendolen earlier in the story, left unexplained by George Eliot in the episode of the dead face and fleeing figure, now acquires an explanation, as the contours of the inner map are traced with clearer definition.

The prose takes on an intensity and creative energy unparalleled in the rest of the book:

> in no concealment had she now any confidence: her vision of what she had to dread took more decidedly than ever the form of some fiercely impulsive deed, committed as in a dream that she would instantaneously awake from to find the effects real though the images had been false: to find death under her hands, but instead of darkness, daylight; instead of satisfied hatred, the dismay of guilt; instead of freedom, the palsy of a new terror - a white dead face from which she was for ever trying to flee and for ever held back.[64]

Her unconscious destructiveness was forcing itself into the conscious and everyday chambers of her mind, and, lacking the internal resources, at this point, to contain and digest the experience, was driving her mad. She becomes obsessed with the fear of wrong-doing. In the episode of Grandcourt's actual death, the mental intensity of Gwendolen's guilt and fear is described in terms which re-evoke and re-echo those split-off, hallucinatory aspects of her inner terror which have come up repeatedly in the course of the novel. The almost exact repetition of words from earlier waking nightmares makes clear the simultaneity of inner and outer experience, the difficulty of discriminating, at this crisis, where the wish and where the reality reside.

The culmination of that self-disapproval which becomes the wakening of the new life within her, lay in her sense of remorse – no longer represented by the kind of easy penance that had characterized the aftermath of the murder of the canary, but described now in terms of a deep inner change – the capacity to face the truth. When, after the drowning, she pours out to Deronda, in a fragmented and semi-delirious account, her mental confusion, her guilt, her gambling, the dead face, the fear of wickedness, she says, 'I saw my wish outside me . . . there was the dead face, dead, dead.'[65] The elements that the reader has been made aware of through image and association are finally brought to consciousness in Gwendolen's mind. She moves to a quite different understanding of herself-in-the-world – from being centre stage in the 'narrow theatre which life offers',[66] to a sense that 'her horizon was but a dipping onward of an existence with which her own was revolving'.[67] Gwendolen could begin to experience 'some of that peaceful melancholy which comes from the renunciation of demands for self, and from taking the ordinary good of existence . . . as a gift above expectation'.[68]

The shift in Gwendolen from careless supremacy, to the terror of stored-up retribution, to the capacity to feel genuine remorse – the shift, that is, from the 'sea-green serpent' to the 'storm-beaten white doe' – occurs in the context of Deronda's mind. For these changes are incomprehensible without the nature of Deronda passing through her life, his character through her soul. From the opening interrogatives of Deronda's reflections, as he watches the 'Nereid in sea-green robes' at the gaming table, the mysterious relationship between them shapes the action of the book – the internal processes, that is, of the development of Gwendolen's mind.

> Was she beautiful or not beautiful? and what was the secret of form or expression which gave the dynamic quality to her glance? Was the good or evil genius dominant in those beams? Probably the evil; else why was the effect that of unrest rather than undisturbed charm? Why was the wish to look again felt as a coercion and not as a longing in which the whole being consents?[69]

Standing at the game of life, where 'our gain is another's loss'.[70] Gwendolen feels as troubled by Deronda's eyes upon her as she had been in the casino. From the beginning 'in some mysterious way', he had become 'part of her conscience',[71] taking hold, from the first, on her mind, 'as one who had an unknown standard by which he judged her'.[72] The gambling metaphor becomes the focus for her guilt. Deronda's redeeming of her necklace carries a weight of meaning which resides at the heart of the enigmatic quality of the relationship:

> Why she should suddenly determine not to part with the necklace was not much clearer to her than why she should sometimes have been frightened to find herself in the fields alone: she had a confused state of emotion about Deronda – was it wounded pride or resentment, or a certain awe and exceptional trust? It was something vague and yet mastering, which impelled her to this action about the necklace. There is a great deal of unmapped country within us which would have to be taken into account in an explanation of our gusts and storms.[73]

On the threshold of beginning her life, at the end of the novel, she identifies him with the 'struggling regenerative process in her which had begun with his action'.[74] In redeeming the necklace he had initiated the process of redemption of parts of her personality. She experienced him as a mysterious influence, not part of herself and yet not apart from herself. Despite her initial proud resistance, Gwendolen becomes increasingly receptive to Deronda's influence and the way in which he functions creatively on behalf of her internal objects. Her experience of him shifts from a coercive judgemental presence – at first part of a persecutory then of an encouraging conscience, to a childlike dependency on him (the 'unreflecting openness, nay, the importunate pleading, with which she expressed her dependence on him';[75] 'You must tell me then what to think and what to do . . .')[76] and finally, to the capacity to live physically separately but emotionally infused with the qualities of his being: 'It is better – it shall be better with me because I have known you'.[77]

The process is, as George Eliot constantly makes clear, a mysterious one unfathomable even by Grandcourt's exquisite capacity to intuit and control. He was aware of, yet unable to master 'the inward action between them'.[78] Gwendolen was herself conscious of an 'uneasy transforming process – all the old nature shaken to its depths'.[79] 'No chemical process shows a more wonderful activity than the transforming influence of the thoughts we imagine to be going on in another'.[80] Deronda's mental presence is able to hold these various projections of persecutory judgement, of fear, of infantile need, and ultimately of hope – his slight relations with her having, 'by some hidden affinity, bitten themselves into the permanent layers of feeling'.[81] He gradually became the representative, or the internal container, for the belief in a recoverable nature, in Gwendolen's capacity to change both through the experience of remorse, and through caring for 'what is best in thought and action – something that is good apart from the accidents of your own lot'.[82] Deronda offered a mind within whose dependable internal space Gwendolen could begin to take back those projected parts, face them as belonging to her own personality and struggle towards a better life. For he possessed that receptiveness which had 'a rare and massive power, like fortitude'.[83] His presence in her mind was 'an awakening of a new consciousness'. George Eliot describes the relationship in terms which were to become characteristic of the reciprocal process of the analytic relationship.

> her feelings had turned this man . . . into a priest; a sort of trust less rare than the fidelity that guards it. Young reverence for one who is also young is the most coercive of all: there is the same level of temptation, and the higher motive is believed in as a fuller force – not suspected to be a mere residue from weary experience.
>
> But the coercion is often stronger on the one who takes the reverence. Those who trust us educate us. And perhaps

in that ideal consecration of Gwendolen's, some education was being prepared for Deronda.[84]

Central to this quality of receptiveness is precisely the aspect of Deronda which has most troubled critics – his lack of personality. He is characterized by an extraordinary absence of egocentricity, lingering 'in a state of social neutrality',[85] and longing for a 'fixed habitation for his wandering energy'.[86] He is intensely inner-directed (like Wordsworth and Keats, early deprived of his mother he perhaps cleaved all the more to his internal object). His ego would seem to be purposely indistinct: lying in his skiff by the Thames river bank, he finds himself

> forgetting everything else in a half-speculative, half-involuntary identification of himself with the objects he was looking at, thinking how far it might be possible habitually to shift his centre till his own personality would be no less outside him than the landscape . . . [87]

Deronda's actual character and life circumstances are wholly opaque to Gwendolen. It is with those internal qualities available to others, which initiate and sustain the processes of change in them, that the novel is primarily concerned. In being able to adopt a foreign culture without being *of* it, Deronda carries an emotionally adequate carapace without endangering his endo-skeleton (what Hamlet did not manage to do). Indeed the perfection of his social carapace is part of his ability to function as he does – a manifest ability to adapt two-dimensionally without sacrificing three-dimensionality.

It seems essential that he be a Jew – that he carry internally, in his blood, the sufferings of the centuries and the capacity to survive them. He also carries the 'inexorable sorrow' of the circumstances of his own birth which 'had given bias to his conscience, a sympathy with certain ills, and a tension of resolve in certain directions, which marked him off from other youths . . . '[88] He is described as having 'a meditative yearning after wide knowledge' which diffused ambition 'for prize acquirement in narrow tracks'[89] and a 'meditative interest in learning how human miseries are wrought';[90] 'an activity of imagination on behalf of others'.[91] He was attracted to rescuing people 'telling upon their lives with some sort of redeeming influence'.[92] At Cambridge he found his 'inward bent towards comprehension and thoroughness'

THE CHAMBER OF MAIDEN THOUGHT

diverging from the standard curriculum, for he sought 'insight into the principles which form the vital connections of knowledge'.[93] His relationship with Hans Meyrick has elements in it which become far more developed with Gwendolen – elements, that is, of the transference object. To Deronda, Hans poured himself out – he 'seemed to take Deronda as an Olympian who needed nothing':[94] Deronda functioned for him as 'an ideal'.[95] Indeed he literally became Hans's eyes – the eyes which gained his scholarship – a foretaste of the inward way in which he became the eyes of Gwendolen's mind. The whole characterization is one of immense inner strength, a strength which developed out of the surviving of internal and external calamities to be drawn on by others to help survive the traumas of their own lives.

In terms of literary and psychoanalytic models of the mind, George Eliot's achievement resides in her emergence from her philosopher/sociologist/moralist self to being a great psychologist. Written with immense creative power, *Daniel Deronda* embodies the ultimate realization of her ideas about the growth of the mind and the mysterious processes whereby one person can assist the development of another. For Deronda, with priest/analyst-like qualities, is able to carry the transference of others, to bear their love and hatred without taking it personally and reacting to it. His lack of personality is essential to his function in the book – primarily as the bearer of the transference. As in the consulting room, Gwendolen opens herself to Deronda, and changes. He too is wrought upon, but less distinctively. It is in the internal evolution of Gwendolen's personality in relation to him that the chief poetic energy lies – the development of her internal object from being primarily judgmental to being the bearer of aspiration and hope (the different aspects of super-ego and ego ideal).

George Eliot's own evolution is marked by her conception of Deronda as the emotional initiator of a move away from the meaning of morality or growth being to do with the relationship between good and bad, to a vision of impoverished or enriched imaginative life as the path to development. In the course of the novel the idea of good becomes constituted by the experience of the growth of the mind: not Gwendolen's earlier childlike conception of the opposition between goodness and wickedness, but the process of becoming wise through the contact between the developing self's relationship with the developing internal object. Deronda carries the 'principle of self- development' in the novel. The mantle he inherits from Mordecai is ultimately an expression of the realization of that principle in the wider spiritual and imaginative politics of Jewish culture. The mantle he leaves with Gwendolen alters the structure of her mind in the process of becoming wise. In this relationship the function of the internal object is clear as the propagator of values and the instrument of the begetting of wisdom.

Gwendolen has 'to take hold of her sensibility and use it as if it were a faculty, like vision'.[96] Deronda cannot do it for her, he can only try to enable her to do it for herself through the internalization of his internal qualities. It is an ongoing process: 'Now we can perhaps never see each other again. But our minds may get nearer.'[97] 'It is better – it shall be better with me because I have known you'. The end of the novel, like the end of an analysis, is not an 'ending' but a beginning. The whole process has been 'a preparation' for life.[98]

It is in this novel, above all, that the distance may be measured between egotistical omnipotence or grandiosity, and inspired learning from emotional experience under the guidance of internal objects – at the heart of what we have been calling the literary model of the mind.

9

PARALLEL DIRECTIONS IN PSYCHOANALYSIS

> The human nature unto which I felt
> That I belonged, and reverenced with love,
> Was not a punctual presence, but a spirit
> Diffused through time and space, with aid derived
> Of evidence from monuments, erect,
> Prostrate, or leaning towards their common rest
> In earth, the widely scattered wreck sublime
> Of vanished nations.
>
> *(The Prelude)*[1]

In his definitive statement of the life of the mind as 'The Vale of Soul-making',[2] Keats distinguishes between those who are genuinely able to explore the further chambers, the inner recesses and dark passages of what he had earlier called the 'large Mansion of Many Appartments' – human life, and those who stopped thinking, or at least did not 'think into the human heart'.[3] The Soul-*making* emphasis in the experience of life, lies in the capacity to tolerate the perception that 'the world is full of Misery and Heartbreak, Pain, Sickness and oppression'.[4] That knowledge is co-terminous with the realization that it is in apprehending that very reality that the many doors open from the Chamber of Maiden Thought. In a world of Circumstances, it is the Heart which is 'the teat from which the Mind or intelligence sucks its identity'.[5]

In considering how the embodiment in literature of the development of the life of the mind has illuminated the task of psychoanalysis, their congruent goals become apparent: to explore the process whereby truthful emotional experiences evolve and to participate in the growth of the mind. Founded, as it is, in the notion that all cognition is primarily emotion, that knowing is essentially an imaginative experience, 'The Vale of Soul-making' offers a description of the human condition that is shared by the Romantic poets, by mid-nineteenth century writers and late twentieth-century, post-Kleinian psychoanalysts alike. By establishing the necessity of placing emotionality at the heart of the matter, it focuses attention on recognizing the place for meaning and value in human affairs – the absolute values of psychic reality as opposed to the relativity of social values. The promotion of the evolution of such values has always required that thought have its anchorage in feeling. In pursuing this same process in the context of psychoanalytic thinking, we follow the central preoccupation of the great creative artists, to oppose the disassociation of thought from feeling.

In this sense a similarity of *direction* may be asserted between Shakespeare's work, that of Milton, of the Romantic poets, of Emily Brontë and of George Eliot, and the way psychoanalysis has developed. This direction could be characterized by its stress on the necessity of value – whether explicitly or implicitly expressed – and a commitment to an organic principle of growth. ('Organic' does not imply that, given the right conditions, the seed of the human mind will grow, blossom and eventually die, but rather that the mind is a living thing with its own processes of development and principles of growth, related to, but by no means determined by, external conditions.) This way of thinking represents an alternative to the positivist view that all life is ultimately reducible to laws operable in the organic and inorganic world alike (an aspiration which Freud struggled to relinquish).

The congruence of direction between literature and psychoanalysis resides in their both being based in this embracing of emotion as lying at the heart of meaning, symbol formation being the entrée to thinking about meaning. Hence it is reasonable for Shelley to say that the 'poets are the unacknowledged legislators of the world', and for the psychoanalysts to say that the mother/baby relationship determines the direction of development for the child. The congruence has become clear through the work of Bion, who represented the mother's functioning – the primary instrument for the reception of symbol formation – as being, in turn, the basic necessary mode of functioning for the baby. The transference, at the level of the infant/breast relationship, is the vehicle for all fundamental change through psychoanalysis. The 'thinking' breast becomes the unconscious 'legislator' of the baby's world. The symbolizing processes of the artist and his or her relationship with the community involve a similar reciprocity – through the symbolic value of the work – to the relationships alike between mother and baby and between therapist and patient.

Bion's theory is that symbol formation is initially a function of the internal object rather than of the self. Alpha function, as he calls it, is first a capacity on the mother's part, stemming from her internal object. It is experienced as the breast, or the 'thinking' breast. In good circumstances she aids in the establishing of, and gives form to, the baby's object – that is when the mother is able to hold, and transform, the baby's mental state, and when the manner and matter of the baby's projections are not too overwhelming. The creating of symbols as the basis for thinking remains a function of that internal object. Most behaving, thinking, speaking, even dreaming, occurs with received symbols. Individuality, however, lies in the generating of autonomous, idiosyncratic symbols – in giving form to 'Ideas, in the highest sense of that word' (Coleridge), in finding a 'local habitation and a name'. It is in embracing these idiosyncratic symbols of emotional experience, initially made available in dreams, that the individuality of each person evolves through self-creative thinking. These 'Ideas' embody 'the shaping spirit of Imagination'. The alternative is to operate with received symbols which are utilized as signs for adaptation, risking the imposition of preconceptions and the insistence that the world, or the world of the mind, conform to them rather than allowing the ideas to modify the mind.

'The Vale of Soul-making' is the symbol Keats has offered, available for having meaning poured into it. For what is shaped by Imagination with the use of symbols is an idea of the world and of self-in-the-world. We contribute to shaping the world in accordance with that vision of self-in-the-world, the nature of which it is the shared task of the patient and therapist to illuminate. In Deronda's case, this process involved thinking himself out of his egocentricity into being-in-the-world – such that 'his own personality would be no less outside him than the landscape'.[6]

In the process of analysis, the patient's essential self, that is the experiencing rather than the adaptive self (the endo-skeletal as opposed to exo-skeletal personality), becomes available for understanding through the symbolic content of the 'dream' being transformed into the symbolic form of language by the interpretation. For this to be achieved, the therapist has to 'follow' the material – holding a candle behind the individual, the better to illuminate what lies before, rather than shining a directive, pedagogic 'light' in front, to lead. ('Does my way of seeing it help you to see it more clearly your way?') For the patient in the consulting room, the development of such capacity for understanding lies in the opportunity to engage with the mind of a therapist who is genuinely open to the idea of carrying the transference image. This function of carrying the transference, by which the therapist aids the forward movement of the patient's development and thus does not repeat the disappointments and disillusionments of past figures, is dependent on the therapist's openness to being apprehended as bearing internal qualities which s/he knows, having overcome egocentricity, s/he not only does not, but in their particularity cannot, possess. With Deronda, for example, there is a far more rich sense of the qualities which are attributed to him than of those which he actually has. The mind's self-creation occurs according to the degree of truthfulness existing in the relationship between subject and internal object.

In *Middlemarch,* the crisis and culmination of the growth of Dorothea's mind is expressed in terms of this same symbolic congruence between subject and object. Her development in the course of the novel is from short-sighted aspiration of a projective kind to a much broader and more humble vision of the nature of humanity and of her place therein. She undergoes her final, and profoundest, disillusionment when,

> with a consciousness which had never awakened before, she stretched out her arms towards [that bright creature whom she trusted] and cried with bitter tears that their nearness was but a passing vision: she discovered her passion to herself in the unshrinking utterance of despair.[7]

George Eliot describes how Dorothea did not linger long 'in the narrow cell of her calamity, in the besotted misery of a consciousness that only sees another's lot as an accident of its own'.[8] Rather,

> She opened her curtains, and looked out towards the bit of road

that lay in view, with fields beyond, outside the entrance-gates. On the road was a man with a bundle on his back and a woman carrying her baby; in the field she could see figures moving – perhaps the shepherd with his dog. Far off in the bending sky was the pearly light; and she felt the largeness of the world and the manifold awakenings of men to labour and endurance. She was part of that involuntary, palpitating life, and could neither look out on it from her luxurious shelter as a mere spectator, nor hide her eyes in selfish complaining.[9]

Dorothea's catastrophic change, which she embraced and accepted, initiated for her a wider vision of the world and altered her experience of herself and her place therein, thus changing her understanding of the relationship between the two. (Dorothea has an inner strength which enables her to undergo these traumatic experiences and to learn from them. It may be that her orphaned state stimulated her to develop certain capacities by cleaving the more to her internal mother. Gwendolen, by contrast, who existed in a mutually childlike emotional dependency with her mother needed a mediating figure to enable her to undergo similar experiences.)

The regenerative process in Dorothea is expressed through her emotional apprehension of external reality, uncluttered by the author's imposition of preconception or by the intrusion of sentimentalism. The author simply describes Dorothea's mental processes. Her character's internal landscape has been opened up to aspects of experience to which she had hitherto been blind, ones which had had no place in 'that part of her world which lay within park palings'.[10] In this kind of writing no self-consciousness as to the nature of the relationship between subject and object obtrudes; none of the confusion which clouds questions of perception and so-called 'objectivity', so well put by Coleridge: 'The cameleon darkens in the shade of him who bends over it to ascertain its colours.'[11] For in the process of Soul-making, of becoming more known to herself, Dorothea's experience finally takes her back to 'the teat from which the Mind or intelligence [could] suck its identity'. The links of relatedness, as George Eliot makes clear elsewhere – particularly in *The Mill on the Floss*, stem from the 'mute dialogues', as Wordsworth describes them, which a baby holds with his mother's heart; from that 'infant sensibility' which is 'the Great birthright of our Being'[12] – akin to George

Eliot's 'landscape of childhood' as the imagination's mother-tongue.[13]

George Eliot's definition of imagination in one of her last essays offers a vivid description of the best of her own writing, where the symbolic representations of experience are expressed in a decreasingly discursive and more idiosyncratic and active way. The words might also be taken to describe, with equal clarity, the nature of the psychoanalytic process:

> Powerful imagination is not false outward vision, but intense inward representation, and a creative energy constantly fed by susceptibility to the various minutiae of experience, which it reproduces and reconstructs, in fresh and fresh wholes; not the habitual confusion of provable fact with the fictions of fancy and transient inclination, but a breadth of ideal association which informs every material object, every incidental fact, with far reaching memories and stored residues of passion, bringing into new light the less obvious relations of human existence.[14]

Writing after the completion of the last novel, George Eliot here offers a formulation about the relationship between art and life towards which her entire *oeuvre* had been moving. It is about vision and the making-available-of-vision. Art, poetry, symbol formation/alpha function are to do with 'making vision available'. The nature of the reciprocity between mother and baby is a relationship *vis-à-vis* the world in which the mother's understanding and vision are presented to the baby. Powerful imagination may similarly be described as manifest in the evolution of the analytic process – the unconscious transaction of transference and counter-transference. The patient and analyst or therapist may thus observe, and try to comprehend, the process, and, in a sense, yield themselves to it. Resistance or defence in either tend to take up their positions against the emotional experience and its forward movement, that is, against development. George Eliot's description may be taken as a statement about the orientation of therapist and patient – together observing and trying to understand the shared emotional experience. It is a mutual experience in which, as George Eliot says, 'The coercion is often stronger on the one who takes the reverence. Those who trust us educate us.'[15]

To be an honest baby requires an honest breast – a flexible

container which is able to change and adapt without losing its essential integrity. Only so can the individual be open to, in terms of having the courage to undergo, catastrophic change. In the course of the experience meaning emerges through the shared symbolic process of the interpretative mode. The capacity of patient and therapist alike to tolerate the transference/counter-transference process is akin to Keats's 'Negative Capability', 'when man is capable of being in uncertainties, Mysteries, doubts, without any irritable reaching after fact and reason' – the quality which, above all, went to form a Man of Achievement.[16]

The final dream of a young model, Sarah, who was facing a premature interruption of therapy for external reasons, rather beautifully indicated that some such process was beginning to occur. Sarah had sought help for her depression – desperate to break a pattern of relating to men in which she found herself in a state of clinging dependency, masochistically unable to separate until, like a climbing plant, she had some alternative supporting structure to which to attach herself.

The pain of mutual relinquishment in the final sessions had been acute. Being the fourth of six siblings, her life had, from the first, constituted a type of group experience, in which the Basic Assumption mentality described by Bion predominated: attitudes were stereotyped around notions defined either by their acceptability, or by their opposition, to the dominant culture of the group at the time. Leaving therapy was yet another in a long series of premature weanings, evoking intense feelings of desolation, loss, and anger – her early experiences all too emotionally immediate.

In this dream, *she found herself in the ante-chamber of a large and beautiful house. There were doors which opened into the interior, dark passages leading off to which she felt she had access and was on the point of entering, but felt uncertain and apprehensive. This small room was itself lovely. Panelled, as in her childhood home, with many recesses and alcoves in which there were exquisite, precious objects – china ornaments, glass, wood carvings. The room was pervaded by a smell of spices – myrrh and frankincense, she thought. Her eyes alighted on one object in particular, a blue glass bowl of extraordinary fragility and beauty. She gazed at it half believing that it belonged to her and that she had the right to take it with her, yet feeling too that that might be to steal. A tall, dark, mysterious woman entered apparently the owner. As they looked at each other, Sarah 'knew' that the object was indeed her own.*

This 'knowledge' was essentially, as she said at the time, an imaginative experience rather than an aspect of reality. Evidence of the prematurity of her leaving lies, perhaps, in the uncertainty about to whom the bowl belonged. Was it really hers or was it that of the tall dark woman? Yet there did seem to have occurred an awakening of 'the thinking principle within', impelling her beyond the ante-chamber. The context made it clear that it derived from having been enabled, albeit briefly, to have an experience of the mysterious psychoanalytic process as a breast which awoke in her an imaginative vision of her ordinary self-creative potential. The house evoked memories – the internal landscape of the parental home – memories and 'shared residues of passion' which she could now 'use' rather than merely bitterly 'recall'; 'Those shadowy recollections', as Wordsworth put it in the *Immortality Ode*,

> Which, be they what they may
> Are yet the fountain light of all our day,
> Are yet the master light of all our seeing

– those 'memories in feelings', as Klein called them, the 'mother tongue of our imagination'.

Sarah's sense that the bowl was related to the imminent possibility of moving into the main part of the house was an aspect of an awakened vision 'into the heart and nature of Man', as Keats had described it in his 'Mansion of Many Appartments'.

The pervasive perfumes offered intimations both of a new birth and of mourning. In beginning to allow herself, with apprehension, to depend on the internal object to help her carry 'the burden of the Mystery', it seems that she was also beginning to relinquish the external pseudo-supportive structures which had characterized her relations hitherto. She was standing at a threshold, mourning a loss, fearful that she had brought it about, but willing to draw on an internalized resource – the blue glass bowl. The dream is full of possibility. Yet there is a shared apprehension, related to the premature leaving of the Chamber of Maiden Thought aspect of the transference. Perhaps she was going into the dark passages inadequately equipped, having internalized less the strong, functional qualities of the object than its non-functional fragility and preciousness. The therapist might be apprehensive as to what exactly Sarah was taking away – the image of the bowl was ambiguous, either ready to be filled with meaning, or simply, empty.

This worrying ambiguity was absent from the dream material of a second patient, 34-year-old Stephen, whose therapy was able to take its course over a number of years. A successful young academic, he had always used intellectuality as an effective defence against a range of infantile anxieties, above all, against the pain of intimacy. Knowledge as a form of power rather than as a source of understanding had long provided a serviceable carapace – this knowledge gradually including the latest psychoanalytic theory, particularly those aspects which he thought most interested his therapist. His quest for knowledge had a quality which was more in tune with a desire to possess and occupy than to understand; to steal secrets and with them innoculate himself against pain, rather than genuinely to take in, and identify internally with, the functions of the object.

This state of mind is well caught in an brief early dream. The contrast to another dream some three years later, which drew on similar images, measured a long period of intense struggle with his fledgling self. The different use of the same image in each dream encapsulates the nature of the developmental process which is described here – something of the possibility of coming out of projective identification, overcoming grandiosity, of risking adventure rather than selling for ambition – in keeping with the ways in which Dorothea and Gwendolen were finally able to place themselves in the world.

In the early dream, *there were beautiful glass spheres, contained each in its own convex cup – spheres which he smashed with a heavy ball-bearing, gathering the broken pieces into a mixing bowl and putting the ball-bearing on top, with a complacent air of 'what a good boy am I'.* In this competitive caricature of analytic work, the self-congratulatory 'good boy' Stephen was able to deceive himself as to the cup-filling confection – as if it constituted an actual cake/breast rather than a mockery of the psychotherapeutic method.

After three more years of hard work an external event occurred, aptly described by Stephen as 'a bombshell', for it introduced a mode of perception and a quality of feeling the capacity for which had only ever been hinted at before. The eruption of a long quiescent skin condition, eczema, coincided with a visit to his home in Ireland, during the weekend when the eldest of his three younger sisters was due to give birth. Tormented over this weekend by his infantile feelings of distress, among other things at the recurrence of the very symptom which had originated at the birth of this same sister thirty-two years earlier, he had the following dream: *he resided in the place where children are before being born – existing as protoplasmic blobs, suspended in a bluish pink atmosphere above cups – themselves seemingly attached, as if by a line of some sort, to a lily pad on the surface of the water. The children were talking together. One conversation was distinct, between himself and an unborn girl. They were discussing his fear of death: 'If you are born you have to die', he said, 'and that feels too terrifying.' She disagreed – the real courage lay in allowing yourself to be born in the first place. Once you'd done that you had already taken care of the fear of death. Dying didn't seem anything like so bad afterwards. What you had to do was meet the cup, get down into it and be born. Then you could bear the rest. With that she did get down into the cup and went ahead, leaving Stephen lingering behind, fearful, and yet infused with courage and expectancy.*

This dream seems rather a remarkable representation of the birth of the mind, the hitherto unborn parts of Stephen's personality – the bluish, pink dawning of the thinking principle. It seems to place the Chamber of Maiden Thought prior to birth (recovered at the breast with all the dark passages). The foetus feels encouraged to proceed by the capacity to hold a dialogue with the part of the self which now knows that the cup constitutes a safe internal container – linked both to internal worlds and external by way of the lily pad/umbilical cord. Held in that container Stephen could allow himself to consider being born – to 'think', in Bion's sense of a preconception meeting a realization – engaging with the cup of life, the internal mother – and thereby being able to proceed with his development. The cup had now become a genuinely containing object in which his mind might be fledged and set on a course of self-creation. The contrast with former states of mind is well caught in George Eliot's description of that between being egotistically enclosed within a mind which takes the world 'as an udder to feed the supreme self', [17] and forming a sense of connectedness with all ordinary human existence:

It is an uneasy lot at best to be what we call highly taught and yet not to enjoy: to be present at this great spectacle of life and never to be liberated from a small hungry shivering self – never to be fully possessed by the glory we behold, never to have our consciousness rapturously transformed into the vividness of a thought, the ardour of a passion, the energy of an action, but always to be scholarly and uninspired, ambitious and timid, scrupulous and dim-sighted[18]

– encased within what she elsewhere calls, 'that troublous fitfully-illuminated life'.[19]

In the vast imaginative worlds of her novels, some characters manage to be born just as, in the process of novel writing, George Eliot's creative capacity was born – decreasingly insistent on imposing preconceptions and discursively moralizing, but committed rather to an ethical position related to understanding the truthfulness of the world within, that 'unmapped country' where the mind is given space to breathe and create itself, 'through the medium of the Heart in a world of Circumstances'. The experience of catastrophic change initiates a process of self-development whereby the mind may become possessed by the glory we behold and not remain shut up within its own short-sighted egotistical enclosure.

In Bion's theory, change involves the birth of a new idea which, in turn, entails the relinquishing of the old form: in order to be born a letting-go has to occur to allow for the transformation of the existing state of mind, or the superimposition upon it of the new idea – the internal catastrophic change. The process, as Keats clearly states, is impelled from within – it is not a matter of wilful fantasizing (Coleridge's 'Fancy'), but one which depends on a capacity for growth and change initiated by the internal object.

In the period between Stephen's two dreams it seemed that a shift had taken place – the necessity of coming out of his projective identification and previous states of mind had become apparent. The second dream shows his trepidation about emerging and having to face both the fact that his younger sister had so obviously moved ahead of him in development, and the situation which had bowled him over in childhood, the birth of the next sibling. This shift was marked (not brought about) by the 'bombshell' of the birth of his nephew; 'marked' because that event occurred in a psyche which seemed prepared also to be born, to suffer the consequences of leaving the manic projective identification. With that event his shell of false identity was felt to have shattered – the shell of 'Custom' and 'Memory', with which he had resisted growth and its associated turbulence, and into which he had withdrawn from any experience of joy or passion.

With Keats, the poems become the serial representation of the changing internal container. An aesthetic reciprocity is established between internal and external objects whereby a new container of meaning is evolved by way of the mind's development. So too with George Eliot, the successive novels may be thought of in terms of her efforts to find a container for meaning – a meaning which clearly did not reside in the contemporary theories of the mind and psychology with which she was so familiar, but which became increasingly located in the internal aspects of her characters' existence, albeit finely tuned by the vicissitudes of their external life and by wider cultural and historical phenomena. The function Deronda performed internally for Gwendolen is George Eliot's most evolved expression of the process whereby a mind's development is initiated and assisted by the changing quality of the internal object. For Deronda was himself wrought upon by Gwendolen's experience, of her life and his impact upon it. He was able to 'receive' that experience without being overtaken by her feelings; to digest her pain and hand it back to her as food for thought.

With the patients described, the contrast is clear between Keats's notion of creative knowledge – which both Sarah and Stephen were struggling towards – and the 'consequitive reasoning',[20] whereby each had lived their lives hitherto. Thinking in these creative terms (as opposed to pseudo-thinking which may amass 'knowledge' as information or fact) is mind-building, soul-making – a process which involves the struggle between the impelling nature of the desire to be born, Coleridge's 'innate principle of self-development', and the resistant pull away from the fear and pain of the unknown, represented as death.

The central metaphor for the interlocking of internal and external lives in *Middlemarch* is the web. Soul-making too belongs to the ordinariness and the beauty of the spider spinning her web, making from her own inwards her own airy citadel. Stephen was slowly becoming 'schooled' in learning to spin from his own inwards, not to suck his knowledge from the entrails of host objects, as was his wont in 'Alien' identifications in days gone by. Similarly, Sarah had to struggle to weave her internal web, or fashion and strengthen her beautiful glass bowl, such that she could feel some confidence that her mind was being born, or fledged – outgrowing its previous identity. For each, the Basic Assumption conformity, with family configurations in Sarah's case, and with ambitious, social expectations of academic success in Stephen's, provided an exo-skeletal mentality which had confined, rather than protected, their respective personalities.

Bion describes catastrophic change as an internal group process whereby these basic assumptions are disrupted by that part of the personality, 'the mystic', which receives the new idea, or the new concept. Internal change has to occur in the personality in order for this new idea to be assimilated. Sarah had clung to the shifting surfaces of the fashion world, moving from relationship to relationship, continuously adhered to the dessicated structures of unions already past, despite knowing that their life had long since drained away. Stephen had remained enslaved to the academic hierarchy, despite conscious attempts to dismantle those structures (literally, as he once put it, to remove the mantle of his beetle/self), that aspect of the superstructure which commanded both his obedience and his illicit contempt.

Each case makes it clear that development in life, or the evolution of the psychoanalytic experience is not a continuous linear process. They both suffered, rather, the impact of certain nodal points (leaving therapy prematurely and the crisis of 'birth', respectively) which constituted growth points, or 'epochs', as George Eliot would describe them. Uncertainly in Sarah's case, and more confidently in Stephen's, these epochs initiated a move forward in development. Each had become able to 'receive' back projections which had been worked on in the therapeutic relationship, making it possible, thereby, to make use of their experience and to suffer the internal change consequent upon it.

In *The Prelude*, Wordsworth addresses the twin processes of projection (as an ordinary and necessary mode of communication) and receptivity, which epitomize the creative act and which describe the literary model of the human mind as a thing whose characteristic activity is self-creation. The lines could equally well convey the reciprocity of the relationship between therapist and patient – both being 'willing to work and to be wrought upon' – by the analytic process.

> That is the very spirit in which they deal
> With all the objects of the universe;
> They from their native selves can send abroad
> Like transformations, and from themselves create
> A like existence, and, whene'er it is
> Created for them, catch it by an instinct;
> Them the enduring and the transient both
> Serve to exalt; they build up the greatest things
> From least suggestions, ever on the watch,
> Willing to work and to be wrought upon,
> They need not extraordinary calls
> To rouze them, in a world of life they live
> By sensible impressions not enthralled
> But quicken'd, rouz'd and made thereby more apt
> To hold communion with the invisible world.
> (XIII.91–105)

In the clinical material described, we find the infant soul on the threshold of exploring the life of the mind, at the point of acceptance of the Chamber of Maiden Thought – and the dark passages that lead off it – able, now, to perceive the man with the bundle on his back, the woman carrying her baby; hopefully to spin from their own inwards an airy citadel. Previous identities have had to be shed, and reborn in the bowl or the cup of the internal object – born of aesthetic reciprocity, inspired by that internalized process, whereby the goddess 'Psyche' can be recognized as the deity of the mind's truthfulness.

EPILOGUE

Poetry is in essence a symbolization of the spaces and tensions of mental life; it shows the poet in the process of discovering the world of his own mind, and the consequent drama of identifications between self and objects. Its primary intent is symbolic expression, not communication; unhindered by the fear of not being understood by its audience, and propelled by the duty to transcribe the internal dictates of its Muse, it has an inexhaustible meaningfulness. This is also the cause of its mystery and inscrutability, which speaks directly to its readers' internal objects or superego, but still requires that they work on their own processes of identification to establish an internal dialogue between self and objects which can receive and digest the poet's symbolization. In this way the 'poetic' quality epitomized in poetry and art can be assimilated into other genres or modes of experience, in literature and in life. The poetic literature discussed in this book could be considered the 'master of all our seeing' (in Wordsworth's words) – a source to which we may continually return for the rejuvenation of our own self-creativity, and the enrichment of our own internal objects. The model of mental spaces, qualities, and functions interacting in literature is not a didactic or 'superinduced' one (in Coleridge's term) but is evolved from within, so can always offer fresh insights into the problem of how the mind creates itself – the overriding concern of psychoanalysis, overshadowing its concern with specific types of psychopathology. Psychoanalysis, in endeavouring to help the individual discover and promote the growing shape of his own identity, focuses on patterns of internal communication between the self and its objects: not with a view to attainting a plateau of normality, but rather to establish a mode of development which will carry it through further 'catastrophic changes' (in Bion's term),[1] as yet unknown and unsymbolized. These changes are not only the classical transition points of individual development (infancy, latency, etc. – the seven ages of man), but all the infinitesimal points of growth which contribute to the mind's structural complexity, derived from emotional experiences which have been effectively metabolized through symbol formation.

Often a work of literature has a specific flavour of some historical phase in development. Thus *The Prelude*, for example, celebrates the primal unity of mother and infant surrounded by 'clouds of glory'; *Lear* images a cataclysmic weaning process, as does *Paradise Lost*. *The Winter's Tale* illuminates the young child's despair over the new baby, and the wintry sleep of latency; the young (oedipal) child also surges up in *Hamlet* and in *The Ancient Mariner*, in the face of marriage. *Wuthering Heights* analyses the transitions to and from adolescence; *Lycidas* also is concerned with the adolescent's sense of exclusion and vulnerability to gangsterism. The *Ode to Psyche* describes the experience of falling in love; *The Tempest* the different turbulence of middle age; in addition both *The Tempest* and *Paradise Lost* have a distinct quality of closeness to prenatal life, and the imminent concept of being born. The characteristic flavour of each of these phases illuminates the psychoanalytic archetypes. However, their significance is probably secondary to the formal, structural impact of the poetry on our own minds (or at least, on our minds' superego). The mind as island, moor or vale is a phenomenological field in which emotional experiences are continually occurring, requiring to become known to outer levels of consciousness in a symbolic form such that they can be thought about; in this way an unknown 'thought' can penetrate the existing structure of the mind and expand it. This is a process which depends on types of internal identification between the self and its objects or deities, both of which are potentially available for development or evolution. In particular, it depends on the quality of 'aesthetic reciprocity' (Meltzer) between self and object:[2] on the mind's ability to contain the complex projective–introjective identifications which result from the inevitable emotional tumult (love, hate, and thirst for knowledge, in Bion's formulation) of this experience of being understood, changed and developed. This 'post-Kleinian' model of thinking has very definite and substantial origins in the literary models of the mind presented in this book, with their related philosophical repercussions. They show in each case the struggle of the thinker to be shaped by the thought, rather than vice versa.

In Shakespeare, then, we see clearly how in *Lear*, catastrophic change must mean 'death to the existing state of mind' (in Bion's phrase), and the last vestiges of an idealized reunion with Cordelia must pass away, along with infantile omnipotence, if the new type of king is to emerge (the man who does not want adulthood's glamour, but accepts its responsibility). Hamlet is prevented from the fulfilment of his new princeship (the 'thought' which is trying to gain entry to the mind of Denmark) by his internal and external struggles with intrusive types of projective identification; he fails to establish aesthetic reciprocity with either of his female containing figures until it is too late within the lifetime of his own story. Richard, by the end of the play, has arrived on the threshold of this 'Chamber of Maiden-thought' (Keats) after his struggle with narcissism and relinquishment of a Wordsworthian inheritance of godlike infancy. *Macbeth* illustrates the mind's regression into a negative state of emotional 'non-existence' (as Bion or Blake would put it), as a result of perversion – in this case, the perversion of femininity within the hero by his wife. Because of this, thinking cannot take place, and thoughts (the mind's children) cannot be born; they are replaced by hallucinations (Bion's 'hallucinosis') and the delusory future of ambition. *Troilus and Cressida* pursues the anti-poetic condition through its manifestations in propaganda, cyncism and pornography; the manic manipulation of society's basic assumptions by Ulysses has police-state undertones, and fails spectacularly in its official function of keeping order.[3] In *The Winter's Tale*, the mother-goddess restores fertility to the mind whose wintry omnipotence had treated the Muse as a puppet; with the help of art, internal communication and symbolic receptivity are re-established – comprising what Bion or Paulina would call an 'act of faith'. In *A Midsummer Night's Dream*, Shakespeare dramatizes the unconscious mind creating its own gods through extraordinary juxtapositions (identifications) outside the scope of its rational ruling intelligence; and *The Tempest* takes the insignificance of the self in creativity to its logical conclusion: the artist becomes obsolete once he has established the birth of a mind beyond himself, a postnatal reality beyond the island's prenatal one. The 'cloud-capp'd tow'rs' dissolve into the 'brave new world'. In *Paradise Lost*, Milton conveys this process through a two-generation narrative structure (often implicit in Shakespeare), which clarified for future poets the interdependence of thinking and of mental evolution. Satan's endurance of aesthetic conflict carries him beyond the devil's infantile omnipotence, and colours the creative 'death' with which he fertilizes God's second generation, the inhabitants of Eden. He becomes Adam and Eve's first thought. In thus rejecting the demands of a potentially gangsterish basic assumption mentality (related to an authoritarian God), Milton had to place his reliance on a strengthened feminine Muse, established in *Lycidas*. This poetic internal organization is the foundation for the 'paradise within', in which God is known 'in dreams', not by commandments. Thus the mind's objects, enriched by experience, evolve alongside the mind as a whole.

The brave new worlds won by Shakespeare and Milton provided not only emotional complexity (in Shakespeare, of an infinitely varied 'Protean' nature), but also models for a creative thinking process, the mind's self-development. From these, as much as from their own selves' experience, the Romantics derived their principles of creativity. Blake made explicit the 'marriage of contraries' (emotional tensions) necessary in work which was 'imaginative' or 'visionary' as opposed to merely 'allegorical' (translation). He stressed the intensity of imaginative observation, as in Freud's description of the spotlight of consciousness focusing attention on internal realities.[4] Then the creative 'contrary' emotional network is contrasted with 'single' or 'negative' vision, the mind imprisoned by its own perversity: as in Bion's grid of negative values, which opposes L, H, K (Love, Hate and Knowledge, all interdependent) with –L, H, K. Bion's negative grid refers to propaganda, cynicism, stupidity. Blake located the mind's enemies didactically in terms of envy, materialism, rationalization, and sentimentality – all forms of 'error' – instead of the traditional pride, disobedience, unbridled passion, etc. However, Blake's expression of his theory has a cryptic, defensive quality rather than a truly pedagogic one like Coleridge's. Coleridge was perhaps the most seminal philosopher of poetic experience, after Plato himself. He made it clear that the mind was able to progress in accordance with its innate poetic quality – a 'principle of self-development' which was co-extensive with the realms of symbol formation and with realization in terms of organic, symbolic forms. This link between internal relations was the key to knowledge-as-being or as becoming: knowledge as principles rather than as information. The mind's ability to 'be' (which is inevitably, to be progressive) depends on whether it is organized mechanically (narcissistically, in psychoanalytic terms) or symbolically (according to its object-relations). The mind, like a work of art, should be formed by its evolutionary principle not by superinduced requirements. This principle – the 'shaping of imagination' – finds expression in 'ideas', which Coleridge saw not as something *invented* by the mind, but as something *perceived* by it when suitably oriented. Ideas do not appear discursively but 'in a symbol' – the product of internal contact with 'the god-like within us'.

To convey things symbolically is the function of poetry and the poetic principle within us. Nobody modelled this function more stunningly than the early Wordsworth, for the Romantic generation. His symbolization of the infant poetic spirit both cradled and driven onwards by love and awe of its internal objects manifest in nature's landscape, exemplifies the mating of a 'preconception' with a 'realization' in perfect aesthetic reciprocation – which fulfils the post-Kleinian psychoanalytic definition of 'the first thought'. Wordsworth, however, relinquished the requisite emotional tumult involved in this, and took early retirement in the arms of the establishment, both internal and external. It was Keats who took up the poetic burden which Wordsworth had set down: learning from his forebears' experience that any model for creative thinking which he might evolve from within, must be able to withstand the disorienting, painful, catastrophic implications of these experiences of emotional tumult. Shakespeare, Milton and Wordsworth all contributed to the qualities of his internal objects. Hence his inspired formulation of the 'Vale of Soul-making', which accepts and assimilates thwartings of the 'identity' and schools it into becoming 'a soul'. In line with this is 'negative capability' – the ability to tolerate frustration – and the innate 'thinking principle' which 'imperceptibly impels' the infant ego towards those

EPILOGUE

unknown mental spaces beginning with the 'Chamber of Maiden Thought', each with their as yet unrealized gods. Keats also saw clearly that this model for encouraging the mind to 'create itself' had implications for the 'salvation' of society as a whole: that it need not rely helplessly upon its great outstanding geniuses, such as Shakespeare and other 'seldom appearing Socrates', to pull it out of the mire. Even the most snail-like, vulnerable mind has the potential to become 'fledged' and explore the dark passages of its own mind without fear. Humanity could become a 'grand democracy of forest trees' if individual identities could likewise discover the goddess Psyche, and be inspired by her in the Vale of Soul-making. In establishing this internal communication between self and objects, creating its own gods from the 'faded hierarchy' of previous ones, the mind is itself created, and the brain fledged with new-grown thoughts.

Like Keats, Emily Brontë in her medium of poetic prose recognized that the mind had to evolve its own gods in response to its emotional experiences, in order to see it through a period of catastrophic change. These gods are not evolved omnipotently according to idealized archetypes; on the contrary, such archetypes are really false gods, projections of self-idealization. In this case it is the standard Romantic hero who is first degraded, then re-made, during the course of the drama. In *Paradise Lost*, the possibility of conceiving a child was the idea or thought which was trying to gain entry to Eden's quiescent mind; in *Wuthering Heights*, a parallel two-generation story, it is the conception of a real working marriage which is seeking for symbolization in the mental landscape of the moor: a marriage which is neither perverse, dolls'-house, nor fragilely status-dependent. To achieve this, Emily Brontë rewrites the story of her internal ancestors. Her painful point of entry to a creative drama is her identification with the anti-hero Lockwood, who is romanticizing but most un-Romantic, and whom her idealized selfhood would have despised. The identification with him represents the necessary vertex of apparent humiliation or degradation which accompanies the ego's relinquishment of omnipotence; it literally fells itself to have become de-graded, eroded – in Coleridge's words, 'dissolving to recreate'. Once this necessary orientation of being prepared to 'learn from experience' (Bion) has been achieved, the story can fulfil its internal necessity and the mind can evolve. The culmination of the drama is the struggle between omnipotence and symbol formation: the core of the writer's own struggle. Through symbol formation, which is co-extensive with a new inspired relationship between the self and its objects, the idea of a real marriage is relayed.

In the wider narrative structures of George Eliot's novels the developmental processes, which in the poetic mode are essentially ones of intense inner concern, are given an outer dimension in the lived experience of the protagonists over time. The myriad ways in which the individual's emotional predicament is inseparably bound to the familial, community, and cultural medium lie at the heart of the novels. Limiting social conditions, in particular, impede growth or, indeed, arrest it altogether. But the determining factors in the mind's capacity to develop increasingly take the form of internal destructive forces, for example, dishonesty, pedantry, sanctimony, philistinism, self-deception, hypocrisy, conformity. These mental characteristics or modes of being, implemented by the psychological processes of what would now be described as splitting, denial, and projective identification, are averse to emotion itself, and are, therefore, fundamentally anti-developmental.

George Eliot is concerned with society and with the society of the mind. Her creative energy becomes focused on the relationship between the personality's carapace – the exo-skeletal structure for navigating the social system – and the endo-skeleton, or personality proper, composed of internal 'characters', bearing qualities which may themselves develop and thereby the better serve the growing personality, thus constituting the seat of the mind's developmental potential. For some of the characters the impelling pressures towards social adjustment offer a welcome quietus to mental life. Others, coming out of their predominantly projective mode, relinquish their narcissistic position and accept a more object-related place in the world: guided by internal principles of growth, they enter the dark passages of uncharted experience.

These internal principles remain essentially mysterious, but what finally become clear are the ways in which the process of learning from experience is assisted by the nature of relationships with internal and external objects, in so far as they are able to carry the transference image. In *Daniel Deronda* this conception of the nature of psychic growth evolves in the context of what, in the traditional novel, would have become a love affair. Here, however, resistance to the erotic possibilities of the relationship is part of the growth, essential to its continuance. It involves painful relinquishment, but leaves open infinite potential for coming-to-knowledge, based in aspiration towards a vision that has been made available as a different kind of being-in-the-world. There is no doubt but that individual development is felt to be bound to imaginative processes which are lodged in this vision of authentic cultural and spiritual evolution. Richness of imagination becomes a force which can shape the world.

The conception of such a relationship brings these ideas closer to the work of the consulting room where, in the transference relationship, the creative potential of the individual patient may be encouraged through a process analogous to the state of 'reverie' which Bion describes the mother as offering her baby. The baby 'with his soul/Drinks in the feelings of his Mother's eye!', as Wordsworth suggests (*The Prelude*, II, 236–40) and experiences 'A virtue which irradiates and exalts/Objects through widest intercourse of sense'. In addition, in good circumstances, the baby participates in a 'thinking' process. It has its mental chaos received, made sense of, and returned to it in a form that has been rendered meaningful through the mother's capacity for symbol formation, and therefore available to be thought about.

Thus the patient is offered the opportunity to recognize and try to integrate disowned aspects of the personality, constituting a new 'idea' of the self. The receiving of the new idea entails the relinquishing of the old one. A turbulent reorganization of the personality is initiated, involving a reducing of splitting processes and a re-assimilation of parts that have been relegated through projective identification and have to be recovered, or 'redeemed'.

For at the centre of this theory of development is the distinction between the capacity to engage with emotion, and the aversion to doing so. The processes of splitting and projection function as part of that aversion, rigidifying the exo-skeletal structure such that the inner life is cut off both from other aspects of itself and from communication with the outside world, leaving the endo-skeleton starved of the emotional experience that would feed its developing self. The dawning potential for emotional engagement, on the other hand, is initiated by the essentially creative process of symbol formation, through the individual's imaginative capacities, enabling the kind of thinking and learning to take place whereby internal conflicts may be addressed in terms of their true meaning. The kind of 'knowledge' thus acquired is at the heart of the mind's capacity to grow.

The model of mind described here not only finds symbolic expression for the factors which encourage or inhibit development but itself becomes integral to that creative growth. The processes that initiate and stimulate the external tradition of the developing human consciousness, 'The Spirit of Poetry', are the same as those by which the individual mind develops. The writers discussed in this book represent that tradition and illustrate its essential features. As their preoccupation with the nature of creativity and the growth of the mind reworks itself in the theory and practice of psychoanalysis and psychotherapy, individuals are deriving from their experience, and developing a framework for, a mode of thinking which recreates what has gone before in a form appropriate for its time and purpose.

NOTES AND REFERENCES

Long poems and plays are referred to by line number; prose by page number.

1 SHAKESPEARE: A LOCAL HABITATION AND A NAME

Shakespeare's plays are quoted from the Arden editions: *King Richard II*, ed. P. Ure (1956, 1961) London: Methuen; *A Midsummer Night's Dream*, ed. H. Brooks (1979), London: Methuen; *Hamlet*, ed. H. Jenkins (1982), London: Methuen; *Troilus and Cressida*, ed. K. Palmer (1982), London: Methuen; *King Lear*, ed. K. Muir (1952, 1964) London: Methuen; *Macbeth*, ed. K. Muir (1951, 1962), London: Methuen; *The Winter's Tale*, ed. J.H.P. Pafford (1963), London: Methuen; *The Tempest*, ed. F. Kermode (1954, 1964), London: Methuen.

1. The term 'stool' had the same faecal connotations in Shakespeare's day as in our own (OED).
2. Most editors emend the original punctuation of this passage, placing a colon instead of a comma between 'afire with me' and 'the King's son' because they cannot believe that Ferdinand could be described as being on fire (see *The Tempest*, p. 23, note 212). This interference flattens the poetry; also it is traditional to be 'on fire with love' (as with the cherubim).
3. Keats, letter to Woodhouse, 27 October 1818, *Letters*, ed. R. Gittings (1970), Oxford University Press, p. 157.

2 MILTON: THE MIND'S OWN PLACE

Milton's poetry is quoted from *Poetical Works*, ed. D. Bush (1966), Oxford University Press.

1. Blake, *The Marriage of Heaven and Hell, Complete Writings*, ed. G. Keynes (1957, 1972), Oxford University Press, pl. 6, p. 150.
2. This and the following quotations are taken from the facsimile of the *Trinity College Manuscript* (Cambridge), ed. W.A. Wright (1972), Menston: Scolar Press, pp. 6–7.

3 'At a Vacation Exercise in the College', ll. 1–6.
4 *Of Education*, in *Areopagiticia and Of Education*, ed. K.M. Lea (1973), Oxford University Press, pp. 54–5.
5 Re. this passage, Coleridge wrote: 'How awful is the power of Words! how fearful often in their consequences when merely felt not understood! but most awful when both felt and understood!' (*Notebooks*, ed. K. Coburn (1957), London, Routledge & Kegan Paul, vol. 3, no. 3287). He also praised 'that good and necessary word "sensuous"', as distinct from 'sensual, sensitive, sensible', etc. (*Notebooks*, vol. 2, no. 2442).
6 *Of Education*, in *Areopagiticia and Of Education*, ed. K.M. Lea (1973), Oxford Universitry Press, p. 48.
7 Keats's Oceanus is Milton; see *Hyperion*, II.167–243.
8 Keats, marginalia to *Paradise Lost*, in *Poetical Works and Other Writings*, ed. H. and M. Buxton Forman (1883, 1938–9), London: Reeves & Turner, vol. 3, p. 21.
9 Ibid., p. 20. (For the 'Negative Capability' passage itself, see letter to G. and T. Keats, 21, 27 December 1817.)
10 See Coleridge on Milton and Shakespeare as the
> two glory-smitten summits of the poetic mountain . . . the one Proteus of the fire and the flood; the other attracts all forms and things to himself, into the unity of his own IDEAL. All things and modes of action shape themselves anew in the being of Milton: while SHAKESPEARE becomes all things, yet for ever remaining himself
(*Biographia Literaria*, ed. A. Symons (1906), London: Dent, p. 172.)
11 Keats, marginalia to *Paradise Lost*, in *Poetical Works and Other Writings*, ed. H. and M. Buxton Forman (1883, 1938–9), London: Reeves & Turner, pp. 29–30.
12 J. Phillips, in *Early Lives of Milton*, ed. H. Darbishire (1932), London: Constable, p.33.
13 Melville (1851/1972), *Moby Dick*, Harmondsworth: Penguin, p. 482.
14 See this volume p. 105, note 25.

3 BLAKE: THE MIND'S EYE

Blake's poetry and prose are quoted from *Complete Writings*, ed. G. Keynes (1966), Oxford University Press.

1 See *Jerusalem* (engraved 1804–20), pl. 42, 35.
2 'A Vision of the Last Judgement', in *A Descriptive Catalogue of Pictures* (1810 edn), pp. 92–5, *Writings*, p.617.
3 *The Marriage of Heaven and Hell* (1793), pl. 11, *Writings*, p. 153.
4 *Jerusalem*, pl. 77, *Writings*, p. 717.
5 *The Marriage of Heaven and Hell*, pl. 14, *Writings*, p. 154.
6 See for example *Jerusalem*, pl. 17, 41–3 and pl. 54, 7–8; *The Marriage of Heaven and Hell*, pl. 16, *Writings*, p. 155.
7 *Jerusalem*, pl. 45, 13.
8 Letter to T. Butts, 6 July 1803, *Writings*, p. 825.

NOTES AND REFERENCES

9 *Jerusalem*, pl.3, *Writings*, p. 621.
10 Quoted by K. Raine (1970), *William Blake*, London: Thames & Hudson, p. 109.
11 *Jerusalem*, pl. 98, 18–19.
12 Epilogue to 'The Gates of Paradise', 1793–1818.
13 *Jerusalem*, pl. 13, 52.
14 *The Marriage of Heaven and Hell*, pl. 3, *Writings*, p. 149.
15 *Jerusalem*, pl. 17, 33–4.
16 *The Marriage of Heaven and Hell*, pl. 10, *Writings*, p. 152.
17 *Jerusalem*, pl. 31, 7.
18 'A Vision of the Last Judgement', p. 68, *Writings*, p. 604–5.
19 Ibid., p. 85, *Writings*, p. 613.
20 Ibid., pp. 87, 92–5, *Writings*, pp. 615, 617.
21 *The Marriage of Heaven and Hell*, pl.12, *Writings*, p. 153.
22 'Inscription in the Autograph Album of William Upcott' (1826), *Writings*, p. 781.
23 *The Marriage of Heaven and Hell*, pl. 14, *Writings*, p. 154.
24 *Jerusalem*, pl. 10, 20.
25 *Milton*, pl. 26, 26–7.
26 *Jerusalem*, pl. 46, 11.

4 WORDSWORTH: THE VISIONARY GLEAM

Wordsworth's poetry and prose are quoted from *Poetry and Prose*, ed. W.M. Merchant (1969), London: Rupert Hart-Davis.

1 See Coleridge, *Biographia Literaria*, ch. 22, for criticism of Wordsworth.
2 Preface to *Lyrical Ballads* (1800), *Poetry and Prose*, p. 231.
3 Preface to *Poems* (1815), *Poetry and Prose*, p. 243.
4 Preface to *Lyrical Ballads* (1800), *Poetry and Prose*, pp. 224, 222.
5 Ibid., p. 229.
6 Ibid., p. 229.
7 Ibid., p. 230.
8 Ibid., p. 222.
9 Ibid., pp. 223–4.
10 Coleridge, letter to Godwin, 25 March 1801, *Letters*, ed. E.L. Griggs (1956), Oxford: Clarendon Press, vol. 2, p. 714.
11 Coleridge, letter to Poole, 6 April 1799, ibid. vol. 1, p. 274.
12 See Keats's review of his friend Reynolds' satire on Wordsworth in his journal-letter to George and Georgiana Keats, 14 Feb. – 3 May 1819, *Letters*, ed. R. Gittings (1987), Oxford University Press, p. 242.
13 Keats, letter to Reynolds, 3 February 1818, ibid., p. 60.

5 COLERIDGE: PROGRESSIVE BEING

Coleridge's poetry is quoted from *Poetical Works*, ed. E.H. Coleridge (1969), Oxford University Press.

1 Lecture 11, 'Lectures on Judgement, Culture and Literature' (1818), in *Lectures 1808–1818 on Literature*, ed. R.A. Foakes (1987), London: Routledge, vol. 5, part ii, p. 193.
2 Letter to Godwin, 25 March 1801, *Letters*, ed. E.L. Griggs (1956), Oxford: Clarendon Press, vol. 2, p. 174.
3 See *Biographia Literaria* (1817), introd. A. Symons (1906), London: Dent.
4 Letter to Sotheby, 19 July 1802, *Letters*, ed. E.L. Griggs (1956), Oxford: Clarendon Press, vol. 2, p.814.
5 Letter to Green, 25 January 1828, ibid., vol. 6, p. 723.
6 Letter to J. Gillman, Jr., 22 October 1826, ibid., vol. 6, p. 631.
7 *Notebooks*, ed. K. Coburn (1957), London: Routledge & Kegan Paul, vol. 3, no. 4047.
8 See Coleridge's preface to 'Kubla Khan', *Poetical Works*, pp.295–6.
9 *Notebooks*, ed. K. Coburn (1957), London: Routledge & Kegan Paul, vol. 1, no. 87.
10 Letter to Wedgwood, 16 September 1803, *Letters*, ed. E.L. Griggs (1956), Oxford: Clarendon Press, vol. 2, p. 991.
11 Emily Brontë, *Wuthering Heights* (1847), ed. D. Daiches (1965), Harmondsworth: Penguin, p. 120.
12 Notes on Shakespeare (1808), in *Shakespeare Criticism*, ed. T.M. Raysor (1960), London: Dent, vol. 1, p. 188. See also *Biographia Literaria* on Shakespeare and Milton as twin summits of the 'poetic mountain' (introd. A. Symons (1906), London: Dent, p. 172; see also this volume, p. 66, note 10).
13 *Notebooks*, ed. K. Coburn (1957), London: Routledge & Kegan Paul, vol. 2, no. 2086.
14 *Shakespeare Criticism*, ed. T.M. Raysor (1960), London: Dent, vol. 1, p. 198.
15 *Notebooks*, ed. K. Coburn (1957), London: Routledge & Kegan Paul, vol. 2, no. 2444.
16 Ibid., vol. 2, no. 3158.
17 *Biographia Literaria* (1817), introd, A. Symons (1906), London: Dent, pp. 159–60.
18 Ibid., p. 159.
19 Ibid., p. 77.
20 *The Statesman's Manual* (1817), *Lay Sermons*, ed. R.J. White (1972), London: Routledge, pp. 23–4.
21 Ibid., pp. 30–1.
22 Essay 7, Second Section, *The Friend* (1818), ed. B.E. Rooke (1969), London: Routledge, vol. 1, p. 473.
23 Ibid., Essay 10, p. 500.
24 *The Stateman's Manual* (1817), *Lay Sermons*, ed. R.J. White (1972), London: Routledge, pp. 23–4.
25 Ibid., p. 50.
26 Ibid., p. 29.
27 Letter to Clarkson, 13 October 1806, *Letters*, ed. E.L. Griggs (1956), Oxford: Clarendon Press, vol. 2, p. 1196.
28 *Notebooks*, ed. K. Coburn (1957), London: Routledge & Kegan Paul, vol.3, no. 3825.

29 Essay 4, Second Section, *The Friend* (1818), ed. B.E. Rooke (1969), London: Routledge, vol. 1, p. 451, and the whole of this section on 'method'.
30 *Biographia Literaria* (1817), introd. A. Symons (1906), London: Dent, pp. 155–6.
31 *Notebooks*, ed. K. Coburn (1957), London: Routledge & Kegan Paul, vol. 3, no. 4418.
32 *The Statesman's Manual* (1817), *Lay Sermons*, ed. R.J. White (1972), London: Routledge, p. 50.
33 *Notebooks*, ed. K. Coburn (1957), London: Routledge & Kegan Paul, vol. 3, no. 4418.
34 *The Statesman's Manual* (1817), *Lay Sermons*, ed. R.J. White (1972), London: Routledge, p. 114.
35 *Notebooks*, ed. K. Coburn (1957), London: Routledge & Kegan Paul, vol. 2, no. 2373.
36 *Biographia Literaria* (1817), introd. A. Symons (1906), London: Dent, p. 131.
37 *Notebooks*, ed. K. Coburn (1957), London: Routledge & Kegan Paul, vol. 3, no. 3632.
38 See this volume, p. 59, note 5. Coleridge called Plato 'Milton's Darling', and pointed out Milton's 'platonizing spirit' (letter to Sotheby, 10 September 1802, *Letters*, ed. E.L. Griggs (1956), Oxford: Clarendon Press, vol. 2, p. 866).

6 KEATS: SOUL-MAKING

Keats's poetry is quoted from *Poems*, ed. M. Allott (1970), London: Longman.

1 Keats, *Letters of John Keats*, ed. R. Gittings (1987), Oxford University Press, p. 95.
2 Ibid., p. 95.
3 Letter to G. and T. Keats, 21 February 1818, ibid. p. 69.
4 Letter to Reynolds, 3 May 1818, ibid., p. 95.
5 Ibid., p. 93.
6 Journal-letter to George and Georgiana Keats, February–May 1819, ibid., p. 230.
7 See his sonnet 'On First Looking into Chapman's Homer'.
8 Letter to Reynolds, 18 April 1817, *Letters*, ed. R. Gittings (1987), Oxford University Press, p. 7.
9 Letter to Haydon, 10, 11 May 1817, ibid., pp. 13–14.
10 Letter to Hunt, 10 May 1817, ibid., p. 10.
11 Letter to Taylor, 27 February 1818, ibid., p. 70.
12 Letter to Hessey, 8 October 1818, ibid., pp. 155–6.
13 Letter to Reynolds, 9 April 1818, ibid., p. 85.
14 Journal-letter to G. and G. Keats, February–May 1819, ibid., p. 218.
15 Keats likewise condemned Wordsworth for the 'sketchy intellectual landscape' and 'comfortable moods' which were not a 'search after

Truth' (ibid., p. 31). Keats's hostility to Byron was in part returned (see *Don Juan*, XII.60), presumably because Keats stirred Byron's feelings of guilt in relation to poetry. Yet Byron was equally aware of the mask of intellectual pseudity: compare their identical satirization of Castlereagh in *Don Juan*, IX.49 and *Letters*, ed. R. Gittings (1987), Oxford University Press, p. 78.
16 Letter to Taylor, 23 August 1819, ibid., p. 280.
17 Letter to Bailey, 14 August 1819, ibid., p. 277.
18 Letter to G. and G. Keats, 17–27 September 1819, ibid., p.325.
19 As reported by his friend Severn (*The Keats Circle*, ed. H.H. Rollins, cited by W.J. Bate, *John Keats*, New York, Oxford University Press, 1966, p.688); see also letter to Fanny Brawne, 1 March 1820, *Letters*, ed. R. Gittings (1987), Oxford University Press, p. 365.
20 Letter to Dilke, 20, 21 September 1818, ibid., p. 153.
21 Letter to Haydon, 10, 11 May 1817, ibid., p. 12.
22 Letter to Rice, 24 March 1818, ibid., pp. 77–8.
23 Letter to Haydon, 10, 11 May 1817, ibid., pp. 11–12.
24 Letter to Rice, 24 March 1818, ibid., p. 77.
25 Keats's marginalia to *Paradise Lost*, in *Poetical Works and Other Writings*, ed. H. and M. Buxton Forman (1883, 1938–9), London: Reeves & Turner, vol. 3, p. 21.
26 Letter to F. Brawne, February 1820, *Letters*, ed. R. Gittings (1987), Oxford University Press, p. 361; and letter to Bailey, 3 November 1817, ibid., p.33.
27 Letter to G. and T. Keats, 21, 27 December 1817, ibid., p.42.
28 Marginalia to *Paradise Lost*, in *Poetical Works and Other Writings*, ed. H. and M. Buxton Forman (1883, 1938–9), Reeves & Turner, vol. 3, pp. 19, 28.
29 *Endymion*, I.779; see letter to Taylor, 30 January 1818, (*Letters*, ed. R. Gittings (1987), Oxford University Press, p. 59) in which he refers to this passage as a 'stepping of the Imagination towards a Truth'.
30 See for example letter to Reynolds, 3 May 1818, ibid., p. 92.
31 Ibid., p. 92.
32 Shakespeare's 'Venus and Adonis', cited in Keats's letter to Reynolds, 22 November 1817, ibid p. 40.
33 Letter to Haydon, 8 April 1818, ibid., p. 83.
34 See marginalia to *Paradise Lost*, IV.268–72 and VII.32–38, in *Poetical Works and Other Writings*, ed. H. and M. Buxton Forman (1883, 1938–9), Reeves & Turner, vol. 3, p.27.
35 Letter to Reynolds, 3 May 1818, *Letters*, ed. R. Gittings (1987), Oxford University Press, p. 93.
36 Letter to Bailey, 22 November 1817, ibid., p. 37.
37 Letter to Reynolds, 19 February 1818, ibid., p. 66.
38 Letter to Bailey, 22 November 1817, ibid., p. 37.
39 Letter to Reynolds, 19 February 1818, ibid., p. 66.
40 Letter to G. and T. Keats, 21, 27 December 1817, ibid., p. 43.
41 Emily Brontë uses the same word (penetralium) in a context of identical emotional significance; see *Wuthering Heights*, ed. D. Daiches (1965), Harmondsworth, Penguin, p. 46.

NOTES AND REFERENCES

42 See letter to T. Keats, 25–27 June 1818, *Letters*, ed. R. Gittings (1987), Oxford University Press, p.103.
43 See Keats's sonnet 'On Visiting the Tomb of Burns', quoted in ibid., p. 109.
44 'Read me a lesson, muse', quoted in ibid., p. 148.
45 Journal-letter to G. and G. Keats, February–May 1819, ibid., p. 224.
46 See ibid., pp. 230–1, 243–4.
47 Ibid., pp. 249–51.
48 Letter to Reynolds, 24 August 1819, ibid., p. 282.

7 EMILY BRONTË: METAMORPHOSIS OF THE ROMANTIC HERO

1 *Wuthering Heights* (1847), ed. D. Daiches (1965), Harmondsworth: Penguin, ch. 3, p. 67.
2 Shelley, *A Defence of Poetry* (written 1821), quoted from *Shelley's Poetry and Prose*, ed. D.H. Reiman and S.B. Powers (1977), New York: Norton, p.508.
3 See 'Adonais', Shelley's epitaph for Keats. Both Shelley and Byron seemed to regard Keats with a certain ambivalence as the most promising son-of-the-Muse in a new world, and reacted characteristically. Keats's hostility to Byron was overt; but he was also careful to avoid the seductions of the self-idealizing aspect of Shelley's generosity.
4 Journal, 23 November 1813, *Letters and Journals of Lord Byron*, ed. L. Marchand, London: Murray, 1974–80, vol. 3, p. 216. Emily Brontë would have read Byron's letters and journals in Thomas Moore's *Life of Byron* (1833).
5 Byron, 'Detached Thoughts' no. 96, *Letters and Journals*, ed. L. Marchand, London: Murray, vol. 9, p. 45.
6 *Wuthering Heights*, ch. 33, p. 353.
7 Ibid., ch. 3, p. 70.
8 Ibid., ch. 15, p. 196.
9 Ibid., ch. 16, p. 204.
10 See ibid., ch. 7, p. 102, and ch. 1, p. 45.
11 Ibid., ch. 4, p. 77.
12 Ibid., ch. 5, p. 84.
13 Ibid., ch. 8, p. 110.
14 Ibid., ch. 12, p. 163.
15 Ibid., ch. 9, p. 122.
16 Ibid., ch. 9, p. 122.
17 Ibid., ch. 14, p. 189.
18 Ibid., ch. 29, p. 318.
19 Ibid., ch. 30, p. 325.
20 Ibid., ch. 21, p. 250, and ch. 34, p. 365.
21 Ibid., ch. 25, p. 289.
22 Ibid., ch. 28, p. 315.
23 Ibid., ch. 29, p. 321.

24 Ibid., ch. 33, p. 352.
25 Ibid., ch. 29, p. 321.
26 Ibid., ch. 29, p. 321.
27 Coleridge, *Biographia Literaria*, ed. A. Symons (1906), London: Dent, pp. 16–17.
28 For the 'final bound' see Emily Brontë's poem-within-a-poem, 'He comes with western winds', *Poems*, ed. C.W. Hatfield (1941), New York: Columbia University Press, pp. 238–9.
29 *Wuthering Heights*, ch. 31, p. 334.
30 Ibid., ch. 31, p. 334.
31 Ibid., ch. 33, p.352.
32 Ibid., ch. 33, p. 353.
33 Ibid., ch. 34, p. 358.
34 Ibid., ch. 33, p. 354.
35 Ibid., ch. 34, p. 366–7.
36 Chaucer, *Troilus and Criseyde* (1385), II.36–7.

8 GEORGE ELIOT: THE UNMAPPED COUNTRY

George Eliot's novels are quoted from the Penguin Classics editions: *Adam Bede* (1859), ed. S. Gill (1985), Harmondsworth; *The Mill on the Floss* (1860), ed. A.S. Byatt (1985), Harmondsworth; *Silas Marner* (1861), ed. Q.D. Leavis (1985), Harmondsworth; *Middlemarch*, (1871–2), ed. W.J. Harvey (1985), Harmondsworth; *Daniel Deronda* (1876), ed. B. Hardy (1986), Harmondsworth. *The Lifted Veil*, originally 'The Hidden Veil' (1859), Blackwoods, is quoted from Virago Modern Classics (1985), London. *Impressions of Theophrastus Such* (1879) is quoted from the Cabinet Edition (1878), Edinburgh and London. Letters are quoted from *The George Eliot Letters*, ed. G.S. Haight (1954–55), 7 vols, New Haven: Yale University Press, hereafter cited as *Letters*.

1 *Daniel Deronda*, ch. 33, p. 431.
2 *Letters*, vol. 6, pp. 216–17.
3 *Letters*, vol. 3, p. 383.
4 *Letters*, vol. 3, p. 227.
5 *Middlemarch*, ch. 20, p.235.
6 'Bain's Psychology', *Dissertations and Discussions* (1867), London, vol. 3, p. 120.
7 *Biographia Literaria*, ed.G. Watson (1965), London: Dent, p.61.
8 A.N. Whitehead (1926), *Science and the Modern World*, reprinted (1985), London: Free Association Books, p. 96.
9 Ibid., p. 94.
10 *Letters*, vol. 1, p. 247.
11 *Letters*, vol.2, p. 299.
12 *Letters*, vol. 4, p. 300.
13 *Daniel Deronda*, ch. 33, p. 431.
14 E. Simcox (1881), 'George Eliot', *The Nineteenth Century*, vol. 9, p. 780, writes: 'Languages, music, literature, science, and philosophy,

interested her alike: it was early in this period [1840s] that in the course of a walk with a friend she paused and clasped her hands with a wild aspiration that she might live "to reconcile the philosophy of Locke and Kant!" Years afterwards she remembered the very turn in the road where she had spoken it.'

15 *The Mill on the Floss*, ch. 2, Book 7, p. 628.
16 See this volume p.102.
17 Keats, *Letters*, ed. R. Gittings (1987), Oxford University Press, p. 93.
18 *The Mill on the Floss*, ch. 5, Book 3, p. 320.
19 'Worldliness and Other Worldliness', *Westminster Review* (1857), vol. 67, p. 30. The details of this Kantian influence are described by G.H. Lewes, writing, it seems, in close collaboration with George Eliot, in 'The Principles of Success in Literature', *Fortnightly Review* (1865) vol. 1, 85–95; 185–96; 572–89; 697–709; vol. 2, 257–68; 689–710.
20 A.N. Whitehead (1926), *Science and the Modern World*, reprinted (1985), London: Free Association Books, p.12.
21 *Adam Bede*, ch. 16, p. 217.
22 Preface to *Lyrical Ballads* (1800), *Poetry and Prose*, ed. W.M. Merchant (1969), London: Rupert Hart-Davies, p.224.
23 Preface to *Sordello* (1863), *Works* (2 vols), ed. John Pettigrew (1981), Harmondsworth: Penguin, p. 150.
24 *Notebooks*, ed. K. Coburn (1957), London: Routledge & Kegan Paul, vol. 3, no. 4265. See this volume, p. 106.
25 *Letters*, vol. 5, p. 380. *The Lifted Veil* was first published in the Cabinet Edition in 1878, together with *Silas Marner* and 'Brother Jacob'.
26 *Letters*, vol. 3, p. 118.
27 *Letters*, vol. 3, p. 24.
28 *Letters*, vol. 3, p. 23.
29 *Letters*, vol. 3, p. 41.
30 *Letters*, vol. 3, p. 111.
31 *Theophrastus Such*, ch. 13, p. 188.
32 *Letters*, vol. 3, pp. 128–9.
33 *Letters*, vol. 3, p. 360.
34 *Letters*, vol. 4, p. 300.
35 *Letters*, vol. 3, p. 371. The experience seems to have been that described by Keats: 'the simple imaginative Mind may have its rewards in the repetition of its own silent Working coming continually on the spirit with a fine suddenness – to compare great things with small . . .' Letter to Bailey, 22 November 1817, *Letters*, ed. R. Gittings (1987), Oxford University Press, p. 37.
36 *Letters*, vol. 5, p. 374.
37 *Letters*, vol. 3, p. 427.
38 *Letters*, vol. 3, p. 382.
39 *Letters*, vol. 1, p. 34.
40 *Silas Marner*, ch. 17, p. 221.
41 Ibid., ch. 13, p. 171.
42 Ibid., ch. 2, p. 65.
43 Ibid., ch. 2, p. 65.

44 Ibid., ch. 10, p. 129.
45 Ibid., ch. 14, p. 185.
46 Ibid., ch. 14, p. 190.
47 Ibid., ch. 14, p. 180. In her introduction to the Penguin edition, Q.D. Leavis makes explicit links with Bunyan's *Pilgrim's Progress*; see especially, pp. 13–14.
48 *Impressions of Theophrastus Such*, ch. 13, p. 197.
49 See this volume, p. 85.
50 *Middlemarch*, ch. 16, p. 194. The role of imagination in Lydgate's researches describes creative endeavour in general terms in language as appropriate to the psychoanalytic process as to the literary.
51 *Middlemarch*, ch. 20, p.226.
52 *Daniel Deronda*, ch. 42, p. 590.
53 *Middlemarch*, ch. 21, p. 243. A change in understanding is described as a capacity 'to conceive with that distinctness which is no longer reflection but feeling – an idea wrought back to the directness of sense, like the solidity of objects'.
54 *Daniel Deronda*, ch. 14, pp. 185–6.
55 Ibid., ch. 4, p. 72.
56 Ibid., ch. 4, p. 72.
57 Ibid., ch. 6, p. 87.
58 Ibid., ch. 7, p. 91.
59 Ibid., ch. 6, p. 94.
60 Ibid., ch. 6, p. 95.
61 Ibid., ch. 2, p. 47.
62 Ibid., ch. 35, p. 477.
63 Ibid., ch. 54, p. 737.
64 Ibid., ch. 54, p. 737–8.
65 Ibid., ch. 56, p. 761.
66 Ibid., ch. 6, p. 94.
67 Ibid., ch. 69, p. 876.
68 Ibid., ch. 69, p. 866.
69 Ibid., ch. 1, p. 35.
70 Ibid., ch. 29, p. 383.
71 Ibid., ch. 35, p. 468.
72 Ibid., ch. 35, p. 484.
73 Ibid., ch. 24, p. 321.
74 Ibid., ch. 65, p. 841.
75 Ibid., ch. 65, p. 841.
76 Ibid., ch. 36, p. 501.
77 Ibid., ch. 70, p. 882.
78 Ibid., ch. 47, p. 656.
79 Ibid., ch. 35, p. 477.
80 Ibid., ch. 35, p. 477.
81 Ibid., ch. 29, p. 380.
82 Ibid., ch. 36, p. 502.
83 Ibid., ch. 40, p. 553.
84 Ibid., ch. 35, p. 485.

NOTES AND REFERENCES

85 Ibid., ch. 16, p. 220.
86 Ibid., ch. 32, p. 413.
87 Ibid., ch. 17, p. 229.
88 Ibid., ch. 16, p. 215.
89 Ibid., ch. 16, p. 217.
90 Ibid., ch. 16, p. 219.
91 Ibid., ch. 16, p. 218.
92 Ibid., ch. 28, p. 369.
93 Ibid., ch. 16, p. 220.
94 Ibid., ch. 16, p. 221.
95 Ibid., ch. 16, p. 224.
96 Ibid., ch. 36, p. 509.
97 Ibid., ch. 69, p. 878.
98 Ibid., ch. 65, p. 839.

9 PARALLEL DIRECTIONS IN PSYCHOANALYSIS

1 The lines from Wordsworth's *Prelude* (1850 edition) are quoted by George Eliot as the Epigraph to Chapter 69 of *Daniel Deronda*, Penguin Classics (1986), p. 864.
2 *Letters of John Keats*, ed. R. Gittings (1987), Oxford University Press, p. 249.
3 Ibid., pp. 95–6.
4 Ibid., p. 95.
5 Journal-letter to G. and G. Keats, February–May 1819, Ibid., p. 250.
6 *Daniel Deronda*, Penguin Classics (1986), ch. 17, p. 229.
7 *Middlemarch*, Penguin Classics (1985), ch. 80, p. 844.
8 Ibid., ch. 80, p. 845.
9 Ibid., ch. 80, p. 846.
10 Ibid., ch. 77, p. 829.
11 *Aids to Reflection* (1905), Edinburgh: Grant, p. 70.
12 See Wordsworth's *Prelude*, II.240–7.
13 *The Mill on the Floss*, Penguin Classics, ch. 5, Book 1, p. 94.
14 *Theophrastus Such*, London, Cabinet Edition (1978), ch. 13, p. 197.
15 *Daniel Deronda*, ch. 35, p. 485.
16 Letter to G. and T. Keats, 21, 27 December 1817, *Letters*, *p. 43*.
17 *Middlemarch*, ch. 21, p.243.
18 Ibid., ch. 29, p. 314.
19 Ibid., ch. 30, p. 324.
20 Letter to Bailey, 22 November 1817, *Letters*, ed. R. Gittings (1987), Oxford University Press, p. 37.

EPILOGUE

1 For Bion's model of the thinking process, see W.R. Bion (1970), *Attention and Interpretation*, London: Tavistock; also 'A Theory of Thinking' (1962), reprinted in *Second Thoughts* (1967), London:

Maresfield. See also entries in R.D. Hinshelwood (1989), *A Kleinian Dictionary*, London: Free Association Books.

2 See D. Meltzer and M.H. Williams (1988), *The Apprehension of Beauty*, Perthshire: Clunie Press; and Meltzer (1986) *Studies in Extended Metapsychology: Clinical Applications of Bion's Ideas*, Perthshire: Clunie Press.

3 See Bion (1961), *Experiences in Groups*, London: Tavistock, for his analysis of group behaviour, including the 'specialized work group' organizing function (exemplified by Ulysses).

4 Freud, letter to L. Andreas-Salome, cited in Bion (1970), *Attention and Interpretation*, London: Tavistock, p.57.

SELECTED BIBLIOGRAPHY

Primary sources are given in the 'Notes and References'. The following is a brief and idiosyncratic selection of critical reading which we hope may provide an entrée for the reader's further explorations.

Adam, I. (ed.) (1975) *This Particular Web. Essays on Middlemarch*, Toronto: University of Toronto Press.
Allott, K. (1969) 'The Ode to Psyche', in K. Muir (ed.) *John Keats: A Reassessment*, Liverpool University Press.
Barfield, O. (1974) 'Coleridge's Enjoyment of Words', in J. Beer (ed.) *Coleridge's Variety*, London: Macmillan.
Barton, A. (1980) Introduction to *Hamlet*, Harmondsworth: New Penguin Shakespeare.
Bate, W.J. (1966) *John Keats*, New York: Oxford University Press.
—— (1968) *Coleridge*, Cambridge, Mass.: Harvard University Press.
Bayley, J. (1968) 'Time and the Trojans', in P. Martin (ed.) *Troilus and Cressida: A Casebook*, London: Macmillan.
Bick, E. (1968) 'The Experience of the Skin in Early Object Relations', in M. Harris Williams (ed.) (1987) *The Collected Papers of Martha Harris and Esther Bick*, Perthshire: Clunie Press.
Bion, W.R. (1962) *Learning from Experience*, London: Tavistock.
—— (1970) *Attention and Interpretation*, London: Tavistock.
—— (1975) *A Memoir of the Future. Book One: The Dream*, Rio de Janerio: Imago Editora.
—— (1977) *Book Two: The Past Presented*, Rio de Janeiro: Imago Editora.
—— (1978) *Book Three: The Dawn of Oblivion*, Perthshire: Clunie Press.
—— (1982) *The Long Weekend, 1897–1919*, Abingdon: Fleetwood.
Bishop, J. (1959) 'Wordsworth and the "Spots of Time"', reprinted in W.J. Harvey and R. Gravil (eds) (1972) *The Prelude: Casebook*, London: Macmillan.
Brooks, C. (1947) 'The Naked Babe and the Cloak of Manliness' (on *Macbeth*), and 'Wordsworth and the Paradox of the Imagination', in *The Well Wrought Urn*, New York: Dobson & Harcourt, Brace & World Inc.
Daiches, D. (1957) *Milton*, London: Hutchinson.

Erdman, D. (1954) *Prophet Against Empire* (on Blake), Princeton University Press.
Fender, S. (1968) *Shakespeare: A Midsummer Night's Dream*, London: Edward Arnold.
Frye, N. (1965) *The Return of Eden: Five Essays on Milton's Epics*, London: University of Toronto Press.
—— (1967) *Fools of Time: Studies in Shakespearean Tragedy*, Oxford University Press.
Hartman, G.H. (1964) 'The Via Naturaliter Negativa' reprinted in M.H. Abrams (ed.) (1972) *Wordsworth: Twentieth Century Views*, Englewood Cliffs, N.J.: Prentice-Hall Inc.
Hazlitt, W. (1817/1906) *The Characters of Shakespeare's Plays*, London: Dent.
Holmes, R. (1982) *Coleridge*, Oxford University Press.
—— (1989) *Coleridge: Early Visions*, London: Hodder & Stoughton.
James, H. (1907) Introduction to *The Tempest* reprinted in D.J. Palmer (ed.) (1968) *The Tempest: A Casebook* London: Macmillan.
Jones, P. (1975) *Philosophy and the Novel: Philosophical Aspects of Middlemarch, Anna Karenina, The Brothers Karamazov, A la recherche du temps perdu and of the methods of criticism*, Oxford: Clarendon Press.
Kermode, F. (1960) 'Adam Unparadised' reprinted in A.E. Dyson and J. Lovelock (eds) (1973) *Paradise Lost: A Casebook*, London: Macmillan.
Klein, M. (1975) *The Writings of Melanie Klein*, 4 vols, London: Hogarth.
Klein, M., Heimann, P., Isaacs, S., Riviere J. (1952) *Developments in Psycho-Analysis*, London: Hogarth.
Knight, G.W. (1931) 'The Milk of Concord: an essay on life-themes in *Macbeth*', and 'The Prophetic Soul: a note on Richard II', in *The Imperial Theme*, London: Methuen.
—— (1947) 'Great Creating Nature' (on *The Winter's Tale*) reprinted in K. Muir (ed.) (1968) *The Winter's Tale: A Casebook*, London: Macmillan.
Knights, L.C. (1943) 'Bacon and the Seventeenth-Century Dissociations of Sensibility' reprinted in *Explorations*, London: Chatto & Windus.
—— (1965) 'Idea and Symbol: Some hints from Coleridge', in *Further Explorations*, London: Chatto & Windus.
Langer, S. (1942) *Philosophy in a New Key*, Cambridge, Mass.: Harvard University Press.
—— (1953) *Feeling and Form*, London: Routledge & Kegan Paul.
Leavis, F.R. (1948) *The Great Tradition. George Eliot, Henry James, Joseph Conrad*, London: Chatto & Windus.
Leavis, Q.D.R. (1985) Introduction to *Silas Marner*, Harmondsworth: Penguin Classics.
Lewes, G.H. (1865)'The Principles of Success in Literature', in *Fortnightly Review*, I: 85–95, 185–96, 572–89, 697–709, II: 257–68, 689–710.
Lewis, C.S. (1941/1969) *A Preface to Paradise Lost*, London: Oxford University Press.
Macleish, A. (1960) *Poetry and Experience*, Harmondsworth: Penguin.
Mack, M. (1952)'The World of *Hamlet*', reprinted in J. Jump (ed.) (1968) *Hamlet: A Casebook*, London: Macmillan.
Mahood, M.M. (1957/1961) *Shakespeare's Wordplay*, London: Methuen.

SELECTED BIBLIOGRAPHY

Meltzer, D. (1975) 'Adhesive Identification', in *Contemporary Psycho-Analysis*, II, pp. 259–310.
—— (1978) *The Kleinian Development*, Perthshire: Clunie Press.
—— (1984)*Dream Life*, Perthshire: Clunie Press.
—— (1986) *Studies in Extended Metapsychology: Clinical Applications of Bion's Ideas*, Perthshire: Clunie Press.
Meltzer, D. and Harris Williams, M. (1988) *The Apprehension of Beauty*, Perthshire: Clunie Press.
Money-Kyrle, R.E. (1952) 'Psycho-Analysis and Ethics', reprinted (1978) in *The Collected Papers of Roger Money-Kyrle*, Perthshire: Clunie Press.
—— (1961) *Man's Picture of his World: A psycho-analytic study*, London: Duckworth.
—— (1978) 'Cognitive Development', in *The Collected Papers of Roger Money-Kyrle*, Perthshire: Clunie Press.
Murry, M. (1936) 'Shakespeare's Dream' (on *The Tempest*), reprinted in D.J. Palmer (ed.) (1968) *The Tempest: A Casebook*, London: Macmillan.
Nurmi, M.K. (1956) 'Blake's Revisions of "The Tyger"', reprinted in M. Bottrall (ed.) (1970) *Songs of Innocence and Experience*, London: Macmillan.
Pater, W. (1889/1910) 'Shakespeare's English Kings', in *Appreciations*, London: Macmillan.
Prickett, S. (1970) *Coleridge and Wordsworth: The Poetry of Growth*, Cambridge: Cambridge University Press.
Raine, K. (1970) *William Blake*, London: Thames & Hudson.
Read, H. (1947) *The True Voice of Feeling*, London: Faber.
Rhode, E. (1987) 'Life Before Words', *Encounter*, LXIX, pp. 47–52.
Richards, I.A. (1950/1977) Introduction to *The Portable Coleridge*, Harmondsworth: Penguin.
Rossiter, A.P. (1961) 'Unconformity in Richard II', in *Angel with Horns*, London: Longman.
Samuel, I. (1947) *Plato and Milton*, New York: Cornell University Press.
—— (1949) 'Milton on Learning and Wisdom', *Proceedings of the Modern Language Association of America*, 64.
Sperry, S. (1973) *Keats the Poet*, Princeton University Press.
Stokes, A. (1954) 'Form in Art', in M. Klein, P. Heimann, R.E. Money-Kyrle (eds) *New Directions in Psycho-Analysis*, London: Tavistock.
—— (1963) *Painting and the Inner World*, London: Tavistock.
Summers, J.H. (1962) *The Muse's Method: An Introduction to Paradise Lost*, Cambridge Mass.: Harvard University Press.
Trilling, L. (1955) *The Opposing Self*, London and New York: Viking Press.
Whalley, G. (1947) 'The Mariner and the Albatross', reprinted in K. Coburn (ed.) (1967) *Coleridge: A Collection of Critical Essays*, Engelwood Cliffs, N.J.: Prentice-Hall Inc.
Williams, M.H. (1981) *Inspiration and Milton and Keats*, London: Macmillan.
—— (1987) *A Strange Way of Killing: The Poetic Structure of Wuthering Heights*, Perthshire: Clunie Press.
Wilson, S. (1984) 'Character Development in *Daniel Deronda*: a

psychoanalytical view', in *The International Review of Psycho-Analysis*, XI (2).

Woodhouse, C.M. (1982) 'How Plato Won the West', in M. Holroyd (ed.) *Essays by Divers Hands*, London: Royal Society of Literature, vol. 42.

NAME INDEX

Aristotle 147

Bion, Wilfred 171, 172, 176, 179, 180, 182, 185, 187, 189, 191
Blackwood, John 149, 154
Blake, William 2, 5, 70–81, 83, 86, 87, 90, 105–6, 112, 113, 114, 119, 128, 140, 186, 187; 'Auguries of Innocence' 70; 'Infant Sorrow' 75; *Jerusalem* 70–1, 73, 77, 81; 'London' 72–3; *The Marriage of Heaven and Hell* 71, 74, 76; *Milton* 77–8, 79; 'The Tyger' 79–81; 'A Vision of the Last Judgement' 75, 76
Brontë, Emily 4, 101, 126–42, 171, 185, 189
Browning, Robert 148
Bunyan, John 157
Byron, George Gordon 3, 112, 129–31

Chaucer, Geoffrey 142
Coleridge, Samuel Taylor 119, 138–9, 141, 144, 145, 146, 172, 174, 180, 181, 184, 187–8; *The Ancient Mariner* 96, 97–101, 104; *Biographia Literaria* 93, 103, 106, 108, 138–9, 144; 'Epitaph' 100; *The Friend* 104–5; 'Kubla Khan' 97; *Notebooks* 102, 103, 106, 107, 108; Shakespeare criticism 102; *The Statesman's Manual* 104–5, 107; 'To William Wordsworth' 93

Darwin, Charles 143–4

Eliot, George 6, 7, 143–69, 171, 173–5, 179–81, 182, 190–1; *Adam Bede* 147–8; *Daniel Deronda* 149, 159–69, 181, 190–1; *The Lifted Veil* 149, 150–3; *Middlemarch* 158–9, 173–4; *The Mill on the Floss* 146, 148; *Romola* 153; *Silas Marner* 149, 153–8

Freud, Sigmund 171, 187

Kant, Immanuel 145, 146, 147
Keats, John 2, 3, 4, 46, 51, 64, 66, 93, 94, 109–25, 128, 142, 167, 170, 177, 180, 181, 188–9; 'La Belle Dame Sans Merci' 121, 122; the 'creative creates itself' letter 111; *The Fall of Hyperion* 120, 122; *Hyperion* 112, 116–17, 121, 122, 123; 'life as allegory' letter 112; 'maiden thought' letter 109–20, 170, 177; 'negative capability' letter 119, 176; 'Ode on a Grecian Urn' 118, 122; 'Ode to Psyche' 122–4; 'Read me a lesson, Muse' 120; 'soul as

spider's-web' letter 118, 181;
'vale of soul-making' letter
   121, 124, 170, 172
Klein, Melanie 177

Locke, John 145, 146

Meltzer, Donald 185
Melville, Herman 67
Mill, John Stuart 144
Milton, John 2, 3, 4, 5, 53–69, 71,
   74, 81, 89–90, 92, 96, 109,
   111, 112, 113, 114–17, 120,
   132; *Of Education* 59, 108;
   'Hail Native Language' 58–9;
   Letter to a Friend 57; *Lycidas*
   59–62, 68; the 'Nativity Ode'
   57–8; *Paradise Lost* 53–7, 61,
   62–9; *Paradise Regained* 57;
   'Sonnet 19' 57

Plato 2, 37, 105

Shakepeare, William 2, 4, 8–52, 101–2, 111, 112, 113, 115–16, 157, 171, 186, 189; *Hamlet* 21–7; *King Lear* 32–8; *Macbeth* 38–43; *A Midsummer Night's Dream* 15–21; *Richard II* 9–15; *The Tempest* 8, 47–52; *Troilus and Cressida* 27–32; *The Winter's Tale* 43–6
Shelley, Percy Bysshe 128–9, 171

Tennyson, Alfred, Lord 144

Whitehead, Alfred North 144, 148, 152
Wordsworth, William 3, 82–94, 95, 97, 109, 113, 116, 148, 154, 155, 157, 158, 167, 174, 177, 184, 188, 191; *The Excursion* 93; the 'Immortality Ode' 82–4, 86; 'Laodamia' 94; Preface to the *Lyrical Ballads* 84–5; *The Prelude* 86, 87–93, 94, 170, 182–3, 191; 'On Westminister Bridge' 86–7

SUBJECT INDEX

The location of the ideas used in this book, whether specified explicitly in the text or not, is here given in order of appearance in the text; the ideas themselves are listed alphabetically.

aesthetic conflict, aesthetic reciprocity
Richard gives up one idea of beauty along with the crown 12–13; the network of contrasts 'married' via Bottom and Titania 17–19; Hamlet's confusion over beauty and ugliness *re* Ophelia's 'paint' 24, resolved through Yorick's skull 26; thought initially experienced as sickness 24 (also Coleridge 95); Lear splitting his object then reintegrating 33, 37; Leontes' struggle to relate Perdita and Hermione 46; the link between Ariel and Caliban 47–8; Milton's scar-faced Satan 55, and the 'hateful siege of contraries' 64; Blake's 'marriage of contraries' versus sterile 'negatives' 71, 74; poetic ambiguity of the Tyger 79; Wordsworth in 'Westminster Bridge' 86–7, and *The Prelude* 90, 92, then ultimately recoils from the conflict 85, 93; Coleridge's ugly/beautiful watersnakes 101; Coleridge and Blake 107; Keats on Milton 114, and on Shakespear's 'snail' 115; complexity of Keatsian ideal of Beauty 117–18, 120; Heathcliff and Satan 132; love and hate in *Wuthering Heights* 134; relationship between Silas Marner and Eppie 156–7; as symbolic congruence in *Middlemarch* 173–4; between mother/baby, therapist/patient, artist/community 171–2; shared symbolic process of the interpetive mode 176; the mind's development assisted by the changing quality of the internal object 181; *see also* internalisation; symbol formation

basic assumption mentality
The chivalric code of *Richard II* 9, 14; 'law' in *A Midsummer Night's Dream* 16; the ready-made prince outgrown by Hamlet 22; Ulysses fails to control the basic assumption groupings of the Greeks 28; the world of battle-values in *Macbeth* 38; the devils' debate and party in *Paradise Lost* 54; the gangster 'rout' in *Lycidas* and *Paradise Lost* 61; Blake's reversal of labels on social codes of value 74; Coleridge on

'awaking' from this 'negative state' 108; Keats on 'negative capability' as the means for overcoming the tyranny of basic assumptions 119; Lockwood unlocks the moor-mind in *Wuthering Heights* 127; in conformity with family configurations or with social and academic expectations 182; *see also* identity, externally supported; knowledge, mechanical

catastrophic change
The 'translations' of *A Midsummer Night's Dream* 19, and *Winter's Tale* 45; Gloucester and Lear become vehicles for the evolution of Edgar 35; Leontes' 'recreation' during his catastrophic winter 43; foundations of *The Tempest*'s 'brave new world' 51; Satan initiates the new world of *Paradise Lost* 54, 65; Coleridge's 'transcendental philosophy' 106, and the 'chrysalid' mind on the verge of metamorphosis 108; Keats on the evolution of Psyche 123; the two-generation story in *Wuthering Heights* corresponds to Coleridge's idea of 'absolute genius' 139–40, and prepares for 'times of tumult' 142; Eppie's impact on Marner 156; Dorothea's 'epochs' 158–9, 174; Gwendolen's capacity to face her inner experience 164; assisted by the 'transference' relationship with Deronda 168; initiating a process of self-development 180; *see also* omnipotence, loss of; symbol formation

identification (the emotional bond between self and other)
adhesive or narcissistic, as Richard with England 9–10; Adam and Eve with Eden and Heaven 53; Wordsworth's self-idealisation 83, 94; Heathcliff and Catherine before the separation of puberty 132; Silas Marner's emergence from 154; Gwendolen's 'Spoiled Child' self 161–2, 163
internalising identifications: see internalisation
intrusive-projective identification, as probing the mystery in *Hamlet* with the Mousetrap and the Queen's arras 24–5; Hamlet himself trapped by his fathers 24; Ulysses and the ideology of war 28–30; Macbeth and his wife 39–40; Milton's wariness of his own possible false intrusion 61; Blake on false projections of the selfhood 72; Heathcliff's desecration of Catherine's coffin, and delusory power 137–8; characterised by Latimer's personality 151
projective-introjective identification as a function of aesthetic reciprocity: *see* aesthetic conflict; internalisation

identity, internally support *versus* externally supported
Richard exchanges 'hollw crown' for inner drama 13–14; Theseus exchanges 'law' for imagination 19; Lear throws off his 'lendings' 35; Macbeth becomes dependent on his false dress 39; Antigonus sheds court-clothes and Autolycus covets them 46; different types of 'prosperity' in *The Tempest* 50; reliance on external show in *Troilus and Cressida* 29; Milton's devils disguise 'pain and anguish' with a husk of culture 55; the link of hands between Adam, Eve and the angel symbolising internal support 69; Blake on unreal coverings of vision

SUBJECT INDEX

72; Wordsworth's 'shades of the prison-house' 83; and his own shield of sanctimony 94; Coleridge on knowledge-as-being 102–4; Keats on 'cutting a figure' as distinct from being 'figurative' 112, and on proving knowledge 'on the pulses' 111, 117; Lockwood's complacency shattered by his dream 127; Heathcliff's 'spectre of a hope' versus Edgar's 'living hope' 137; commanding versus absolute genius 139–41; Eppie takes the place of the Silas Marner's gold 154, 156–7; collapse of Gwendolen's external supports 163–4; relationship between internal and external in Deronda 167–8; as evidenced in Sarah and Stephen's dreams 176–7, 178–9; contrast between endo-skeletal and exo-skeletal personalities 191–2; *see also* knowledge; self-creativity

imagination
see knowledge, organic or imaginative

infant-self embodying the **thirst for knowledge** (the exploratory and evolutionary self)
The Shakespearean hero 8, 14–15; the ruler Theseus becomes a learner 15, 20; Hamlet's struggle for identity 23, 27; Lear's infant self 33–4, 37; the murdered 'babe' in *Macbeth* 40; Perdita and 'things new-born' 45; Miranda and Caliban as children of Prospero 47; Satan and God's new 'creatures' 55; evolution in Milton 63; Blake's 'infant sorrow' 73, and 'little children of Jerusalem' 73, 75; the newborn infant of the 'Immortality Ode' 82; Coleridge's metaphor of the chrysalis 107–8; Keats's 'leviathan' infant appetite 110, and Chamber of Maiden Thought 108–9; infant poet as 'snail' 115, 'fledged' by symbolic forms 115, 124; as 'witless elf' in the birthplace of poetry, Fingal's Cave 120; 'schooling' the intelligence in the vale of soul-making 121; Lockwood's exploratory curiosity 127; Earnshaw unwraps the infant Heathcliff 133; Catherine's child-ghost 126–7, 137; Dorothea's development out of short-sighted aspiration 173–4; Sarah's 'blue glass bowl' dream 176; Stephen's 'unborn children dream' 179; being 'schooled' by the internal object 181; patients becoming 'fledged' 182; *see also* knowledge; self-creativity

inner world
Richard's prison 13; the wood of *Midsummer Night's Dream* 16; Hamlet's 'undiscovered country' 24; Bohemia in *The Winter's Tale*; contents destroyed in *Macbeth* 40–1; island of *The Tempest* 47; Milton and 'the mind's own place' 54; 'things invisible to mortal sight' 56; the 'paradise within' 69; Blake's Jerusalem and deities in the human breast 70–1; Wordsworth's Nature 88–9; the Ancient Mariner's seascape 98–9, and 'terra incognita' 106; the Chamber of Maiden Thought 109–10, 'terra incognita 114, and soul a 'world of itself' 122; the dream-chamber of *Wuthering Heights* 126, moor-mind 128, and Heathcliff's 'heaven' 138; Dorothea leaves the mind-within-park palings 173–4; Gwendolen's 'unmapped country' 161–4; Sarah's ante-chamber to the mind's 'Mansion' 176–7; Stephen's place for 'unborn children' 179

inspiration

Richard, time and music 14; Bottom and Edgar as inspired prophets 19, 35; 'seeing feelingly' in *Lear* 35; renewed life in Hermione 46; the Arielisation of relationships in *The Tempest* 48–50; Satan in the serpent 65–7; the angel in *Lycidas* 62; vulnerability when waiting for inspiration 57, 60–1; the artist as secretary to authors in eternity 72; Blake's tiger-light 79; the path of light traced by the sheepdog in *The Prelude* 91–2; the Mariner's water-snakes 100–1, and the fountain of reason 104; Keats inspired by Milton and Shakespeare 112–15; 'awakened eyes' in 'Psyche' 122; Edgar inspired by Catherine 136, then Heathcliff via the 'eyes' of the younger generation 137, 140; *see also* internalisation

internal object(s), combined object, poetic Muse

The Muse as director or legislator of the infant self 5–6; need for change in Richard's idea of his mother-space 12; Bottom and Titania as combined dream-legislators for Theseus and the lovers 17; internal object degraded in the world of *Troilus and Cressida* 28–9, and Macbeth's witches 39; Hermione as Muse 44; Milton's developing relation with his muse from 'native language' onwards 56–62; Blake's paternalistic internal family 70, 76; Wordsworth's Nature 90–2; Coleridge's Albatross/moon, taking revenge as Life-in-Death 100; his 'Parent Mind' in symbol formation 105; Keats on the 'Genius of Poetry' 111, and internal objects from Apollo to Psyche 112–23, including fear of the Belle Dame 121; 'our Prime Objects' 129, 132; Catherine as Muse in *Wuthering Heights* 134; Eppie's function for Silas Marner 157; Deronda's for Gwendolan 165–6, 169; the 'blue glass bowl' 176–7; *see also* infant self

internalisation

Richard internalises time 14; Bottom's revelation and Theseus' struggle 19–20; Hamlet internalises the Ghost's infant sorrow 23, and Ophelia Hamlet's madness 25; Lear internalises his daughter-mothers 37, and Leontes his wife and daughter 43, 46; Ferdinand and Alonso internalise Ariel 48, 50; Prospero acknowledges Caliban 51; Milton finds lost aspects of himself in *Lycidas* and internalises a strengthened Muse 60; Satan internalised by Eve then Adam 67; Blake's poem is shaped by the tiger's 'fearful symmetry' 80; Wordsworth internalises features of nature 88; Coleridge searching for ways to describe the process of internalisation 105–7; Keats internalises the experience of his poetic forebears 111–17; internalising Psyche results in a 'working brain' 124; Hareton is the means for Heathcliff's internalisation of Catherine 138; the principle of growth represented for Silas Marner by Eppie 156–7; Gwendolen's relationship with Deronda 165–7, 169, 181; introjective identification in the 'blue glass bowl' dream 176–7; shift in Stephen from projective to introjective identification 178–9

SUBJECT INDEX

knowledge, organic or imaginative *versus* mechanical or omnipotent
Theseus and Hippolyta on imagination and fancy 16, 20; Hamlet's conventional versus 'undiscovered' roles 22–3; Lear and Gloucester learning to see feelingly 35; Macbeth's loss of imagination 40–1; Prospero abandons the 'vanity of his art' for the unknown new world 51; Milton's theory of poetic learning 59, and inspired serpent with 'tongue organic' 66; Blake on imagination versus reason, vision versus allegory 72, 75; Coleridge on the 'shaping spirit of imagination' 84, and knowledge as becoming 104–5, evolved versus impressed 118, organic versus mechanical 102; knowledge's 'terra incognita' 106; Keats on the mystery and allegory of inner life 112, versus 'consequitive' conclusions 118–19; on how the creative creates itself 111; unlike the Belle Dame, Psyche is known rather than possessed 122; Byron's analysis of the emptiness of non-being 130; Lockwood's 'unknown Catherine' finally known not possessed 141–2; Coleridge on 'absolute' as opposed to 'commanding' genius 138–9, in relation to Heathcliff 140–1; an opposition lying at the heart of George Eliot's work 144–7; exemplified in *The Lifted Veil* 151–2; Stephen's omnipotent relationship to knowledge 178; *see also* identity; infant-self; self-creativity

omnipotence, grandiosity (the delusion of controlling the inner world and its objects)
Richard's narcissism 11; Theseus, Egeus and false aesthetics 16; Hamlet, Polonius and sterile wordplay or acting 24, 26; Greeks and Trojans 28–30; Lear's infantile omnipotence 33; Macbeth's delusion of knowing the future 41; Leontes' tyranny 44; cynicism of Antonio and Sebastian 49; Prospero's omnipotence 50; Milton's devils 54–5 and struggle with his own will and doctrine 57, 65; the cryptic Blake 77, despite his disapproval of men's 'systems' 71; Wordsworth's self-idealisation, promoted by Coleridge 92–3; Coleridge on mechanical aesthetics and false philosophy 102–3; shooting of the Albatross and its consequences 99; Keats on 'irritable reaching after fact and reason' 119, and on doctrine in Milton 114; egotism and the lap-dog/false baby motif in *Wuthering Heights* 132; Heathcliff's tyranny and self-imprisonment 137; Coleridge on 'commanding genius' 139; Latimer's conviction of his creative powers 152; the struggle against it in *Middlemarch* 159; contrast with learning from experience 169; Stephen's 'cup' dream 178; *see also* basic assumption mentality

omnipotence, loss of (the prelude to self-creativity)
Richard in the 'prison' of his inner world 13; Theseus turns his back 16; Lear throws off his lendings 35, and relinquishes his idealised cave 37; Hamlet formulates the sense of thought-sickness associated with loss of omnipotence 24; Leontes hands over to Paulina 46; Prospero's farewell 51; Milton places trust in the Muse 59; Coleridge on 'remorse' 96, and the Mariner's rejuvenation 101; on 'absolute' versus 'commanding' genius 138–9; Keats on thought-sickness 110,

215

THE CHAMBER OF MAIDEN THOUGHT

negative capability 119, Scottish mist 120, and Saturn's loss of power 116–17; Lockwood's fever 127; Emily Brontë's new way of writing 128; Heathcliff's 'strange way of killing' 138; Dorothea's experience in Rome 159; the culmination of Gwendolen's self-disapproval 163–4; contrast between Stephen's 'cup' and his 'unborn children' dreams 178, 179, 180–1

perversion

Cynicism, pornography and social manipulation in *Troilus and Cressida* 28–30; perversion of femininity in *Macbeth* 39–40, resulting in faecal hallucinations 41; Blake on 'error' and sanctimony 81; Hindley's degradation 154; exorcism through 'moral teething' 134–5; Byron's 'jar of atoms' in lieu of internal objects, and Heathcliff's 'collection of memoranda' 130; *see also* internal object degraded; omnipotence

self-creativity

Richard discovers the means 14; Theseus places his 'house' in the hands of the fairies for procreation 21; Hamlet glimpses the undiscovered country in the skull 26; Lear's self-creativity through death 37; Leontes re-creates himself via Paulina 44, 46; the process of prosperity in *The Tempest* 50–1; Milton a voyager in his own epic 56; Blake on 'vision' as the developmental force 71; Coleridge on the 'principle' of self-development' 105, and growth of consciousness 106; Wordsworth on the growth of a poet's mind 87; Keats on how 'the creative must create itself' 111; 'fledging' 115, 120; soul-making 121; breeding thoughts in 'Psyche' 124; *Wuthering Heights* establishes the principle of self-development 141–2; the change in Silas Marner 155–6; carried by Deronda as a principle, to be lived by Gwendolen 169; the function of the transference in assisting the process 173, 190–1; *see also* identity; infant-self; knowledge

social development

The changing idea of kingship in *Richard II* 9–10, and *Hamlet* 21–2; governor and workman in *Midsummer Night's Dream* 21, and *Winter's Tale* 45; Ulysses' failure to maintain the status quo 29; lack of social development in *Macbeth* 42; unforeseeable development of the *The Tempest's* new world 51–2; end of the rule of Heaven and Hell in *Paradise Lost* 53, 68–9; Blake on their 'marriage' 71; social ills represent the obscuring of vision in 'London' 73; Coleridge on the need for imagination not dogmatism in all aspects of life 103; Keats on the 'grand march of intellect' 110, 'grand democracy of forest trees' 118–19, and 'faded hierarchy' of pre-Psyche gods 123; a marriage which can survive the end of the church and times of tumult 142

SUBJECT INDEX

symbol formation
Emotional reality finds a 'local habitation and a name' 20; achieved by Hamlet through Yorick's skull 26 (versus anti-symbolic space of the Mousetrap 24); Macbeth loses his capacity for symbol formation 41, but ultimately symbolises his predicament 30–1; Hermione's statue awoken by 'faith' 46; Prospero's cloud-capped towers 51; symbols presented by the Muse in *Paradise Lost* 56; the drama of Satan and Eve 66–7; clouds of symbolic potential surround the expulsion from Eden 68–9; Blake's house for the passions 78, exemplified in 'The Tyger' 79–80; theory absent in Wordsworth's Preface 85; symbol formation in *The Prelude* 89–92; Coleridge on symbol formation and the equivalence of form and meaning 102–5; Keats's spatial description of symbol formation 115; on the relation of the sense of beauty to symbolic congruence between self and objects 118–19; 'breeding' symbols in the 'Ode to Psyche' 124; Heathcliff completes Catherine's 'existence beyond herself' and achieves symbol-formation with its 'thousand forms' 140–1; the entrée to thinking about meaning 171; a function of the internal object 172; making vision available 175; lodged in the unconscious transaction of transference and countertransference 175; in the model of the mother/baby relationship 172, 191